Contents

WHEAT: BREADS AND DESSERTS   24

SOYBEANS   37

Recipes for
Self-sufficient
Living

Recipes for
Self-sufficient Living

Kay Martineau
Marlynn Phipps
Sally Hornberger

SHADOW MOUNTAIN
Salt Lake City, Utah

©1984 Deseret Book Company
All rights reserved
Printed in the United States of America
First printing March 1984

Shadow Mountain Press is an imprint of
Deseret Book Company, P.O. Box 30178,
Salt Lake City, Utah 84130

Library of Congress Cataloging in Publication Data
Martineau, Kay.
   Recipes for self-sufficient living.

   Includes index.
   1. Cookery. I. Phipps, Marlynn. II. Hornberger,
Sally. III. Title.
TX652.M293   1984   640   84-3117
ISBN 0-87747-955-0 (pbk.)

CORN AND MEXICAN DISHES   50

VARIETY GRAINS   57

DRIED BEANS AND LEGUMES   66

PASTA AND CRACKERS   71

DAIRY PRODUCTS AND EGGS　81

DRYING, CURING, AND SMOKING　99

GRAVIES, SOUPS, AND SAUCES   111

SWEETS AND CONFECTIONS   117

SOAPS AND COSMETICS   122

EQUIVALENTS, SUBSTITUTES, AND MISCELLANEOUS TIPS   133

INDEX   139

Preface

There is a feeling of security in knowing you can create appetizing and nutritious meals at very little cost. With a variety from six basic groups—grains and legumes, flavorings and seasonings, shortening or fat, sugar or honey, eggs or substitutes, and garden fruits and vegetables—you can create almost any dish. There are many delightful ways to use these basics and save money.

We feel that homemakers are grasping for ways to save money and still serve nutritious, appetizing meals without the additives and preservatives of store-bought food.

We offer recipes and methods of preparing food that are easy for almost any homemaker. We have sought ways to use foods or leftovers that are often wasted.

For economic or health reasons, many people search for nutritious recipes without meat. We have included simple meatless recipes that still have the satisfying look and taste of meat.

This book is designed to go hand in hand with food storage. We believe that hard times will come to most families at some time in their lives, whether in the form of ill health, accidents, disasters, or depression. For those who are prepared, the recipes in this book can help them create delightful meals at very little cost. There is security in knowing a family can be provided for regardless of economic situations.

Repeatedly serving the same foods can be very discouraging. During hard times the first things most people miss are luxuries. We know that the nice things can still be made available—steak, whipped cream, desserts, even a nice-smelling bar of soap— all from the basics. Don't do without but make do creatively.

We sincerely hope this book will help you as much as it has helped us in preparing attractive, appetizing, and nutritious meals. These are truly recipes for self-sufficient living.

Seasonings and Flavorings

Herbs and Spices

Flavoring with herbs and spices is an art that can make mealtime a wonderful experience. When you look at your spice shelf, you are looking at exotic products from all areas of the world. By airplane, freighter, train, or truck, they cross the continents to your kitchen. They come from all parts of plants: roots, bark, stalks, leaves, buds, fruits, and seeds.

Use of seasonings is basically a matter of taste, conditioned by each person's taste buds. They should always be used sparingly so as to accent or enhance the food, not to destroy or hide the natural flavors. A wise cook will use just a pinch, then taste. Properly seasoned food can be a delight to the eyes and stimulating to the senses. Herbs and spices make food more economical by making it more palatable and easier to digest.

The word *spices* encompasses four basic categories:

Spices are derived from the bark, root, fruit, or berry. Most spices come from the hot, humid tropics.

Herbs are leaves of low-growing shrubs in temperate climates. They grow in abundance in sunny lands and low countries.

Seeds come from lacy annual plants.

Seasonings are combinations or blends of the above.

Salt is not listed in the four categories, yet it is one of the most essential of all seasonings. It is neither an herb nor a spice, but a mineral. Our food would be very bland without this ingredient.

Preserving Herbs and Spices

Harvesting and Drying: Drying is the most popular way to preserve the flavor and fragrance of herbs and spices. When harvesting, be sure you don't take too much of the plant while it is young, or it will become weak. Select only the fresh, healthy leaves, and cut out those that are yellowed or dead.

Herb Leaves: The leaves should be cut when the plant is at its highest with essential oils, when buds are forming just before blossoming. Cut the leaves early in the morning, after the dew has dried, but before the sun brings out the oils. Cut several inches of stem. If the leaves are dusty, rinse quickly with cool water and then shake off excess water.

To hang-dry, gather a bunch of herbs together and tie the ends. Hang upside-down (oils in stems will flow into leaves) in a warm, dry, well-ventilated place away from direct sunlight. To prevent dust and bugs from getting into the leaves, cover them with a brown paper bag, perforated to allow air to circulate. This method is best for basil, oregano, sage, marjoram, savory, horehound, and mint. Thyme, parsley, and rosemary are best dried by removing the leaves and drying on racks outdoors or in food dryers.

Herb Flowers: Harvest flowers when the blossoms first open and are fresh. Dry them in food dryers.

Herb Seeds: Harvest seeds when the heads turn color, just before they open and scatter. Cut off entire head and drop it in a bag. If you hang-dry the seeds, they will fall off into the bag. If you dry on racks, rub the seeds between your hands when the pods are dry. The seeds will fall out of the pods.

Roots: The roots should be dug up during the plant's dormant stage (fall and winter). Remove only a few roots from each plant, trying not to injure the plant. Roots can be left whole or sliced and dried on racks in a food dryer. Always store herbs and spices in tightly sealed jars and keep out of direct sunlight. Dry them as whole as possible to retain the flavor.

Freezing: Herbs such as basil, tarragon, chives, dill, and parsley can be frozen. Dip them in boiling water a few seconds; then remove and cool in ice water. Remove the stems and place the leaves in air-tight containers and freeze.

A Guide to Herbs, Spices, and Seasonings

The fun of adding new spices to your cooking and baking can last a lifetime. Whether you are a new cook or one who has been cooking for years, the anticipation of preparing something new can still give you a thrill. There is hardly a dish that can't be improved with a pinch of this and a dash of that.

The following charts will give you some tips on flavoring dishes with a variety of spices. You will want to experiment, adding small amounts at a time. Soon you will develop a cooking personality all your own.

Herbs, spices, and seasonings, all made from natural ingredients

Figure 1. Blends

	SEASONING SALT	SMOKED SALT	ITALIAN SEASONING	CURRY POWDER	CHILI POWDER
APPETIZERS AND SOUPS	Use to season vegetable soup or chicken broth.	Add a pinch to split pea, bean, lentil, or vegetable soups.	Add a sprinkle to vegetable tomato, or bean soups.	Add a pinch to cream cheese for canapés.	Add a dash to vegetable or meat soups.
MEATS AND POULTRY	Sprinkle lightly on chops or hamburgers. Use to season gravies.	Mix 1 teaspoon in hamburgers. Sprinkle on pork, veal, roasts, steaks, and spareribs.	Add to lasagna, spaghetti sauce, casseroles, or pizza.	Add to marinades for lamb, beef, chicken, or game.	Use in casseroles, meat loaf, or hamburgers. Use in Mexican dishes.
EGGS AND CHEESE	Add to omelets, scrambled or deviled eggs.	Add to omelets or deviled eggs.	Sprinkle lightly on scrambled eggs.	Blend into deviled eggs or egg salad.	Add a dash to scrambled eggs or cheese dips.
FISH	Use to season coating for fish.	Add a pinch to fish chowder. Add to fried oysters and fish fillets.	Add a pinch to butter used for basting broiled or baked fish.	Sprinkle on broiled or baked fish. Use in creamed shrimp or tuna and serve over rice.	Use in cocktail sauce for seafood. Use to season shrimp or oysters.
SALADS	Use in vinegar dressings.		Add to French dressing. Sprinkle lightly over tossed salad.	Add to egg or chicken salads.	
VEGETABLES	Sprinkle on raw vegetables.		Add a dash to tomatoes, eggplant, or onions.	Use to season sauce for creamed vegetables.	Add a dash to cheese sauce for vegetables. Add a dash to corn, rice, or lima beans.
SAUCES	Use in dips and sauces for meats and vegetables.	Add to cream sauce, barbecue sauce, or marinade.	Use in sauces for fish or Italian dishes.	Add ½ teaspoon curry to 2 cups cream sauce.	Use in basting sauces for meats. Use in sauces for vegetables.

Figure 2. Spices

	ALLSPICE	CINNAMON	CLOVES	GINGER	LEMON PEEL
APPETIZERS AND SOUPS	Add a dash to pea or tomato soups. Add to spaghetti, barbecue, or brown sauces.	Add to fruit punch, eggnog, or hot chocolate.	Add to fruit punch, spiced cider, or cranberry juice. Add a pinch to split pea or potato soups.	For zest try a pinch in bean soup.	Use in cream sauces.
MEATS AND POULTRY	Add to pot roasts, stews, veal, pork, lamb, or meat loaf. Add a pinch to gravies.	Sprinkle lightly on ham, lamb, or pork chops. Add to corned beef, lamb, or beef stew. Use in stuffing for goose.	Stud baked ham or pork roast with whole cloves. Use ¼ teaspoon in meat loaf.	Add ½ teaspoon with salt and pepper to season meat. Good on poultry, lamb, and pot roast. Add to stuffings.	Use in gravies for veal, chicken, or lamb. Add to glazes for ham or marinades for pot roast or veal.
EGGS AND CHEESE		Add ½ teaspoon to milk and eggs for French toast.			
FISH	Add to fish while poaching.	Use in court-bouillon for fish or shellfish.	Add to court-bouillon for fish and shrimp.	Sprinkle lightly on fish before baking or broiling. Use in barbecue or basting sauces for fish.	Sprinkle lightly on fish or add to court-bouillon.
SALADS OR FRUIT	Sprinkle lightly on fruit salad or fruit compote.	Add a dash to applesauce, baked apples, or fruit salads. Sprinkle on cottage cheese.		Sprinkle on pear halves.	Sprinkle lightly on green salads or add to salad dressings or seasonings.
VEGETABLES	Sprinkle lightly on sweet potatoes.	Add a dash to butter for squash, sweet potatoes, or beets.	Add sparingly to Harvard beets, sweet potatoes, tomatoes, or squash.	Add a dash to candied sweet potatoes, glazed carrots, or winter squash.	Use on chard, spinach, or beets.
DESSERTS	Add spicy flavor to mincemeat, fruit cake, plum pudding, pumpkin, chiffon, or apple pies.	Add a teaspoon to pumpkin, apple, peach, cranberry, cream, or custard pies. Sprinkle over vanilla ice cream.	Add spice to prune, applesauce, or fruit cakes. Use in molasses cookies or spiced muffins.	Use in gingerbread, steamed puddings and bread, or rice puddings. Sprinkle lightly on honeydew melon.	Use in chiffon and angel cakes. Add to custards, bread puddings, sauces, and meringues. Add to breads, rolls, or muffins.

Figure 2. Spices

	MACE	MUSTARD	NUTMEG	PAPRIKA	CAYENNE PEPPER
APPETIZERS AND SOUPS	Add a dash to tomato juice, oyster stew, or cream of chicken soup.	Add to dips for chilled shrimp and lobster tails. Add ¼ teaspoon to cream of celery, mushroom, bean, or lentil soups.	Sprinkle in eggnog or spiced drinks. Add a dash to chicken and cream soups.	Garnish soups and appetizers.	Use in seafood appetizers. Add to vegetable juices or soups.
MEATS AND POULTRY	Use ¼ teaspoon to season veal, lamb chops, or sausage. Add a pinch to chicken a la king. Add to marinades for veal or chicken.	Use in raisin sauce for ham. Blend 1 teaspoon in hash or hamburgers. Add to stews, pot roast, or coating mix for chicken.	Try ½ teaspoon in meat loaf. Mix ¼ teaspoon in Swedish meat balls or cream sauce for chicken.	Add 1 teaspoon to butter for basting chicken or making cream sauces or gravies. Use in flour coating mixtures.	Add a dash to stews, casseroles, roast, or meat sauces.
EGGS AND CHEESE		Add to cheese and egg recipes.	Sprinkle on scrambled eggs.		Add a dash to egg dishes.
FISH	Sprinkle lightly on trout before frying or broiling. Add to fish sauces.	Add to deviled crab. Add to sauces for fish or casseroles.	Add a dash to stuffing for fish or fish croquettes.	Use in dipping mixture for fish. Add to butter for basting.	Sprinkle on baked or broiled fish.
SALADS OR FRUIT	Sprinkle on spiced fruit, fruit salads, or cooked apples. Add ¼ teaspoon to French dressing.	Add to French dressing or mayonnaise. Add to vinegar dressings for cole slaws. Add to dressings for potato, macaroni, or chicken salads.	Add a dash to dressing for fruit salads.	Add ¼ teaspoon to French dressing, cooked salad dressing, or sour cream dressing.	Add a pinch to salad dressings.
VEGETABLES	Sprinkle lightly on buttered carrots, cauliflower, squash, or swiss chard. Add to cream sauces for vegetables.	Add ¼ teaspoon to scalloped potatoes. Mix with butter and use on cabbage, Brussels sprouts, asparagus, or broccoli.	Sprinkle on carrots, green beans, spinach, squash, or candied sweet potatoes.	Use as a garnish or seasoning in vegetables.	Add a dash to baked bean, tomato, or eggplant dishes. Add to creamed onions.
DESSERTS	Add a dash to chocolate pudding or sauce. Use in spice cake, applesauce, or popovers. Use in pie crust for peach or cherry pies.		Sprinkle lightly over ice cream, rice pudding, or custards, or add to whipped cream. Add to apple, pumpkin, or nut pie fillings.		

Figure 3. Herbs

	BASIL	CARAWAY	DILL SEED	MARJORAM	OREGANO
APPETIZERS AND SOUPS	Add ¼ teaspoon to tomato juice or bouillon. Add to vegetable and minestrone soup.	Add to cream cheese for spreads, dips, or stuffed celery.	Blend with deviled ham for canapés. Add ¼ teaspoon to cream cheese for dips and spreads.	Add just a pinch to vegetable soup during final cooking hour.	Add a pinch to tomato juice or tomato soup.
MEATS AND POULTRY	Add ½ teaspoon of beef stew. Good in spaghetti and pizza sauces.	Add to beef, lamb, or oxtail stews. Sprinkle over roast pork, pork chops, pork sausage, or spareribs.	Add to boiled beef, lamb, or corned beef. Add a few seeds to lamb stew or pork roast.	Add to stuffings. Sprinkle on veal, pork, and beef. Add to cooking liquid for poultry, veal, or lamb.	Add to meat loaves, stews, hamburger, and stuffings. Add to meat sauces for spaghetti and pizza. Add to poultry cooking liquid.
EGGS AND CHEESE	Add a pinch in scrambled eggs and omelets.	Add to cheese spreads. Combine with cottage cheese.	Add 1 teaspoon to cottage or cream cheese for sandwich spread.	Add to scrambled eggs, souffles, and omelets.	Add a pinch to scrambled eggs, omelets, or soufflés.
FISH	Crumble in a little lemon juice and drizzle over fried, broiled, or scalloped fish.		Sprinkle on all fish, especially salmon and shrimp. Add to cooking water when poaching fish.	Sprinkle lightly over baked, broiled, or creamed fish.	Combine with butter to serve on shellfish.
SALADS	Good in tomato and seafood salads. Sprinkle on cottage cheese, fresh tomatoes, or cucumbers.	Add to potato and tomato salads, or sliced cucumbers in vinegar. Sprinkle on cole slaw or beet salad.	Use in vegetable, avocado, cucumber, seafood, cole slaw, or potato salads.	Add a dash to French dressing or sprinkle on sliced tomatoes. Good in tuna and chicken salads.	Add to herb salad dressing. Add ¼ teaspoon to tuna fish, potato salad, or tomatoes.
VEGETABLES	Add ¼ teaspoon to eggplant, squash, green beans, tomatoes, broccoli, asparagus, while cooking.	Use crushed or whole in cooked cabbage, carrots, sauerkraut, turnips, green beans, potatoes, or onions.	Add ¼ teaspoon to cooked green beans, beets, turnips, cauliflower, squash, or sauerkraut.	Add a pinch to mushrooms, carrots, peas, spinach, zucchini, or eggplant while cooking.	Add to cooking water for zucchini, eggplant, tomatoes, string beans, and peas.
BREADS	Mix with butter for herbed bread or add to bread dough.	Sprinkle on or add to rolls, rye or pumpernickel bread, or bread sticks.	Sprinkle on rye bread, rolls, or add to bread dough.	Blend into butter and spread on French bread. Good in biscuit and bread doughs.	Sprinkle on pizza or Italian sandwiches.

Figure 3. Herbs

	BAY LEAVES	ROSEMARY	SAVORY	THYME	SAGE
APPETIZERS AND SOUPS	Add a leaf to vegetable, minestrone, or tomato soups.	Try ¼ teaspoon in split pea, spinach, minestrone, or chicken soups.	Add a pinch to consomme, lentil, pea, bean, potato, or fish soups.	Use in gumbo, clam chowder, or pea, or vegetable soups. Add a pinch to tomato juice.	Add ¼ teaspoon to consomme, cream soup, or chowder.
MEATS AND POULTRY	Add to cooking water for pot roast, corned beef, stews, and venison.	Add to lamb, veal, or beef roast. Add to poultry or stuffing seasoning. Try in beef stew or ham loaf.	Add ¼ teaspoon to pot roast, meat loaf, or poultry stuffing.	Add to fricassee or roast chicken or turkey.	Use in sausage, meat loaf, stews, or stuffings. Rub lightly on pork, veal, or lamb before roasting.
EGGS AND CHEESE	Add to custards and creams.	Add a pinch to scrambled eggs or omelets.	Blend in ¼ teaspoon for scrambled or deviled eggs.	Sprinkle on scrambled eggs, omelets, or deviled eggs.	Sprinkle lightly on cottage or cream cheese for a sandwich spread.
FISH	Put in bouillon for poaching fish.	Use in stuffing for fish or sprinkle lightly before baking or broiling fish. Try with salmon.	Use to garnish or add a dash to baked or broiled fish.	Sprinkle lightly on fish before broiling or baking. Use in stuffing.	Add a dash to melted butter for basting broiled fish.
SALADS		Combine 1 teaspoon in French dressing or in mayonnaise for potato or chicken salad.	Add a pinch to vegetable or potato salad.	Use in tomato and aspic salads.	
VEGETABLES	Add a leaf to boiling potatoes or carrots.	Add to liquid when cooking green beans, peas, spinach, chard, carrots, or potatoes.	Add to cooking water for zucchini, green beans, peas, sauerkraut, lima beans, or cauliflower.	Add to cooking water for onions, beets, carrots, or asparagus.	Combine ¼ teaspoon with melted butter and pour over eggplant, tomatoes, onions, or lima beans.
BREADS		Add ¼ teaspoon to batter for corn bread, muffins, or dumplings.	Use ½ teaspoon in biscuits or dumplings.	Add ½ teaspoon to liquid used in biscuits or dumplings.	Add a dash to dumplings and biscuits.

Hints for Using Herbs and Spices

1. Add herbs to a hot dish in the last hour of cooking, unless it is a simmering stock. This will keep the flavor from cooking out.

2. For best results, add the herbs after browning, even if a recipe calls for the herbs to be added during or before browning.

3. Experiment with seasonings and combinations before you test your ideas on guests.

4. Always use spices and herbs sparingly. Add a pinch, then taste.

5. When adding herbs to dishes, remember that dried herbs are stronger than fresh herbs.

6. Two teaspoons of fresh herbs equal one-half teaspoon dried herbs.

7. To enhance the flavor of herbs used in salads or dressings, steep the herbs in hot water for a few minutes.

8. Freezing will preserve the flavor of herbs and spices. Do not refreeze after thawing.

9. When using fresh leaves, remove the woody stem and cut leaves into small pieces just before adding to food.

10. When combining herbs, combine the strong-flavored ones, such as sage, rosemary, marjoram, and tarragon, with the milder ones.

11. Dried herbs and spices will lose their flavor and fragrance faster if they are not kept in sealed containers.

12. Generally, one-fourth teaspoon of dried herbs is used for every four servings. A pinch measures approximately one-eighth teaspoon.

13. When using leaves, crush just before adding to a recipe. This will release the flavor.

Equivalents for Herbs, Spices, and Seasonings

Herbs: 2 teaspoons fresh chopped herbs equal 1 teaspoon dried, loosely crumbled herbs or ¼ teaspoon finely powdered herbs.

Bell peppers: 1 tablespoon dehydrated equals 3 tablespoons fresh chopped.

Garlic powder: ⅛ teaspoon equals 1 medium clove garlic.

Garlic salt: ½ teaspoon equals 1 clove garlic plus a small amount of salt.

Lemon or orange peel: 1 teaspoon dried equals 1 teaspoon grated fresh peel or ½ teaspoon extract.

Mustard powder: 1 teaspoon mild equals 1 tablespoon prepared.

Onion powder: 1 tablespoon equals 1 medium chopped onion.

Onion, minced: 1 tablespoon equals 1 small chopped onion.

Dill seed: 1 teaspoon equals 1 head fresh dill.

Creating Your Own Spices, Seasonings, and Condiments

Curry Powder

4½ teaspoons coriander seed
4½ teaspoons ground turmeric
1½ teaspoons peppercorns
1½ teaspoons mustard seed
1½ teaspoons ground ginger
¾ teaspoon cardamom
½ teaspoon cayenne or red chili pepper
¼ teaspoon cumin
¼ teaspoon mace

Combine and powder ingredients in a blender or food processor. Put in an airtight container and store in a cool place.

Kitchen Pepper

6 tablespoons salt
1 tablespoon ginger
1½ teaspoons black pepper
1½ teaspoons ground cinnamon
1½ teaspoons nutmeg
1½ teaspoons allspice
½ teaspoon ground cloves

Combine ingredients. Put in an airtight container and store in a cool place. Use to season pork, beef, and ham.

Meat Loaf Spice

1½ teaspoons salt
3 tablespoons minced onion
1 tablespoon pepper flakes (optional)
⅛ teaspoon black pepper
¼ teaspoon sage
1 teaspoon garlic powder
¼ teaspoon dry mustard
1 teaspoon curry powder
⅛ teaspoon oregano
⅛ teaspoon nutmeg

½ teaspoon turmeric

½ teaspoon paprika

¼ teaspoon sweet basil

1 tablespoon parsley flakes

Combine all ingredients. Put in an airtight container and store in a cool place. Keep spice handy for seasoning meat loaves, casseroles, meatballs, and hamburgers.

Meat Loaf: Combine 2 pounds ground beef, 2 eggs, 1 cup bread or cracker crumbs, ½ cup milk or catsup, and one recipe Meat Loaf Spice (above). Shape loaf and place in casserole dish. Bake at 350° F. for one hour.

Italian Seasoning

1 tablespoon marjoram

1 tablespoon thyme

1½ tablespoons rosemary

½ teaspoon savory (optional)

¼ teaspoon sage

1½ teaspoons oregano

1 teaspoon sweet basil

Combine all ingredients. Put in an airtight container and store in a cool place. Use in making Italian sauces.

Chili Spice

3 tablespoons chili powder

3 tablespoons flour

2½ teaspoons cumin

2½ teaspoons paprika

2½ teaspoons crushed dried red pepper

2½ teaspoons garlic powder

¾ teaspoon oregano

1 teaspoon sugar (optional)

⅛ teaspoon cayenne pepper

1 teaspoon minced onion

Combine all ingredients. Put in an airtight container and store in a cool place. Use to season eggs, soups, rice, sauces, and vegetables, as well as Mexican dishes.

Spaghetti Spice

1 teaspoon parsley flakes

1 teaspoon sugar (optional)

1 tablespoon flour

1 tablespoon grated Romano or Parmesan cheese

1 teaspoon Italian seasoning

1 tablespoon minced onion

½ teaspoon minced garlic

½ teaspoon paprika

1 teaspoon salt

Combine all ingredients. Put in an airtight container and store in a cool place. Use to season spaghetti, lasagna, pizza, and other Italian dishes.

Spaghetti Sauce: Mix a 1-pound can of tomatoes with a 6-ounce can of tomato paste. Add 1 recipe Spaghetti Spice and simmer for 1 hour. If desired, just before serving add browned sausage or Wheat Meat Sausage (see index).

Sausage Seasoning

2 tablespoons sage

2 tablespoons rosemary

2 teaspoons marjoram

2 teaspoons sweet basil

½ teaspoon minced garlic

½ teaspoon minced onion

⅛ teaspoon crushed red pepper

Combine all ingredients. Put in an airtight container and store in a cool place. Use to season sausage or Wheat Meat Sausage (see index).

Macaroni and Cheese Dinner Mix

¼ cup dry cheddar cheese powder

5 teaspoons skim milk powder

¾ teaspoon salt

⅛ teaspoon lemon powder or unsweetened lemon Kool-Aid (optional)

Combine ingredients. Put in an airtight container and store in a cool place. Makes 6 tablespoons mix.

Macaroni and Cheese: Bring 2 quarts water to a rolling boil; add 1½ cups dry macaroni. Cook until tender, approximately 15 minutes. Drain. Add ¼ cup margarine and ¼ cup milk. Stir in 6 tablespoons Macaroni and Cheese Dinner Mix. Makes 3 cups.

Dip 'n Bake for Chicken

1 cup oat flour (see index) or cornflake or cracker crumbs

½ cup flour

3 tablespoons Parmesan cheese

2 tablespoons powdered skim milk

2 teaspoons salt

½ teaspoon pepper

½ teaspoon dry mustard

½ teaspoon sage

½ teaspoon onion powder

½ teaspoon garlic powder

¼ teaspoon marjoram

¼ teaspoon paprika

Combine ingredients. Put in an airtight container and store in a cool place.

Baked Chicken: Cut up one 3- or 4-pound chicken. Dip chicken pieces in a mixture of ⅓ cup milk and 1 beaten egg. Roll in Dip 'n Bake. Arrange chicken pieces in a shallow baking dish. Drizzle ¼ cup butter or margarine over top. Bake at 375° F. for 1 hour.

Dip 'n Bake for Pork Chops

**1 cup oat flour (see index) or cornflake
    or cracker crumbs**
¼ cup Parmesan cheese
2 teaspoons salt
½ teaspoon pepper
½ teaspoon onion powder
½ teaspoon dry mustard
¼ teaspoon thyme
¼ teaspoon marjoram
2 tablespoons dry milk powder

Combine all ingredients. Put in an airtight container and store in a cool place.

Baked Pork Chops: Dip 6 pork chops in a mixture of ⅓ cup milk and 1 beaten egg. Roll in Dip 'n Bake. Arrange in shallow pan and bake at 350° F. for one hour or until tender.

Dip 'n Fry for Fish

**½ cup oat flour (see index) or
    all-purpose flour**
½ cup cornmeal
1 teaspoon baking powder
**⅛ teaspoon lemon powder or
    unsweetened lemon Kool-Aid, or
    ½ teaspoon dried lemon peel**
1 teaspoon salt
½ teaspoon pepper
½ teaspoon dry mustard
**¼ teaspoon each marjoram, rosemary,
    and thyme**

Combine ingredients. Put in an airtight container and store in a cool place.

Fried Fish: Dip 1 pound fish fillets in a mixture of ⅓ cup milk and 1 beaten egg. Coat fish with Dip 'n Fry. Fry in ½-inch-deep hot oil (375° F.) for 2 minutes on each side or until crisp and golden brown.

Seasoned Flour

½ cup flour
½ teaspoon paprika
⅛ teaspoon sage
⅛ teaspoon onion powder

⅛ teaspoon garlic salt
¼ teaspoon pepper
1 teaspoon salt

Combine ingredients. Keep in an airtight container in a cool place. Use to coat meats, poultry, and fish.

Pickling Spice

3 cinnamon sticks
2 tablespoons black peppercorns
2 tablespoons mustard seed
1 tablespoon ground ginger
1 tablespoon dill seed
2 to 4 dried red peppers
2 teaspoons whole cloves
2 teaspoons coriander seed
2 teaspoons mace
2 teaspoons whole allspice
1 teaspoon cardamom seed
6 bay leaves

Combine all ingredients. Put in an airtight container and store in a cool place. Just before using, put required amount in a cloth or spice bag and crush ingredients with a hammer to release the flavor. This spice adds a tangy, peppery taste to pickles without the predominance of cloves and allspice.

Garlic Salt or Onion Salt

Combine ¾ cup coarse salt with ½ cup chopped garlic cloves or ½ cup chopped onions. Mix in blender until a paste forms. Spread on waxed paper and dry in oven or dehydrator at 100° to 140° F. When paste is dry, return to blender and blend into a powder.

Herbed Seasoning Salt

Spread a layer of non-iodized salt on a cookie sheet. Cover the salt with fresh herbs or tops from your garden vegetables. Carrots, beets, turnips, and radishes add a good flavor. (Do not use tomato or potato tops.) Top with another layer of salt. Place the pan in a 225° F. oven for 25 minutes. Remove from oven and break up any lumps. Return pan to the oven and dry for 15 minutes longer, or until the leaves crumble easily. Remove from oven and cool. Powder the leaves and salt in a blender. Add dry lemon peel and other desired dried, ground, or powdered herbs and spices. Put in an airtight container and store in a cool place. Use to liven up salad greens, fresh raw vegetables, dips, dressings, and many cooked dishes.

Marinade or Basting Sauce

1 cup vegetable oil
½ cup vinegar
1½ teaspoons salt
1½ teaspoons pepper
1 clove garlic, crushed
½ teaspoon onion powder
1 tablespoon dried herb or spice
    combination (see variations
    below)
½ teaspoon tenderizer

Combine ingredients. Cover meat and marinate for several hours before cooking.

Variations: For beef marinade, use singly or in any combination bay leaves, dill, oregano, rosemary, savory, thyme. For lamb, use rosemary, mace, sage, coriander, basil, tarragon, cumin, caraway. For pork, use parsley, nutmeg, cumin, fennel seed, rosemary, anise, thyme. For poultry, use ginger, marjoram, turmeric, tarragon, basil, rosemary, sage.

Range-top Dressing Mix for Poultry

1 tablespoon dried chopped onion
1 tablespoon dried chopped celery*
2 teaspoons dried parsley
1½ teaspoons Chicken Soup Base (see
    index) or 2 tablespoons
    granulated bouillon
½ teaspoon sugar (optional)
¼ teaspoon sage
¼ teaspoon onion powder
¼ teaspoon poultry seasoning

Combine ingredients. Put in an airtight container and store in a cool place. To double or triple recipe, use 3 tablespoons plus 1 teaspoon seasoning for every 2 cups of crumbs.

Dressing: Combine 1 recipe dressing mix and 1 ¾ cups water in a saucepan. Add ¼ cup margarine or butter. Bring to a boil. Reduce heat, and simmer six minutes. Add 2 cups dry bread crumbs; cover, and let stand five minutes. Serve.

Corn Bread Dressing: Substitute 2 cups crumbled corn bread for bread crumbs.

Mushroom Dressing: Add 1 small can drained mushrooms, 1 tablespoon soy sauce, and ¼ cup chopped chestnuts.

*If you do not have dried celery, sauté ¼ cup chopped fresh celery in margarine or butter until tender. Add to water when making dressing.

Range-top Dressing Mix for Pork

1 tablespoon dried chopped onion
1 tablespoon dried chopped celery*
1 tablespoon dried parsley
1 teaspoon Chicken Soup Base (see
    index) or granulated bouillon
½ teaspoon Beef Soup Base (see index)
    or granulated bouillon
½ teaspoon sugar (optional)
¼ teaspoon sage
¼ teaspoon turmeric
½ teaspoon onion powder
¼ teaspoon poultry seasoning

Combine ingredients. Put in an airtight container and store in a cool place. To double or triple this recipe, use 4 tablespoons plus 1 teaspoon seasoning mix for every 2 cups crumbs and rice.

Dressing: Combine dressing mix and 1¾ cups water in saucepan. Add ¼ cup margarine or butter. Bring to a boil. Reduce heat, and simmer 6 minutes. Add 1 cup dry bread crumbs and 1 cup instant rice. Cover and let stand 5 minutes. Serve.

*If you do not have dried celery, sauté ¼ cup chopped celery in margarine or butter until tender. Add water when making dressing.

Horseradish

Fresh horseradish is more flavorful than dried horseradish, which develops a bitter taste if kept too long. Fresh horseradish is available in most grocery stores in early fall. It should not be kept for more than three months without being dried.

Peel the skin off the roots and grate or blend. Combine ¾ cup grated horseradish, ¼ cup vinegar, and salt and sugar to taste. This will keep well for 2 to 3 weeks in the refrigerator. One cup cooked, skinned, and grated beets may be added to the horseradish to mellow and sweeten the flavor.

Dry Horseradish

1 tablespoon horseradish powder
2 tablespoons water
½ cup cream, whipped
¼ teaspoon salt

Combine the horseradish powder and the water to make a paste. Add the whipped cream and salt. Chill.

Make Your Own Mustard

Once you have made mustard to fit your own personal taste, you will never want to buy commercial mustard again. Mustard flavoring is a matter of personal preference. The following recipes and ideas may help you create your own unique flavor, tailored to your individual taste.

Make up a small amount of mustard at a time, as the flavor changes rapidly. If the mustard is too hot, you can tone it down with milk, cream, olive oil, or mayonnaise. Vary the flavor by adding crushed garlic, sugar, or a variety of other spices. For a bright yellow color, add 1 teaspoon turmeric.

Mustard

½ cup dry mustard
4 to 6 tablespoons vinegar
½ teaspoon sugar
1 tablespoon melted butter
⅛ teaspoon salt

Make a paste with the dry mustard and vinegar. Add sugar, melted butter, and salt. Blend well.

French Mustard

½ cup tarragon vinegar
1 egg, beaten
3 tablespoons dry mustard
1 tablespoon sugar
1 tablespoon olive oil

Combine all ingredients except olive oil. Cook 3 to 4 minutes, stirring constantly. Remove from heat and cool. Add olive oil; mix thoroughly.

Spiced Mustard

5 tablespoons dry mustard
¼ cup mustard seed
½ cup hot water
1½ cups cider vinegar
½ teaspoon sugar
2 tablespoons flour
⅛ teaspoon cinnamon
⅛ teaspoon cloves
⅛ teaspoon allspice
⅛ teaspoon ginger

Soak dry mustard and mustard seed in hot water for 3 hours. Add remaining ingredients and bring to a boil. Remove from heat and let stand one hour. Blend in a blender or food processor. Cook in a double boiler for 10 minutes or until thick.

Make Your Own Vinegars and Dressings

Apple Cider Vinegar

Put fresh apple juice or sweet cider into a gallon glass jug, crock, or watertight wooden container. Cover the container with several layers of cheesecloth or a loose-weave cloth that will keep the insects and dust out but will allow the air in. Secure the cloth with a string or rubber band. Store in a cool, dark place, undisturbed, for 4 to 6 months. Taste the vinegar after about 4 months. When vinegar is strong enough for your taste, strain and seal in jars.

The cloudy clump of bacteria that forms on the bottom is called "mother." Save this "mother" as a starter for your next batch. Just add it to your container of juice and a little brown sugar or honey, and let it ferment. You will have vinegar in a much shorter time.

Once a lid is placed on your vinegar and air can no longer get in, the fermenting process will stop. Pasteurization will also stop the fermenting process and help your vinegar to keep better. Bring the vinegar to 145° F. and hold at that temperature for 30 minutes. Put in containers. Once the vinegar or "mother" has been pasteurized, you can no longer use it as a starter.

Vinegar used for pickling purposes should have an acidity of 4 to 6 percent. If at all possible, test your homemade vinegar before you use it in pickling to be sure it has the right acidity.

You can strengthen your homemade vinegar by putting it in the freezer. Only the water on top will freeze. Remove the ice before thawing.

For a variation in apple cider vinegar, add ½ cup molasses, honey, or brown sugar for every gallon of apple juice or pulp. This will feed the bacteria and help in the fermenting process. Other fresh fruit and fruit juices can also be added to your apple juice. Stir ingredients in and then do not disturb for two months.

Homemade Table Vinegar

Put 1 gallon distilled water, 1 quart molasses, and 1 pint yeast in a cask or jug. Cover with cheesecloth or muslin and leave in the sun, covering when it rains. In 3 to 4 weeks this will be good table vinegar. If cider is used in place of distilled water, the vinegar will ferment much sooner. In a week it will be very sharp—excellent for pickling purposes.

Very Strong Table Vinegar

Thoroughly mix 1 gallon good cider with 1 pound new honey. Pour in a cask or bottle and let stand for 4 to 6 months. You will have vinegar so strong that it cannot be used at the table without diluting with water. It is the best vinegar for pickling purposes.

Spiced Vinegar

1 tablespoon sugar
1 tablespoon celery seed
1 clove garlic
1 small onion, chopped
½ teaspoon prepared horseradish
  (optional)
1 quart cider vinegar
2 whole cloves
1 teaspoon peppercorns
1 teaspoon nutmeg
½ teaspoon mustard seed

Combine all ingredients and let stand 3 weeks. Strain and use.

Hot Vinegar

Add any of the following to vinegar: hot yellow, green, or red chili peppers or a combination of all three, and cayenne pepper. Optional—horseradish, curry powder, onion. Add 1 to 3 peppers to 1 quart vinegar and steep 3 to 6 weeks. Strain and bottle.

Herbed or Spiced Vinegar

You can use almost any herb or spice to flavor your vinegar. Use ½ cup fresh herbs or ¼ cup dried herbs for every quart of vinegar. Let steep 4 to 6 weeks (unless otherwise indicated in recipe below); then strain and bottle.

For quick flavor, bring the vinegar and herbs to a boil; cool, and allow to steep 2 weeks. It may also be brought to a boil and then simmered 20 minutes. Use immediately, or cap the vinegar and store it.

Basil: Steep for 1 week; then strain and bottle.

Mint: Steep 3 to 6 weeks; bottle and store. This is good in fruit salad dressings.

Dill: Use 3 dill heads or 3 tablespoons dill seed per quart of vinegar. This vinegar is good in potato, bean, or seafood salads.

Garlic: Use 2 or 3 cloves garlic per quart of vinegar. Add ½ teaspoon salt and 1 teaspoon peppercorns.

Tarragon: Use a few sprigs for each quart of vinegar.

Chive: Chop a handful and add to one quart of vinegar.

Celery Vinegar

1 quart vinegar
1 cup celery and tops, chopped
½ teaspoon salt
4 peppercorns

Bring vinegar to a boil and pour over remaining ingredients. Steep for 3 to 4 weeks. Strain and cap.

Cucumber Vinegar

10 large cucumbers, chopped
1 quart vinegar
2 shallots
1 tablespoon salt
2 tablespoons pepper
1 teaspoon cayenne pepper (optional)

Combine all ingredients. Let stand 4 or 5 days. Bring to a boil; then cool. Strain and cap. This vinegar is a nice addition to gravies, hashes, or salads, or to eat with cold meat.

Pineapple Vinegar

Cover sliced pineapple with pure cider vinegar. Let stand 3 or 4 days; then mash and strain. To every 3 quarts juice, add 5 pounds sugar. Bring to boil; boil 10 minutes. Skim carefully until nothing rises to the surface. Cool. Blackberries, raspberries, or any other strong-flavored fruit may be substituted for pineapple. Add 1 tablespoon pineapple vinegar to 1 cup of ice-cold water for a good warm-weather drink.

Raspberry Vinegar

Put 1 quart of raspberries in a dish. Pour over them 1 quart of good vinegar; let stand 24 hours. Strain through a cloth bag, and pour the liquid over another quart of berries. Do this for 3 or 4 days successively: then strain. Sweeten with sugar to taste; bottle and seal. Strawberries can be substituted for raspberries.

French Dressing

1 or 2 cloves garlic
¼ cup vinegar
¾ cup oil
¼ teaspoon salt
¼ teaspoon celery salt
½ teaspoon lemon peel
¼ teaspoon rosemary
1 teaspoon sugar
¼ teaspoon dry mustard
¼ teaspoon pepper
½ teaspoon paprika

Rub garlic on inside of a bowl or jar. Combine remaining ingredients; beat with a fork to blend. Chill.

Herb Salad Dressing

¼ cup vinegar
⅓ cup oil
¼ teaspoon dry mustard
¼ teaspoon salt
1 clove garlic, crushed
1 tablespoon oregano
1 tablespoon lemon peel
1 teaspoon rosemary
1 teaspoon marjoram

Combine all ingredients, mixing well. Chill.

Wheat
Meat

Wheat Meat

Wheat Meat is the term we use for imitation meat made from gluten, the complex mixture of proteins developed when wheat flour doughs are mixed. Gluten holds the yeast bubbles in bread, causing it to rise. When dough is washed in water, the starch and bran are washed away, leaving gluten, an insoluble elastic mass.

Wheat meat can be a nutritious alternative to meat. Prepared properly, it can have the tasty goodness and texture of real meat, making it difficult to tell the difference between the two. Wheat meat is so versatile that it can be made a variety of ways to taste and look like different kinds of meat.

For those who are looking for ways to prepare meatless meals because of cost or diet, wheat meat is an excellent substitute. It not only saves money but also satisfies the craving for meat. Wheat meat will not take the place of a top sirloin steak, but prepared in other ways, it can be made to taste like meat.

Wheat meat or gluten has no cholesterol and is high in protein, an important consideration for people with heart problems and on restricted diets. One-half cup wheat meat has the same amount of protein as three ounces of hamburger, with one-third fewer calories.

Though wheat meat is high in protein, it is not a complete protein; it is lacking in the amino acid lysine. In order to provide this amino acid, foods high in lysine should be served with the wheat meat. Some good sources of lysine are eggs, beans, milk products, nutritional yeast, soy products, and nuts.

At today's supermarket prices, it is becoming increasingly difficult for many families to buy meat. You can use two pounds of whole wheat flour to make 1¼ pounds of wheat meat. If you buy your own wheat and grind it into flour yourself, the savings are even greater. Even partial introduction of wheat meat into your meals will save you money.

Making wheat meat at home is an easy process that requires little time. A batch of raw wheat meat can be made in 15 to 30 minutes. Equipment needed includes a meat grinder, food processor, or blender; a large bowl or dishpan; and a colander.

Raw Wheat Meat 1
(Electric Bread Mixer Method)

**11 cups wheat flour (if white meat is
    desired, use white flour)**

7 cups water

1. Combine flour and water in mixer and mix with a dough hook for 5 minutes.
2. Take as much dough as you can comfortably work with. Place it in a colander sitting in a large bowl or dishpan. Cover the dough with warm water. Wash with in and out movements to loosen the gluten from the bran and starch. Work dough in the same water until it becomes the consistency of bubble gum. Repeat until all dough is used.
3. Hold dough under a small stream of water and rinse until water is clear and dough is elastic and rubbery. Do not try to wash all the bran out. You now have raw wheat meat or gluten.

Raw Wheat Meat 2 (Hand Method)

7 cups wheat flour
3 cups cool water

Mix flour and water into a dough. Pound dough with your fist or rubber mallet until it is smooth and elastic. (This should take 10 to 12 minutes.) Make a dough that is easy to work with, one that is not sticky or too stiff. Follow steps 2 and 3 for Electric Bread Mixer Method (above).

Raw Wheat Meat 3 (No-Knead Method)

7 cups wheat flour
3 cups cool water

Mix flour and water into a dough. Cover with cold water and let rest for 2 to 3 hours. Pour off water and mix until smooth. Follow steps 2 and 3 for Electric Bread Mixer Method (above).

Starch Water

Starch water has many nutrients that should not be wasted. Separate it from the bran and use it to thicken puddings, sauces, gravies, soups, and stews. Use it to replace the liquid in making bread or in baking. Pour it over animal food. Use it to reconstitute powdered milk. It is excellent for making hand lotion and floor wax and for watering plants.

Bran

Allow the starch water to settle. A layer of bran will form on the bottom of the pan, a layer of starch in the middle, and a layer of water on top. Carefully pour off the starch and water. Use the bran in making crackers, breads, and cereal, or in any recipe calling for bran.

When substituting bran for flour in recipes, use 1 cup bran for every 2 cups flour. Bran is a leavening agent and produces extra lightness in bread. It is high in potassium,

Seasoning Wheat Meat

The real secret of making wheat meat taste like real meat is in the seasoning. For this reason, you should read the chapter on seasonings and flavorings. The seasonings are what will make your wheat meat delicious and exciting. Listed here are some spices and seasonings for wheat meat. You should take the basic ideas and experiment until you find one or a combination that suits your family's taste.

1. *Homemade soup base:* For greater versatility, our homemade soup base (see index) is unsalted. This differs from the commercial soup bases or bouillon, which are salted. Because even homemade soup bases will differ in strength, we can only give you an approximation of how much it will take to season your wheat meat. You will have to experiment with seasoning and salts to taste. Use 1 to 2 tablespoons soup base (beef or chicken) to flavor 2 cups wheat meat, firmly packed. Add salt to taste.

To flavor the wheat meat like ham, add 2½ teaspoons each of beef soup base and chicken soup base, and a few drops of smoke flavoring.

2. *Commercial soup base:* These differ in taste. Some will be saltier than others and some are richer in flavor than others. Again, we give you an approximation of how much to use; you will have to experiment with your brand of soup base. In flavoring your wheat meat, add only enough soup base to give the amount of salt you like.

Commercial soup bases can be ordered through a local grocery store, restaurant, or cafe. Restaurant supply houses generally carry them or can order them for you. You may have to order in bulk. If so, ask others to share the expense and product with you. Stores that carry dehydrated foods may carry soup base or be able to order it. Some brands available are S.E.R., Schilling, McCormick, Lipton, and Wyler's. Use 5 tablespoons commercial soup base (beef or chicken) to flavor 2 cups wheat meat, firmly packed.

3. *Bouillon granules:* Bouillon does not have as strong or as good a flavor as homemade or commercial soup bases. It may be used if other bases are not available, or you may mix the granules with other

flavorings. Use 2 tablespoons bouillon granules to flavor each 2 cups wheat meat, firmly packed.

4. *Liquid seasoning:* Soy sauce, Kitchen Bouquet, and Worcestershire sauce can give your wheat meat a darker color and enhance the flavor. Use them in combination with soup base, bouillon, or onion soup mix. Use 1 tablespoon Kitchen Bouquet or Worcestershire sauce to flavor each 2 cups wheat meat, firmly packed. Or use 1 teaspoon soy sauce.

5. *Onion soup mix:* This may be used if nothing else is available. It adds good flavor to the wheat meat, but it can be expensive. Use ½ package onion soup mix for each 2 cups wheat meat, firmly packed.

To test the flavor of your wheat meat after you've added seasonings, make a small patty the size of a half-dollar and fry it in a small pan. Taste; add more seasoning if needed. If wheat meat is too salty, rinse it, dry it in the oven, and start again.

Ground Wheat Meat

Place raw gluten or wheat meat on a greased cookie sheet and bake at 350° F. for 30 to 45 minutes or until you have a porous glob. Remove from the oven and cool. Put wheat meat through a meat grinder or food processor with 1 medium onion and 1 clove garlic. Grind to the consistency of hamburger.

Tomato Wheat Meat Loaf

4 cups ground wheat meat
3½ tablespoons beef soup base
2 teaspoons soy sauce
3 eggs
1 cup bread crumbs
1 medium onion, chopped
1 medium tomato, chopped
1 clove garlic, chopped fine
2 tablespoons catsup
½ teaspoon basil
¼ teaspoon oregano

Combine ingredients, mixing well. Shape mixture in a loaf pan or casserole dish. Top with sauce (below). Bake at 350° F. for 50 to 60 minutes. Makes 6 to 8 servings.

Sauce: Combine ½ cup catsup, ¼ cup water, 2 tablespoons sugar or honey, and 1 tablespoon Worcestershire sauce. Mix well.

Variations: To meat loaf, add ¼ cup chopped green peppers, or ½ cup cubed cheese, or 1 small can drained green chilies and 1 teaspoon chili powder.

Wheat Meatball Stew (p. 20)

Wheat Meat Loaf and Gravy

4 cups ground wheat meat
3½ tablespoons beef soup base
3 eggs
¼ cup flour
¼ cup cornflake or bread crumbs
1 medium onion, chopped fine
2 tablespoons minced onion
¼ teaspoon black pepper
¼ teaspoon sage
⅛ teaspoon garlic powder
¼ teaspoon oregano
⅛ teaspoon nutmeg
2 tablespoons oil

Combine ingredients, mixing well. Shape mixture in a loaf pan or casserole dish. Bake at 350° F. for 50 to 60 minutes or until firm. Top with brown gravy (see index). Makes 6 to 8 servings.

Stuffed Wheat Meat Loaf

4 cups ground wheat meat
3 eggs
2 tablespoons flour
3½ tablespoons beef soup base
1 teaspoon Worcestershire sauce
2 tablespoons oil or bacon drippings
2 tablespoons tomato sauce or catsup
½ cup quick-cooking oats or bread crumbs
1 recipe Meat Loaf Spice (see index)
½ recipe Range-Top Dressing (see index)

Combine all ingredients except dressing. Put half the wheat meat mixture in a greased loaf pan. Cover with dressing, and top with remaining wheat meat mixture. Bake at 350° F. for 30 minutes. Slice and top with brown gravy (see index). Makes 6 to 8 servings.

Stuffed Peppers

3 medium peppers
2 quarts water
2 cups ground wheat meat
½ cup instant rice
4 teaspoons beef soup base
2 teaspoons flour
1 large egg
1 teaspoon Worcestershire sauce
¼ cup bread crumbs
¼ cup catsup

Cut off the tops of peppers, and wash and clean out seeds. Simmer peppers in water for 5 minutes; drain. Mix remaining ingredients together. Stuff peppers and set in a casserole dish. Top with sauce. Bake at 350° F. for 30 minutes.
Sauce: Combine one 8-ounce can tomato sauce, ¼ cup water, ¼ teaspoon salt, and ⅛ teaspoon chili powder. Pour over top of peppers.

Wheat Meat Burgers

2 cups ground wheat meat
1 large or 2 small eggs
2 teaspoons flour
5 teaspoons beef base
1 teaspoon Worcestershire sauce
2 tablespoons oil or bacon drippings

Combine all ingredients except oil or drippings, mixing well. Form into patties and fry in oil or drippings until brown. Serve on hamburger buns with mustard, catsup, onion, pickles, lettuce, and tomatoes.
Variations:
Top with barbecue sauce (for our basic barbecue sauce, see index). Simmer burgers 5 minutes.
Top with brown gravy (see index). Simmer burgers 5 minutes.
Top with a 10-ounce can cream of mushroom soup mixed with ½ cup milk. Simmer burgers 5 minutes.
Top with onion gravy (see index). Simmer burgers 5 minutes.

Chunky Wheat Meat

2 cups ground wheat meat
1 large or 2 small eggs
2 teaspoons flour
5 teaspoons beef soup base
1 teaspoon liquid seasoning, such as Kitchen Bouquet or Worcestershire sauce
2 tablespoons oil or bacon drippings

Combine all ingredients, mixing well. Spread on a greased cookie sheet, and bake at 275° F. for 20 to 30 minutes. Cool. Tear into small pieces to resemble hamburger.
Meat Extender: Add 2 cups Chunky Wheat Meat for every ½ pound hamburger.

Chunky Wheat Meat Sausage

Follow the recipe and procedure for Chunky Wheat Meat, but add 2 teaspoons sausage seasoning (see index) before baking.

Wheat Meatballs

Follow the recipe for Chunky Wheat Meat. Roll into walnut-size balls and bake on a well-greased cookie sheet, turning often to brown. Bake at 275° F. for 30 to 35 minutes. You can also fry meatballs in an oiled skillet until brown or cook in microwave oven until set. Add meatballs to dishes during last 10 to 15 minutes of cooking.

Chunky Wheat Meat Texas Chili

1 medium onion, diced
2 cloves garlic, diced
2 stalks celery, diced
2 tablespoons vegetable oil
1 teaspoon oregano
1 teaspoon pepper
2 tablespoons sugar
2 cups canned tomatoes
3 cans (8 ounces each) tomato sauce
1 cup cooked kidney beans
1 cup cooked pinto beans
1 can diced green chilies
2 cups Chunky Wheat Meat

Sauté onion, garlic, and celery in oil until tender. Add seasonings, sugar, tomatoes, tomato sauce, beans, and green chilies. Bring to a boil; reduce heat and simmer 30 minutes. Add wheat meat and cook 5 minutes. Makes 6 servings.

Sloppy Chunky Wheat Meat

¼ cup finely chopped celery
½ cup finely chopped onion
2 tablespoons vegetable oil
1 tablespoon brown sugar
2 cans (8 ounces each) tomato sauce
1 teaspoon mustard
1 tablespoon vinegar
1 tablespoon Worcestershire sauce
2 cups Chunky Wheat Meat

Sauté celery and onion in oil until almost tender. Add remaining ingredients except wheat meat, and simmer uncovered for 15 minutes. Add wheat meat and serve.

Use for Sloppy Joes, ravioli filling, or spaghetti sauce.

Chunky Chili

2 cups Chunky Wheat Meat
3 cups cooked and drained red kidney
    beans
1 cup chopped onion

½ cup chopped celery
2 cloves garlic, minced
3 tablespoons butter or margarine
1 can (28 ounces) tomatoes, chopped
1½ cups tomato juice
1 cup water
1 tablespoon soup base
1 or 2 tablespoons chili powder
Salt to taste
⅛ teaspoon cayenne

Add wheat meat to beans. In a large skillet sauté onion, celery, and garlic in butter until tender. Stir in bean mixture and remaining ingredients. Bring to a boil; reduce heat and simmer 10 minutes. Makes 6 to 8 servings.

Chunky Wheat Meat Stroganoff

1 medium onion, chopped
3 tablespoons margarine
2 tablespoons flour
1 teaspoon soup base
1 clove garlic, minced
⅛ teaspoon pepper
1 can (4 ounces) mushrooms
1 cup milk
1 cup sour cream or yogurt
2 cups Chunky Wheat Meat
3 cups cooked noodles or rice

In a large skillet, sauté onion in margarine until tender. Stir in flour, soup base, garlic, pepper, and mushrooms. Stir in milk and bring to a boil; reduce heat and simmer uncovered for 10 minutes. Stir in sour cream and wheat meat. Serve over noodles or rice. Makes 4 to 6 servings.

Cabbage Rolls

2 cups water
1 tablespoon vinegar
1 teaspoon salt
1 medium cabbage
1 medium onion, diced
2 tablespoons butter
2 cups cooked rice
2 cups Chunky Wheat Meat
2 cans (10 ounces each) tomato soup
1 soup can water

Bring water to a boil in a 4-quart saucepan. Add vinegar and salt. Core cabbage and add to boiling liquid. Simmer until leaves become soft and are easy to remove.

As leaves become tender, remove them from boiling water and cool.

Sauté onion in butter until tender. Add rice, wheat meat, and 1 can tomato soup. Spoon wheat meat mixture in cabbage leaves and fold over. Stack in a pan or casserole dish. Mix 1 can tomato soup with 1 can water and pour over cabbage rolls. Bake uncovered at 350° F. 45 minutes. Makes 6 to 8 servings.

Chunky Wheat Meat Pie

½ cup diced onion
1 tablespoon butter or margarine
½ teaspoon soup base
⅛ teaspoon pepper
2 cups green beans, cooked
1 cup tomato soup
2 cups Chunky Wheat Meat
5 medium potatoes, cooked
½ cup milk
1 clove garlic, crushed
Salt and pepper to taste
½ cup shredded cheese

Sauté onion in butter until tender. Add soup base, pepper, green beans, and tomato soup. Add wheat meat. Pour into greased casserole dish. Mash potatoes while hot. Add milk, garlic, salt, and pepper to potatoes. Spread over wheat meat mixture. Sprinkle with cheese. Bake at 350° F. 20 to 30 minutes. Makes 4 to 6 servings.

Chunky Hash

1 can (28 ounces) or 3½ cups tomatoes
1 cup chopped green peppers
½ cup chopped onions
½ cup uncooked rice
½ teaspoon beef soup base
½ teaspoon basil
Dash pepper
2 cups Chunky Wheat Meat
1 cup grated cheese

In a skillet, combine all ingredients except wheat meat and cheese. Simmer, covered, until rice is tender. Add wheat meat, top with cheese, and return to heat until cheese is melted. Makes 4 to 6 servings.

Wheat Meat Chili-Roni

2 tablespoons oil
2 medium onions, chopped
1 cup chopped green pepper
1 cup uncooked elbow macaroni
1 can (8 ounces) tomato sauce
1 can (12 ounces) or 1½ cups tomatoes
2 teaspoons chili powder
1 teaspoon salt
⅛ teaspoon cayenne pepper
⅛ teaspoon paprika
1 can (15½ ounces) or 2 cups cooked
   kidney beans
2 cups Chunky Wheat Meat

Heat oil in large skillet. Add onion and green pepper; sauté until tender. Stir in remaining ingredients, except wheat meat. Cover and simmer 20 minutes or until macaroni is tender. Add wheat meat; simmer 3 minutes. Makes 6 servings.

Shepherd's Pie

2 cups Chunky Wheat Meat
1 recipe Brown Gravy (see index)
2 cups mixed vegetables (peas, carrots,
   green beans, onions, celery),
   cooked and drained
3 cups seasoned hot mashed potatoes

Combine wheat meat, gravy, and mixed vegetables. Pour into a 2-quart casserole dish. Top with potatoes. Bake at 400° F. for 20 minutes. Makes 6 servings.

Lasagna

1 tablespoon sugar
1 can (16 ounces) or 2 cups tomatoes
2 cans (6 ounces each) tomato paste
2 cloves garlic, minced
1 teaspoon salt
½ teaspoon pepper
½ teaspoon oregano
1 teaspoon sweet basil
4 cups Chunky Wheat Meat
1 package (8 ounces) lasagna noodles
   or homemade noodles
3 cups cottage cheese
1 tablespoon parsley
⅓ cup Parmesan cheese
1 beaten egg
1 pound Swiss or mozzarella cheese,
   sliced

In a 3-quart saucepan combine sugar, tomatoes, tomato paste, garlic, salt, pepper, oregano, and sweet basil. Simmer uncovered for 30 minutes. Add wheat meat and remove from heat. Cook lasagna noodles as directed on package; drain. Combine cottage cheese, parsley, Parmesan cheese, and egg. In a greased 13″ x 9″ x 2″ baking dish place a layer of noodles; spread with half the cottage cheese mixture, then half the sauce. Add a layer of mozzarella cheese. Repeat with the remaining ingredients. Bake uncovered at 325° F. 20 to 30 minutes. Makes 10 to 12 servings.

Wheat Meatball Stroganoff

2 cups cream of mushroom soup (see index) or 1 can (10 ounces) mushroom soup mixed with ½ cup milk
½ cup water
3 teaspoons soup base
1 cup sour cream or yogurt
12 meatballs made with wheatmeat

Combine soup, water, and soup base in a saucepan. Simmer 10 minutes. Add sour cream and simmer 5 minutes more. Add meatballs and simmer another 5 minutes. Serve with noodles. Makes 4 servings.

Wheat Meatball Stew

2 tablespoons butter or margarine
2 tablespoons soup base
1 quart water
1 tablespoon minced onion
2 teaspoons parsley
1 teaspoon onion powder
2 bay leaves
1 teaspoon Worcestershire sauce
3 medium potatoes, peeled and cubed
1 cup celery, chopped
3 medium carrots, sliced
1 medium onion, quartered
Dash of cayenne
½ cup water
¼ cup flour
12 to 16 meatballs made with wheat meat

Combine butter or margarine and soup base in a large saucepan; stir over medium heat until blended. Add remaining ingredients except the ½ cup water, the flour, and the meatballs. Simmer 20 minutes or until vegetables are tender. Dissolve flour in ½ cup water and add to stew. Cook until thick. Add meatballs and cook until heated through, 2 to 3 minutes. Makes 6 servings.

Spaghetti and Wheat Meatballs

2 tablespoons butter or margarine
2 tablespoons beef soup base
2 cans (16 ounces each) or 4 cups tomatoes
2 cans (6 ounces each) tomato paste
2½ cups water

3 tablespoons minced onion
2½ teaspoons seasoned salt
1½ teaspoons basil
¾ teaspoon oregano
1 teaspoon brown sugar
12 to 16 Wheat Meatballs
1 pound spaghetti
Parmesan cheese

Combine butter or margarine and soup base in a large saucepan; stir over medium heat until blended. Add remaining ingredients except meatballs, spaghetti, and cheese. Simmer for 20 minutes. Cook spaghetti according to package directions. Drain. Add meatballs to spaghetti sauce and cook until heated through, 2 to 3 minutes. Serve spaghetti with sauce and meatballs. Top with Parmesan cheese. Makes 4 to 6 servings.

Wheat Meat Steaks

Raw Wheat Meat (see index)
2 tablespoons soup base
2 cups water
2 tablespoons Worcestershire sauce
2 tablespoons fat or drippings, or bones or scraps of meat
⅓ cup milk
1 egg, beaten
Flour or seasoned coating (below)

Slice ¼- to ½-inch slices of Raw Wheat Meat. Roll or stretch into desired shapes, ⅛- to ¼-inch thick. Combine soup base, water, Worcestershire sauce, and fat or drippings (use bones or scraps of meat for a meatier flavor); bring to simmer. Drop steaks into broth and simmer for 15 to 30 minutes, according to thickness of the steaks. Do not boil. Two cups of broth should be sufficient for 4 to 6 steaks.

When most of the broth has been absorbed, remove the steaks and pat dry with a paper towel. Place steaks on a greased cookie sheet and bake at 325° F. for 20 minutes, or longer if you desire a chewy steak. Cool.

Combine milk and egg. Dip steaks in egg-milk mixture and roll in flour or seasoned coating (below). Fry in hot oil or bacon drippings on each side until brown. Steaks may be used immediately or frozen for later use.

Seasoned Coating: Combine 1 cup bread, cracker, or cornflake crumbs; 1 tablespoon grated Parmesan cheese; 2 tablespoons instant nonfat dry milk; 1 teaspoon paprika; 1 teaspoon pepper; ½ teaspoon onion powder; and 1 teaspoon dry mustard.

Variations: For Chicken-Fried Wheat Meat Steak, top steaks with brown gravy (see index). For Chicken Burgers, flavor steaks with chicken soup base. Serve on hamburger buns, topped with tartar sauce (see index).

For Wheat Meat Cubes or Slices, roll Raw Wheat

Wheat Meat Steaks (p. 21) with Brown Gravy (p. 113) and mushrooms

Meat ¼- to ½-inch thick, and cut into cubes or slices with a knife or scissors. Proceed as for Wheat Meat Steaks. Add to stews or casseroles.

Mock Chicken Legs

Wheat meat cubes, chicken-flavored
    (see Wheat Meat Steaks, above)
2 eggs, beaten
½ cup milk
Cracker crumbs or seasoned coating
Oil or bacon drippings

Place 1-inch cubes of wheat meat on a wooden skewer. Mix eggs and milk. Dip skewer into egg mixture and roll in cracker crumbs or coating. Cook in hot oil or drippings until browned. Cover and steam for 15 minutes. Makes 6 to 8 servings.

Wheat Meat Pepper Steak

2 medium onions, sliced
¼ teaspoon pepper
1 teaspoon soup base
2 tablespoons soy sauce
1 tablespoon Worcestershire sauce
Few drops Tabasco sauce
1 cup water

1 clove garlic, minced
1 can (16 ounces) tomatoes
3 medium green peppers, sliced
1 can (4 ounces) mushrooms
6 Wheat Meat Steaks, sliced into thin
    strips
3 tablespoons cornstarch
¼ cup cold water

Combine in a saucepan all ingredients except steaks, cornstarch, and cold water. Bring to a boil and reduce heat. Simmer 20 minutes. Add steak slices and cook 15 minutes more. Mix cornstarch and cold water and use to thicken steak mixture. Serve over rice or noodles.

Steak Roll-ups

1 teaspoon poultry seasoning
1 cup water
2 tablespoons margarine
1 cup dry bread crumbs
8 medium Wheat Meat Steaks
2 cups mushroom soup (see index) or
    1 can (10 ounces) mushroom soup
    mixed with ⅓ cup milk

Combine poultry seasoning and water in saucepan. Add margarine. Bring to boil; reduce heat and simmer 5 minutes. Add bread crumbs. Remove from heat and let stand 5 minutes.

Place one heaping tablespoon stuffing in center of each steak. Roll steak and secure with a toothpick. Place in a casserole dish and top with mushroom soup (or brown gravy, if you prefer). Cover, and bake at 350° F. for 30 minutes.

Variation: For Chicken Roll-ups, use chicken-flavored steaks. Top with chicken gravy or basic barbecue sauce (see index). Stuff with grated cheese and mushrooms.

Swiss Steak

6 to 8 Wheat Meat Steaks
2 eggs and ¼ cup milk, beaten together
Seasoned flour
Oil or drippings
2 medium onions, chopped
1 clove garlic, chopped
⅓ cup chopped green pepper
2 cups tomato juice
½ teaspoon chili powder
1 teaspoon sugar
⅛ teaspoon rosemary
⅛ teaspoon oregano
⅛ teaspoon basil
1 cup chopped celery

Dip steaks in egg and milk mixture and roll in seasoned flour. Brown in hot oil on both sides. Combine remaining ingredients in saucepan; simmer 20 minutes. Pour over steaks and cook 20 minutes.

Veal Parmesan with Spaghetti

½ cup chopped onion
¼ cup chopped green pepper
2 tablespoons olive oil
1 can (16 ounces) or 2 cups tomatoes
2 cans (8 ounces each) tomato sauce
1 can (6 ounces) tomato paste
1 clove garlic, minced
1 teaspoon dried parsley
1 teaspoon oregano
1 teaspoon sweet basil
1 pound spaghetti
6 medium Wheat Meat Steaks
1 cup grated cheese

Sauté onion and green pepper in oil until tender. Stir in tomatoes, tomato sauce, tomato paste, garlic, parsley, oregano, and sweet basil. Simmer 30 minutes, stirring occasionally. Cook spaghetti according to package directions; drain. Stir half the sauce into spaghetti. Add Wheat Meat Steaks to remaining sauce and top with cheese. Cover pan; simmer 5 minutes. Arrange spaghetti and meat on platter. Makes 6 servings.

Wheat Meat Roast

1 recipe Raw Wheat Meat
3 tablespoons butter or margarine
3 tablespoons beef soup base
2 cups water
1 tablespoon soy sauce
2 tablespoons minced onion
¼ teaspoon garlic powder
½ teaspoon Kitchen Bouquet
Brown gravy (optional)

Shape raw wheat meat into a small ball the size of a roast. Place butter or margarine and soup base in medium saucepan; stir over heat until combined. Add remaining ingredients; bring to a boil. Add roast; simmer 4 hours. Cool. Refrigerate in liquid 8 to 12 hours or overnight. Place on a greased cookie sheet and bake at 300° F. for 1 hour or until a meat texture is obtained. Cool and slice very thin. Cover slices with brown gravy (see index) or dip in gravy and serve on toasted bread or buns.

Wheat Meat Jerky

4 cups water
2 tablespoons fat drippings
2 tablespoons ham base
1 teaspoon garlic powder
1 tablespoon Worcestershire sauce
2 tablespoons beef soup base
1½ teaspoons Kitchen Bouquet
Raw Wheat Meat
2 tablespoons liquid smoke
Hickory salt
Pepper (optional)

Bring water and fat to a boil. Add ham base, garlic powder, Worcestershire sauce, beef soup base, and Kitchen Bouquet. Roll out wheat meat into thin strips. Drop strips in seasoned water. Turn down heat; simmer until wheat meat has absorbed most of the liquid. Add liquid smoke; simmer 5 minutes longer. Remove strips and arrange on a lightly greased cookie sheet. Sprinkle with hickory salt and pepper, if desired. Place in a 275° F. oven; bake until strips are very chewy but not dry. Turn off oven and let strips set until dry.

For bacon-flavored bits, put the dry jerky into a blender and chop, or cut jerky into small pieces with a knife.

Wheat: Breads and Desserts

Cooking with Wheat

Wheat, often called the staff of life, is an important basic item of food storage. In addition to being nutritious, it is also versatile as an ingredient for breads, casseroles, cereals, desserts, and even meat substitutes (see the section on wheat meat).

Wheat is generally either hard or soft. Hard wheat contains the gluten necessary for bread making. Soft wheat, with less gluten, is used in cakes, muffins, pancakes, biscuits, and pastas. Wheat can also be ground in all grades of coarseness, from fine for baking to extra coarse for pilaf or cracked-wheat cereal.

Wheat or bread flour, either white or whole wheat, is high in gluten and is used in recipes in which yeast is also used. Stone-ground whole-wheat flour is ground with stones and should be fine and powdery.

Whole-wheat pastry flour, made from soft wheat, has less gluten than bread flour. It may be ground from soft wheat or purchased at health-food stores. Lower in protein than wheat or bread flour, it is suitable for quick breads, pastries, and pastas, and should be sifted before being used.

All-purpose flour is a blend of hard and soft wheat and may be used in most household baking.

Cake flour is made from soft wheat and has very small particles, making it ideal for finer-textured cakes.

Self-rising flour contains both salt and baking powder, making it convenient to measure. It cannot be used in recipes that call for yeast, however.

Here are some helpful hints for using wheat:

1. Whole-wheat flour should be refrigerated or frozen to preserve the flavor, nutrition, and freshness. Bring the flour back to room temperature for use in recipes calling for yeast.

2. You will get your best results with a finely ground flour. Coarse flour will make a difference in your recipe.

3. Always sift whole-wheat pastry flour before measuring it.

4. One cup wheat will make 1½ cups flour after grinding.

5. Whole-wheat pastry flour can be substituted for all-purpose flour in any cake, cookie, or quick-bread recipe.

6. Scald raw milk before using it in yeast bread recipes.

Whole-wheat Bread (p. 27); Whole-wheat Rolls (p. 27); Italian Bread Sticks (p. 27); French Bread (p. 28)

7. The more yeast you add to bread, the quicker the dough will rise and the greater the nutritional value will be. A yeasty flavor does not result from too much yeast; rather, it is a result of having the dough rise at too warm a temperature.

Nutty Wheat Cereal

3½ cups whole-wheat flour
½ cup brown sugar
1 teaspoon baking soda
1 teaspoon salt
2 tablespoons lemon juice or vinegar
2 cups milk
½ cup raisins (optional)
½ cup nuts (optional)

Combine flour, brown sugar, baking soda, and salt in a large mixing bowl. Combine lemon juice or vinegar and milk; then add to dry ingredients, stirring until blended. Spread mixture ½-inch thick on a greased cookie sheet. Bake at 350° F. for 15 to 20 minutes. Remove from oven and cool. Put into blender or food grinder to make coarse crumbs. Return to oven and toast for 15 to 20 minutes, or until no moisture remains. Add raisins and nuts. Put in an airtight container and store in a dry place.

Leavening Agents

Doughs and batters are leavened by water vapor, air, and carbon dioxide. Vapor is formed from the liquid; air is formed by beating or adding egg whites; carbon dioxide is formed by a chemical reaction of baking soda with acid or by microorganisms.

An acid, such as sour milk, molasses, or fruit juice, is required when using baking soda. The acid releases the carbon dioxide. Baking powder contains the acid required to release carbon dioxide. It is made by mixing baking soda, cornstarch or other diluent, and an acid-reacting material. Good results can be achieved with any of the types of baking powders if they are mixed properly and in the right amounts.

Yeast and sourdough are bacteria leavening agents. The yeast reacts with sugar, producing carbon dioxide and alcohol. The sugar can come from the flour itself or from added sugar.

Baked products sometimes fail to rise properly at altitudes higher than 3,000 feet because of reduced atmospheric pressure, which makes the leavening gases expand more. This stretches the cell walls, causing them to break. Reducing the amount of leavening agent used will increase the strength of the cell walls. This can be done by decreasing the amount of sugar and baking powder used and sometimes by increasing the amount of liquid.

Biscuits and muffins can be made without changing the recipe or with only a slight decrease in baking powder. No adjustments are necessary in yeast products, although rising times may be shorter.

No general rule can be given that will adapt successfully to all cake recipes. However, a guideline is given. You will have to experiment to get the correct proportions. The higher the altitude, the greater the change required.

For altitudes over 3,000 feet, add 2 to 4 tablespoons additional liquid and decrease baking powder by ⅛ to ½ teaspoon. Sugar may also be decreased by as much as 2 tablespoons.

If you reside in an area above 3,000 elevation, contact your local county extension agent for guidance on adapting recipes for high altitudes.

Everlasting Yeast

1 potato, peeled
4½ cups potato water
1½ teaspoons sugar
1 teaspoon salt
1 tablespoon dry yeast

Cook potato in water until tender. Drain, saving the water. Mash potato and add sugar and salt. Cool. Add potato water and dry yeast. Cover and set in a warm place until fermentation has stopped (when no bubbling occurs when jar is shaken). Cover jar loosely and store.

Dried Alum Yeast

2 cups flour
Boiling water
1 teaspoon powdered alum
1 teaspoon salt
2 tablespoons sugar
1 tablespoon dry yeast
½ cup warm water
Cornmeal

Add enough boiling water to flour to make a thick batter. Cool to lukewarm. Add alum, salt, sugar, and yeast dissolved in warm water. Cover and set in a warm place 4 to 6 hours. Stir and add enough cornmeal to make a stiff dough. Spread on a cookie sheet and put in a well-ventilated place out of the sun. To make a powder, crumble with hands or process in a blender. Use 1½ to 2 tablespoons powder in 2 cups warm water for leavening.

Wild Yeast

½ to ¾ cup juniper berries
2 cups flour
2 cups lukewarm water

Put juniper berries in a quart jar. Add flour and water; stir. Screw the lid on loosely to allow the gas from the fermenting berries to escape and yet protect the yeast culture from contamination. Set in a warm place for 2 days or until tiny bubbles appear. Strain to remove berries. Use yeast in recipes calling for yeast. To keep wild yeast active, add flour and water just as you would for sourdough starter.

Hops Yeast Cakes

1 cup dried hops (available at herb
 shops or health food stores)
1 dried yeast cake or 1 tablespoon
 yeast granules
½ cup warm water
1 cup flour
1 cup potato water
1 cup mashed potatoes
2 tablespoons sugar
4 cups cornmeal

Put hops in a small saucepan with just enough water to cover; simmer 1 minute. Strain hops through a sieve; reserve the water. Dissolve yeast in ½ cup warm water. Combine flour and potato water in a pan and mix to form a thick paste. Add dissolved yeast, mashed potatoes, and sugar. Mix well. Add enough hops water to make a medium-soft dough. Let rise until double in bulk. Punch down and work in enough cornmeal to make a stiff dough. Roll out ½-inch thick on a board and cut into 2-inch-square cakes. Dry, turning often. Hang in a cloth bag in a dry place. Use yeast cakes within 6 months. Reserve one yeast cake as the basis for your next batch of yeast.

To use in making bread, add a 2-inch cake of yeast to 2 cups warm water and 1 teaspoon sugar. Mix in enough flour to make a soft sponge for your bread.

Baking Powder

There are basically three types of baking powder: (1) double-acting (such as Calumet, Clabber Girl, Crescent); (2) phosphate (such as Rumford, Dr. Price); and (3) tartrate (such as Royal, Swansdown). Most of the recipes in this book were tested with double-acting baking powder. To adjust recipes for different types of baking powder, use 2½ teaspoons of phosphate or 3 teaspoons of tartrate for every 2 teaspoons of double-acting baking powder called for in the recipe. *(Continued)*

To make your own baking powder, combine 1 part soda to 2 parts cream of tartar and 1 part cornstarch or flour. Use 2 teaspoons of homemade baking powder for every cup of flour called for in recipe.

Breads and Rolls

Gluten Flour

Gluten flour improves volume and elasticity of whole-wheat breads and rolls. Used with lower quality wheat flour, it also gives better results.

To make gluten flour, follow the instructions for making raw wheat meat or gluten (see index).

Place raw gluten in a greased pan or on a cookie sheet. Bake at 350° F. for 30 to 40 minutes. Remove from oven and cool.

Put gluten through a meat grinder or food processor, or grate on a large grate. Spread ground gluten on a cookie sheet and dry in a 200° F. oven or in a dehydrator until no moisture remains.

Grind gluten granules in a stone grinder. Replace ½ cup wheat flour with ½ cup gluten flour for every 10 to 12 cups flour called for in recipe. Or, to ensure the safety of your grinder, mix ½ cup wheat with ½ cup ground gluten and grind in stone grinder. Replace 1 cup wheat flour with 1 cup gluten flour mixture for every 10 to 12 cups flour called for in recipe.

Whole-Wheat Bread

3 tablespoons yeast
½ cup warm water
5 cups hot water
7 cups whole-wheat flour
½ cup gluten flour (optional)
2 eggs (optional)
⅔ cup honey
⅔ cup cooking oil
2 tablespoons salt
6 cups whole-wheat flour

In a small bowl dissolve yeast in ½ cup warm water; set aside. In a large mixing bowl, combine hot water, 7 cups whole-wheat flour, and gluten flour. Beat vigorously with a wooden spoon or electric mixer until smooth. Add yeast mixture, eggs, honey, oil, and salt. Beat until smooth. Add 4 cups whole-wheat flour. Mix well. Let stand 15 minutes; then turn dough out onto a floured board and knead in 1 to 2 cups wheat flour—enough to form a smooth, elastic dough.

Put dough into a greased bowl; cover. Let stand in a warm place for at least 30 minutes or until double in bulk.

Turn onto a greased board and divide into 4 equal portions. Form loaves and place in greased loaf pans. Let rise until double in bulk. Bake at 350° F. for 30 to 45 minutes. Bake 15 minutes longer if you like your bread crusty.

If desired, the dough can be mixed the night before and set in the refrigerator overnight. Substitute cool water for the 5 cups of hot water so the dough will not rise too rapidly.

Whole-Wheat Bread (Mixer Method)

4 tablespoons yeast
¾ cup warm water
7½ cups hot water
10 cups unsifted whole-wheat flour
1 cup honey
1 cup cooking oil
3 tablespoons salt
2 eggs (optional)
½ cup gluten flour (optional)
10 to 12 cups whole-wheat flour

In a small bowl, dissolve yeast in ¾ cup warm water. Combine hot water and 10 cups whole-wheat flour in bread mixer. Mix on low speed while adding honey, oil, salt, and eggs. Mix until well blended; add yeast. Add gluten flour and whole-wheat flour until bread begins to pull away from sides of bowl. Knead dough on low speed for ten minutes. Remove dough from mixer and form into 5 or 6 loaves, depending on size of pans. Cover and let rise until double in bulk, about 30 minutes. Bake at 350° F. for 35 to 40 minutes. For a soft crust, brush tops of loaves with butter or margarine.

Italian Bread Sticks

Roll out Whole-Wheat Bread dough after its first rising. Cut into strips and roll in fine cornmeal. Place on greased cookie sheet and bake at 400° F. for 8 to 10 minutes, or until browned. If desired, brush with beaten egg white and coat with sesame seeds or salt before baking.

Whole-Wheat Buns or Rolls in 60 Minutes

4 cups warm water
1 cup cooking oil
¾ cup sugar or ½ cup honey
6 tablespoons dry yeast
1 tablespoon salt
3 eggs
11 to 12 cups whole-wheat flour

Combine water, oil, sugar or honey, and yeast in a large mixing bowl. Let set 10 minutes. Add salt, eggs, and flour. Shape into dinner rolls, cinnamon rolls, or hamburger buns. Let rise about 10 minutes or until double in bulk. Bake at 375° F. for 15 minutes.

French Bread

2½ cups warm water
1 teaspoon sugar
3 tablespoons dry yeast
7 to 8 cups flour
2 tablespoons softened butter or
    margarine
1 tablespoon salt
Cornmeal
1 egg white
1 tablespoon cold water

In a small bowl, combine ½ cup of the warm water, the sugar, and the yeast; set aside. Combine 1 cup warm water with 1 cup flour and beat until smooth. Add butter or margarine, salt, yeast mixture, 1 cup flour, and remaining 1 cup water. Beat 2 minutes. Stir in enough additional flour to make a stiff dough. Turn onto a floured board and knead until smooth and elastic. Cover and let stand 15 minutes. Cut dough in half, form into loaves, and place on a greased baking sheet sprinkled with cornmeal. Let rise until double in bulk. Gently brush tops of loaves with egg white beaten with cold water. Make shallow slits diagonally across loaves with a sharp knife. Bake at 350° F. for 40 minutes. Cool on rack.

Hamburger or Hot Dog Buns

2 tablespoons dry yeast
½ cup warm water
6 to 7 cups flour
⅓ cup dry milk solids
¼ cup sugar or honey
1 tablespoon salt
½ cup cooking oil or shortening
2 cups hot water

In a small bowl, dissolve yeast in ½ cup warm water; set aside. In a large mixing bowl, combine 2 cups flour, dry milk, sugar or honey, salt, and oil or shortening. Gradually add hot water and beat 2 minutes. Add yeast mixture and beat 2 minutes. Stir in remaining flour to make a stiff dough. Turn out on a floured board and knead until smooth and elastic (8 to 10 minutes). Place in a greased bowl and cover. Let rise in a warm place until double in bulk. Punch down and let rise another 20 minutes. Shape into hamburger or hot dog buns or dinner rolls, if desired, and place on greased baking sheet. Let rise until double in bulk. Bake at 400° F. for 10 to 12 minutes. If desired, brush buns with a mixture of 1 beaten egg white and 2 tablespoons water, and sprinkle with sesame seeds.

English Muffins

1 cup hot milk
2 tablespoons sugar
1½ teaspoons salt
3 tablespoons softened margarine or
    shortening
1 cup warm water
1 tablespoon dry yeast
6 cups flour
Cornmeal

Combine milk, sugar, salt, and margarine in a large mixing bowl. In a small bowl, dissolve yeast in warm water; stir into milk mixture. Add 3 cups flour and beat 2 minutes. Add enough additional flour to make a smooth, elastic dough. Turn onto a floured board and knead 2 minutes. Place in a greased bowl and cover. Let rise in a warm place until double in bulk. Punch down, then let rise an additional 45 minutes. Roll out ½-inch thick on a lightly floured surface. Cut into 3-inch circles. Place on a greased baking sheet sprinkled with cornmeal. Let rise until double in bulk. Heat a greased skillet or griddle. Cook muffins 8 to 10 minutes on each side, or until well browned. Cool on racks. Split in half and toast.

Whole-Wheat Muffins

2 cups whole-wheat pastry flour
3 teaspoons baking powder
½ teaspoon salt
2 tablespoons brown sugar or honey
1 cup milk or sour milk
⅓ cup cooking oil
1 egg

In a large mixing bowl, combine dry ingredients, and form a well. In a smaller mixing bowl, combine milk, oil, and egg; add to dry ingredients. Stir until flour is moistened. Batter will be lumpy. Bake at 400° F. for 20 minutes. Makes 12 muffins.

Blueberry Muffins: Fold in 1 cup frozen, fresh, or well-drained canned blueberries.

Apple-Nut Muffins: Add ¾ cup chopped apples, ½ cup nuts, and ½ teaspoon cinnamon.

Cranberry Muffins: Add 1 cup chopped raw cranberries mixed with ½ cup brown sugar.

Banana Muffins: Reduce liquid to ½ cup. Add ½ cup mashed bananas and ¼ teaspoon nutmeg.

Whole-Wheat Pancakes

2 cups whole-wheat pastry flour, sifted
4 teaspoons baking powder
2 tablespoons sugar
1 teaspoon salt

1½ cups milk or sour milk
¼ cup cooking oil
2 eggs

Combine flour, baking powder, sugar, and salt in a large mixing bowl. Make a well. Combine milk, oil, and eggs, and add to flour mixture. Stir just until moistened. Pour onto a preheated greased griddle or skillet. Cook until cakes are full of bubbles and undersurface is nicely browned. Lift with a pancake turner or spatula and brown the other side. Serve immediately.

Waffles: Increase oil to ¾ cup, and decrease milk to 1 cup. Cook as manufacturer directs for your type of waffle iron.

Light Sweet Rolls

2 tablespoons dry yeast
1 teaspoon sugar
½ cup warm water
1 cup shortening
½ cup sugar
2 teaspoons salt
1 cup boiling water
4 eggs
7½ cups flour
1 cup cold water

Combine yeast, sugar, and warm water in a small bowl; set aside. In a large mixing bowl, cream shortening, sugar, and salt. Add 1 cup boiling water. Cool to lukewarm. Beat in eggs and add yeast mixture. Beat in flour and cold water. Do not knead. Refrigerate 2 hours or more. Roll dough out on floured board. Sprinkle dough with sugar and cinnamon and dot with butter. Roll up as for jelly roll, pressing down edge firmly. Cut into 1-inch slices. Place in a greased baking pan or cookie sheet and let rise until double in bulk. Bake at 400° F. for 12 to 15 minutes.

Pizza Dough

1 tablespoon dry yeast
1 cup warm water
2 teaspoons sugar
1 teaspoon salt
2 tablespoons olive or salad oil
3 to 3½ cups flour

In a large mixing bowl, dissolve yeast in warm water. Add sugar, salt, oil, and 2 cups flour. Beat until smooth. Add additional flour to make a stiff dough. Turn onto a floured board and knead until smooth and elastic, about 5 minutes. Place in a large greased bowl and cover. Let rise about 45 minutes or until double in bulk. Grease two pizza pans or baking sheets. Divide dough in half, and form pizza crust in pans by pressing with palms of hands. Top with desired fillings, and bake at 425° F. for 20 to 25 minutes.

Danish Dumplings

2 cups fine, dry bread crumbs
½ teaspoon cinnamon
½ teaspoon baking soda
Salt and pepper to taste
Sour cream or buttermilk
2 eggs
½ cup chicken broth
Flour

Combine bread crumbs, cinnamon, baking soda, salt, and pepper. Add enough sour cream or buttermilk to soak up crumbs. Mix in eggs and chicken broth. Add enough flour to make a very stiff dough, almost like a biscuit dough. Drop by teaspoonfuls into boiling soup. Dumplings will float to the top when they are cooked.

Croutons

Cut dry, stale bread into ½-inch cubes. Drop into 1-inch deep very hot fat. When cubes are browned, remove and drain. Or butter one side of thin slices of bread and cut into small squares. Put in a baking pan, buttered side up, and brown under broiler.

Cheese Croutons

½ cup butter or margarine
½ cup Parmesan cheese
10 slices old French bread

Combine butter and cheese. Spread on both sides of bread slices; cut bread into cubes. Heat a skillet with enough oil or butter to coat the bottom. Drop bread cubes into hot skillet and cook until toasted. Add more butter or oil to pan, if needed, and shake pan to prevent sticking. Serve croutons on soups or salads.

Sourdough

Sourdough was an important provision for the pioneers; they carried it with them in crocks, valuing it as a solution to their baking problems because there was no fear of dead yeast. Today it is still a popular ingredient in the cuisine of many countries.

Laboratory tests have shown that sourdough contains more protein for its size and weight than just about any other food. It also provides the necessary bacteria to aid in digestion.

Sourdough starters can be never-ending. Some say the older the starter, the better and more tangy the flavor. Sourdough is a natural leavening ingredient and contains no preservatives.

Though sourdough does not spoil easily, it must be well cared for. Here are some suggestions for its use:

1. Never use a metal pot or metal spoon. A wooden spoon is a must for mixing sourdough.

2. Sourdough works best when the room temperature is between 65° and 77° F.

3. When traveling with sourdough, be sure to keep it cool. Heat and pressure will cause sourdough to expand.

4. Allow plenty of room for sourdough to expand. It can more than double in bulk.

5. Foods made with sourdough may be baked in either glass or metal pans.

6. Soda is a leavening agent and is always added last. Bake while the air is in the sourdough.

7. If your sourdough begins to separate, stir it and add a little more flour.

8. Always keep your sourdough covered, but do not keep the lid tightly closed. Sourdough needs to breathe. A small hole in the lid will suffice.

9. Even though it is possible to start more sourdough with just a few teaspoons of old starter, it is better to leave 1 cup of sourdough starter to start a new batch.

10. Sugar is used as a booster to make the enzymes in sourdough work. Too much sugar in foods made with sourdough will make them tough. Soda, not sugar, will sweeten the sourdough.

11. Remove sourdough from the refrigerator and allow it to become bubbly before using.

Sourdough Starter

2 cups flour
1 teaspoon salt
3½ teaspoons sugar
1 tablespoon dry yeast
2 cups warm water

With a wooden spoon, mix all ingredients until smooth. Set in a warm place (approximately 85° F.) away from drafts. Stir several times each day. In about 4 days, the starter will be ready to use. Be sure to save at least ½

cup starter each time you use it. To replenish starter, add equal parts flour and warm water and leave at room temperature for 24 hours. Store in refrigerator.

Sourdough starter should be used once a week. If not, it needs to be replenished. To replenish, add ½ cup flour and ½ cup water to 1 cup sourdough starter. Let stand overnight at room temperature. In the morning, stir and return sourdough to refrigerator.

Sourdough Bread

5 cups sourdough starter
¼ cup cooking oil or shortening
3 tablespoons sugar
1 teaspoon baking soda
1 cup warm water
1 teaspoon salt
Flour

Mix sourdough, oil or shortening, and sugar. Dissolve soda in water and add to sourdough mixture. Stir in salt and enough flour to make dough elastic and smooth. Shape into loaves, place in bread pans, and let set until double in bulk. Bake at 400° F. for 35 minutes. Makes 2 loaves.

Sourdough Corn Bread

1 cup sourdough starter
1½ cups yellow cornmeal
1½ cups milk
2 eggs, beaten
2 tablespoons sugar
¼ cup softened butter or margarine
½ teaspoon salt
1 teaspoon baking soda

Combine sourdough starter, cornmeal, milk, eggs, and sugar in a large mixing bowl. Add butter or margarine, salt, and baking soda, and mix well. Pour into an 8" x 11" greased pan and bake at 450° F. for 30 minutes.

Sourdough Buttermilk Biscuits

2 cups flour
1 teaspoon salt
½ teaspoon baking soda
½ teaspoon baking powder
½ cup margarine
½ cup buttermilk
½ cup sourdough starter
Melted butter

Combine flour, salt, baking soda, and baking powder. With a fork or pastry blender, cut in margarine until mixture resembles coarse cornmeal. Mix buttermilk and sourdough starter with a fork; stir into flour mixture until a soft dough is formed. Turn onto a floured board and knead 15 to 20 times. Roll dough to ½-inch thickness. Cut biscuits with 2-inch cutter and place on a greased baking pan. Brush tops of biscuits with melted butter. Set pan in a warm place for 30 minutes. Bake at 425° F. for 15 minutes.

Sourdough English Muffins

½ cup sourdough starter

1 cup water

⅓ cup instant nonfat dry milk

2½ cups flour

2 tablespoons sugar

¾ teaspoon salt

½ teaspoon baking soda

Cornmeal

In a bowl combine sourdough starter, water, dry milk, and 2 cups flour; mix well. Put a damp towel over mixture and let set at room temperature overnight. In the morning, combine ½ cup flour, sugar, salt, and baking soda. Stir into sourdough mixture and add additional flour if needed (dough should be stiff, not sticky). Turn out onto floured board and knead until smooth and elastic. Roll out ¾-inch thick and cut into 3-inch rounds. Sprinkle cookie sheet with cornmeal and place muffins on sheet. Sprinkle tops of muffins with cornmeal. Let rise 30 to 40 minutes at room temperature. Cook on greased grill at medium heat 8 to 10 minutes on each side, or until well browned. Cool on racks. Split in half and toast.

Sourdough Hotcakes

2½ cups sourdough starter

3 tablespoons sugar

5 tablespoons oil

1 or 2 eggs

1 teaspoon soda dissolved in ¼ cup
　　warm water

Combine first four ingredients and thicken with flour, if necessary. Mix well. Fold in soda and water mixture. *Do not beat after adding soda.* Pour batter onto hot greased griddle or skillet. Cook until cakes are full of bubbles and undersurface is browned. Turn with a pancake turner or spatula and brown the other side. Serve immediately.

Sourdough Pancakes

2 cups flour

1 cup warm water

1 cup sourdough starter

2 tablespoons sugar

1 teaspoon salt

½ teaspoon baking powder

4 tablespoons oil

2 or 3 eggs

½ teaspoon baking soda dissolved in ¼
　　cup warm water

Mix flour, water, and sourdough starter until smooth. Add sugar, salt, baking powder, and oil. Beat in eggs. Fold in soda and water mixture. *Do not beat after baking soda is added.* Preheat and oil griddle or skillet. Pour pancakes onto griddle or skillet and cook until cakes are full of bubbles and undersurface is nicely browned. Turn with a pancake turner or spatula and brown the other side. Serve immediately.

Basic-Mix Breads and Desserts

Basic Mix

10 cups all-purpose or
　　whole-wheat flour

6 tablespoons baking powder

1 cup plus 2 tablespoons instant
　　nonfat dry milk

4½ teaspoons salt

1 tablespoon cream of tartar

2 cups vegetable shortening or
　　1¾ cups lard

Combine all dry ingredients. Cut fat into flour mixture until thoroughly mixed. (Mix will resemble cornmeal.) Store in an air-tight container in a cool place. Yield: 14 cups.

Biscuits

2 cups Basic Mix

½ cup water

Combine Basic Mix and water; stir just enough to make a soft dough. Roll to ½-inch thickness and cut into desired shapes. Place on an ungreased cookie sheet. Bake at 425° F. for 10 minutes. Makes 12 to 14 biscuits.

Drop Biscuits: Increase water to ⅔ cup. Drop batter by spoonfuls onto a greased baking pan or muffin tin. Bake at 425° F. 8 to 10 minutes, or until done.

Dumplings: Increase water to ⅔ cup (or use broth). Drop into boiling stew. Cover and cook 12 minutes.

Muffins

2 cups Basic Mix

4 teaspoons sugar

1 egg

⅔ cup water

Combine Basic Mix and sugar. Beat egg with water and add to mix. Stir just enough to blend ingredients. Bake in greased muffin tins at 400° F. for 20 minutes. Makes 12 muffins.

Banana Muffins: Reduce water to ½ cup. Add to batter ½ cup mashed banana, ¼ teaspoon nutmeg, and ½ cup nuts.

Blueberry Muffins: Add to batter ½ cup fresh, canned, or frozen blueberries.

Apple Muffins: Add to batter ¾ cup chopped apples, ⅛ teaspoon cinnamon, and a dash of nutmeg.

Nut Muffins: Add to batter ½ cup nuts.

Cranberry Muffins: Use 3 tablespoons sugar. Add to batter ½ cup chopped cranberries.

Pancakes

2 cups Basic Mix

1 teaspoon sugar

1 egg

1 cup water

Combine Basic Mix and sugar. Beat egg and water together. Add to dry ingredients, and stir just enough to blend. Pour onto a preheated greased griddle or skillet. Cook until cakes are full of bubbles and undersurface is nicely browned. Turn with a pancake turner or spatula and brown the other side. Serve immediately. Makes approximately 16 4-inch pancakes.

Blueberry Pancakes: Add to batter ½ cup fresh, canned, or frozen blueberries.

Cornmeal Pancakes: Substitute ½ cup cornmeal for ½ cup mix.

Nut Pancakes: Add to batter ¼ cup chopped nuts.

Apple Pancakes: Add to batter ½ cup chopped apple, ⅛ teaspoon cinnamon, and a dash of nutmeg.

Waffles: Add ¼ cup oil with the egg and water. Cook as manufacturer directs for your waffle iron. Makes about 4 large waffles.

Fried Pies

2 cups Basic Mix

½ cup water

Combine Basic Mix and water just enough to form a soft dough. Place on floured board and knead 15 times. Roll into thin dough as for pie crust. (You may also use a pasta maker.) Cut into 5- or 6-inch circles. Place 2 to 4 tablespoons filling (below) on one-half of each circle. Fold dough over and press edges together with a fork dipped in flour. Fry in hot fat (350° F.) 3 minutes, or make holes in crust for steam to escape and bake in 400° F. oven 18 to 20 minutes. Makes 6 pies.

Fruit Fillings: Use any fruit that has been thickened as for pies. Add ¼ teaspoon nutmeg and ½ teaspoon cinnamon.

Pineapple Filling: Mix 4 teaspoons sugar and 2 teaspoons cornstarch; add ⅔ cup drained crushed pineapple. Cook until thick. Cool.

Meat Pies: To ½ cup thickened gravy or sauce, add 1 cup minced, cooked meat (beef, pork, chicken, turkey, or tuna) and 1 cup finely diced cooked vegetables (onions, celery, potatoes, cabbage, carrots, or peas).

Navajo Tacos: Fry circles of dough in hot oil. Top with meat or refried beans, cheese, tomatoes, and lettuce.

Chimichangas: Add Chimichanga meat mixture (see index).

Peanut Butter Cookies

2 cups Basic Mix

⅔ cup sugar

1 cup peanut butter

½ teaspoon vanilla

1 egg, beaten

Combine Basic Mix, sugar, and peanut butter. Stir in vanilla and beaten egg. Mix thoroughly. Shape into 1-inch balls and place on ungreased cookie sheet. Flatten with a floured fork. Bake at 375° F. for 10 to 12 minutes. If desired, add 1 cup chocolate chips. Makes 3½ dozen cookies.

Oatmeal Cookies

2 cups Basic Mix

½ cup brown sugar

½ cup granulated sugar

1½ cups oatmeal

1 teaspoon cinnamon

1 teaspoon nutmeg

1 teaspoon ginger

2 tablespoons water

1 teaspoon vanilla

2 eggs

½ cup raisins

½ cup chopped nuts

Combine Basic Mix, sugars, oatmeal, and spices. Add water, vanilla, and eggs. Mix thoroughly. Add raisins and nuts. Arrange by teaspoonfuls on greased cookie sheet. Bake at 400° F. for 10 to 12 minutes. Makes about 50 cookies.

Brownies

1 cup Basic Mix
½ cup unsweetened cocoa
1 cup sugar
2 eggs, beaten
1 teaspoon vanilla
½ cup chopped nuts

Combine all ingredients; mix thoroughly. Bake in a greased 8-inch square pan at 350° F. for 30 minutes. Cool. Cut in squares. Makes 16 brownies.

Basic Cake

3 cups Basic Mix
1 cup sugar
1 cup water
2 eggs
1 teaspoon vanilla

Combine Basic Mix and sugar. Add water, eggs, and vanilla. Beat 3 minutes. Pour batter into greased 13″ x 9″ pan. Bake at 350° F. for 30 to 40 minutes. Cool on a rack. Frost, if desired.

Applesauce Spice Cake: Increase sugar to 1½ cups, and omit water and vanilla. Add 1 cup applesauce, 1 teaspoon cinnamon, ½ teaspoon nutmeg, and 1 teaspoon cloves.

Banana Cake: Reduce water to ⅔ cup, and add 2 large mashed bananas.

Gelatin Cake: Bake Basic Cake. Cool 10 minutes. Insert a fork into cake ½ inch deep every inch or two. Dissolve one 3-ounce package of flavored gelatin in 1 cup hot water (do not set), and pour over cake while still liquid. Refrigerate 4 hours. Top with whipped cream.

Bundt Cake

3 cups Basic Mix
1 cup sugar
¼ cup water
2 eggs
1 cup sour cream or yogurt
1 package (3 ounces) flavored gelatin

Grease and flour a fluted cake pan. Set aside. In a large mixing bowl, combine Basic Mix and sugar. Add water, eggs, and sour cream or yogurt. Beat 3 minutes. Spoon one-third of the batter into the prepared cake pan. Sprinkle with one-half of the gelatin. Spoon an additional one-third of the batter over the gelatin and sprinkle with the remaining gelatin. Spoon in remaining batter. Bake at 350° F. for 45 to 50 minutes. Cool and remove from pan. Sprinkle confectioner's sugar on cake, if desired.

Basic Chocolate Cake

3 cups Basic Mix
½ cup cocoa
1½ cups sugar
½ teaspoon baking soda
1½ cups buttermilk
2 eggs
1 teaspoon vanilla

Combine Basic Mix, cocoa, sugar, and baking soda. Add buttermilk, eggs, and vanilla. Beat 3 minutes. Pour batter into a greased 13″ x 9″ pan, and bake at 350° F. for 30 to 40 minutes. Cool. Frost, if desired.

Coffee Cake

2 cups Basic Mix
⅓ cup brown sugar
½ teaspoon cinnamon
1 egg, beaten
½ cup water
1½ cups Oat Topping (see index)

Combine Basic Mix, brown sugar, and cinnamon. Add egg and water; stir until ingredients are well mixed. Spread batter in a greased 8-inch square pan. Sprinkle with Oat Topping (see index), and bake at 375° F. for 20 minutes.

Cobbler

¼ cup Basic Mix
¾ cup brown sugar
¼ teaspoon cinnamon
½ cup water
6 cups sliced apples or other fruit
¼ cup butter or margarine

Combine Basic Mix, sugar, cinnamon, and water. Mix thoroughly. Pour into a large oblong baking dish. Arrange fruit on top and dot with butter or margarine. Bake at 375° F. for 40 to 50 minutes.

Pastry and Cakes

Whole-Wheat Pie Crust

1 cup sifted whole-wheat pastry flour
¼ teaspoon salt
5 tablespoons shortening or margarine
1 egg, beaten

Combine flour and salt in a large mixing bowl. Cut in shortening or margarine until mixture is about the size of baby peas. Add egg and stir until dough holds together. Refrigerate for 1 hour. Roll out pastry or press dough evenly over bottom and sides of pie pan. Place foil in pie shell and spread over foil ½ cup dried beans or rice. Bake at 450° F. for 10 minutes. Remove foil and beans or rice, and bake 3 minutes longer. Makes 1 pie shell. Double recipe for a 2-crust pie.

Honey Whole-Wheat Cake

¼ cup sugar (use either granulated or
    brown sugar)
½ cup margarine
½ cup mild honey
1 teaspoon almond extract
2 large eggs
2 cups whole-wheat pastry flour
3 teaspoons baking powder
½ teaspoon mace
½ teaspoon salt
⅔ cup milk

Cream sugar, margarine, and honey together. Add almond extract. Add eggs one at a time, beating well after each addition. Sift dry ingredients together and add to creamed mixture alternately with milk. Bake in a well-greased 8-inch square pan at 350° F. for 30 to 35 minutes. Top with Honey Nut Topping (below). Return to oven and bake 5 minutes more. If desired, top with whipped cream.

Honey Nut Topping: Combine ¼ cup mild honey, ¼ cup brown sugar, ½ teaspoon cinnamon, ¼ cup softened butter, and ½ cup chopped nuts. Spread on warm cake.

Sour Cream Spice Cake

3 eggs
¾ cup honey
1 teaspoon baking soda
1½ cups sour cream
2¼ cups flour
½ teaspoon salt
1 teaspoon cinnamon
½ teaspoon allspice
¼ teaspoon cloves
1 teaspoon vanilla
½ cup nuts
½ cup raisins

Beat eggs and honey together lightly. Mix soda and sour cream, and add to eggs. Sift flour and spices and add to egg mixture. Add vanilla, nuts, and raisins. Pour batter into greased and floured 8″ x 12″ pan. Bake at 350° F. for 40 to 50 minutes. Frost with Caramel Frosting.

Lemon Honey Cake

½ cup margarine
¾ cup mild honey
2 large eggs
2 cups whole-wheat pastry flour
¾ teaspoon baking soda
½ teaspoon salt
2 tablespoons lemon juice
1 teaspoon grated lemon peel
½ teaspoon lemon extract
⅓ cup milk

Cream margarine and honey together. Add eggs one at a time, beating well after each addition. Sift dry ingredients together. Add lemon juice, peel, and extract to milk, and add to creamed mixture alternately with dry ingredients. Pour into two well-greased and floured 8-inch layer-cake pans. Bake at 350° F. for 25 to 30 minutes. If desired, put cake together with Lemon Kool-Aid Pie filling (see index), and frost with Honey Egg-White Frosting.

Cupcakes

1 cup sifted whole-wheat or all-purpose
    pastry flour
¼ cup cornstarch or flour
½ cup sugar
1½ teaspoons baking powder
½ teaspoon salt
⅓ cup softened margarine
1 teaspoon vanilla
½ cup milk or water
2 eggs

In a large mixing bowl, combine flour, cornstarch, sugar, baking powder, and salt. Add margarine, vanilla, and milk or water. Beat until smooth (about 2 minutes). Add eggs and beat 1 minute more. Fill paper cupcake cups or greased muffin cups two-thirds full. Bake at 350° F. for 20 minutes, or until top of cake springs back when pressed with fingertip. Frost with Creamy Vanilla Frosting or Fluffy Frosting or sprinkle with chocolate, butterscotch, or peanut butter chips just before baking. Makes 12 to 14 cupcakes.

Almond Cupcakes: Substitute ½ teaspoon almond extract for vanilla. Bake as directed, and frost with Fluffy Frosting, substituting ½ teaspoon almond extract for vanilla.

Apricot Cupcakes: Substitute 1 teaspoon almond extract for vanilla. Add 1 tablespoon grated orange peel and ½ cup chopped dried apricots. Bake as directed. Frost as desired.

Chocolate or Carob Cupcakes: Add ¼ cup unsweetened cocoa or ¼ cup powdered carob. Bake as directed. Frost with Fluffy Frosting, Creamy Vanilla Frosting, or Creamy Fudge Frosting, or sprinkle with chocolate, carob, or peanut butter chips before baking.

Chocolate Peanut Cupcakes: Add ¼ cup unsweetened cocoa, ¼ cup peanut butter, and ½ cup chopped peanuts. Frost with Peanut Butter Frosting, or sprinkle with peanut butter chips just before baking.

Coconut Cupcakes: Substitute ½ teaspoon vanilla and ½ teaspoon coconut flavoring for vanilla. Add ⅓ cup flaked coconut. Bake as directed, and frost with Creamy Vanilla Frosting or Fluffy Frosting. Sprinkle frosting with coconut.

German Chocolate Cupcakes: Add ¼ cup unsweetened cocoa, ½ cup chopped nuts, and ½ cup grated coconut. Bake as directed. Frost with desired frosting or serve unfrosted.

Lemon Cupcakes: Substitute ½ teaspoon lemon extract and 1 teaspoon lemon peel for vanilla. Bake as directed. Frost with Fluffy Frosting, substituting ½ teaspoon lemon extract for vanilla.

Orange Cupcakes: Substitute ½ cup orange juice for milk, and add 2 teaspoons grated orange peel. Bake as directed. Frost with Fluffy Frosting, substituting ½ teaspoon orange extract for vanilla.

Ginger Cakes

1 cup sifted whole-wheat or all-purpose pastry flour
¼ cup cornstarch or flour
½ teaspoon salt
½ teaspoon baking powder
½ teaspoon baking soda
½ teaspoon ginger
1 teaspoon cinnamon
¼ teaspoon cloves
¼ cup margarine
¼ cup brown sugar
1 egg
½ cup molasses
½ cup hot water

Combine flour, cornstarch, salt, baking powder, baking soda, and spices. In a large bowl beat margarine and sugar until fluffy. Add egg and molasses, and beat until well mixed. Add dry ingredients alternately with hot water. Beat until smooth (about 2 minutes). Fill cupcake cups or greased muffin tins two-thirds full. Bake at 350° F. for 20 minutes, or until top springs back when pressed with fingertip. Frost with Cream Cheese Frosting or sprinkle with chocolate chips just before baking. Makes 12 cupcakes.

Applesauce Cakes: Substitute ½ cup applesauce for molasses, and increase brown sugar to ½ cup. Add ⅓ cup raisins or chopped nuts, if desired. Bake as directed. Frost with Caramel Frosting.   *(Continued)*

Peanut Butter Cakes: Substitute ½ cup chunky peanut butter for molasses. Increase brown sugar to ¾ cup. Frost with Peanut Butter Frosting or sprinkle with chocolate or peanut butter chips just before baking.

Fluffy Frosting

1 egg white
½ cup sugar
¼ cup honey or corn syrup
⅛ teaspoon cream of tartar
2 tablespoons water
½ teaspoon vanilla

In the top of a double boiler combine egg white, sugar, honey or corn syrup, cream of tartar, and water. Beat about 1 minute to combine ingredients. Cook over boiling water, beating constantly, for 5 to 7 minutes or until stiff peaks form. Remove from heat and add vanilla. Beat 1 minute longer. Frosts 12 cupcakes or one 9-inch square cake.

Creamy Vanilla Frosting

3 tablespoons softened butter or margarine
1½ cups powdered sugar
1 tablespoon milk
1 teaspoon vanilla

Beat butter or margarine until fluffy. Add powdered sugar and milk; beat until smooth. Beat in vanilla. Frosts 12 to 14 cupcakes or one 9-inch square cake. Double recipe for 2-layer cake.

Cream Cheese Frosting

3 tablespoons softened butter or margarine
1½ cups powdered sugar
2 teaspoons lemon juice
¼ cup cream cheese
1 teaspoon vanilla
¼ cup chopped nuts (optional)

Beat butter or margarine until fluffy. Add powdered sugar, lemon juice, and cream cheese; beat until smooth. Stir in vanilla and nuts. Frosts 12 to 14 cupcakes or one 9-inch square cake. Double recipe for 2-layer cake.

Creamy Fudge Frosting

3 tablespoons softened butter or margarine
1½ cups powdered sugar
2 tablespoons unsweetened cocoa or carob

2 tablespoons hot water
1 teaspoon vanilla

Beat butter or margarine until fluffy. Add powdered sugar, cocoa or carob, and hot water; beat until smooth. Beat in vanilla. Frosts 12 to 14 cupcakes or one 9-inch square cake. Double recipe for 2-layer cake.

Peanut Butter Frosting

2 tablespoons softened butter or
    margarine
1½ cups powdered sugar
¼ cup peanut butter
1 tablespoon milk
1 teaspoon vanilla

Beat butter or margarine until fluffy. Add powdered sugar, peanut butter, and milk; beat until smooth. Beat in vanilla. Frosts 12 to 14 cupcakes or one 9-inch square cake. Double recipe for 2-layer cake.

Honey Egg-White Frosting

½ cup honey
½ cup sugar

2 egg whites
1 teaspoon vanilla

Combine honey, sugar, and egg whites in the top of a double boiler. Beat 1 minute to blend. Cook over boiling water, beating constantly for 5 to 7 minutes or until stiff peaks form. Remove from heat and add vanilla. Beat 1 minute longer. Frosts one 9-inch layer cake. Double recipe for 2-layer cake.

Caramel Frosting

¼ cup butter or margarine
⅓ cup dark brown sugar
3 tablespoons milk
1½ cups powdered sugar
½ teaspoon vanilla

Melt butter or margarine in a medium saucepan. Add brown sugar and milk and bring to a boil over low heat. Cook 2 minutes, stirring constantly. Remove from heat and cool to lukewarm. Add powdered sugar and vanilla; beat until smooth. Frosts 12 cupcakes or one 9-inch square cake.

Soybeans

Cooking with Soybeans and Soybean Products

Soybeans provide a nutritional, low-cost way to vary your family meals. They are one of the most concentrated, healthful foods known to man, almost as high in quality as meat, eggs, and milk products.

Soybeans are the vegetable source nearest to being a complete protein. They lack the amino acid methionine and should be combined with other sources of methionine, such as wheat, rice, corn, milk, and milk products. Most textured vegetable products (TVP) have had the amino acid blended in, making them a complete protein.

Soybeans have a much higher protein content than many other foods. One-third of a pound of soybeans has as much protein as one pound of ground round—and the soybeans cost one-eighth or less per pound than the ground round. They contain as much vitamins A and B, iron, and phosphorous as cow's milk. Soy milk has slightly less calcium; there-fore, if it is used exclusively, another source of calcium should be found to supplement the diet.

Compared to animal protein foods, soybeans are lower in carbohydrates. One serving (½ cup) of soybeans has 100 calories. They are also low in starch and cholesterol.

Raw soybeans contain an antitrypsin factor that inhibits the digestion of protein. In whatever form you use soybeans, they must be cooked to be digestible.

Powdered soybeans have the ability to absorb and hold moisture. In addition to adding moisture, they improve the flavor and browning quality of breads and rolls; they keep waffles and pancakes from sticking to the pan; and they increase the moisture content in cakes and make cookie dough easier to handle.

Soy flour does not contain gluten or starch to bind mixtures together. Therefore, it cannot be used by itself or in large quantities in bread or yeast products. A good proportion to follow is 2 tablespoons soy flour to 1 cup wheat flour. Do not use more than ¼ cup soy flour per cup of wheat; too much soy flour will make the dough heavy.

In doughs, such as those for cookies, cakes, pancakes, and nonyeast breads, as much as one-half of the wheat flour can be replaced with soy flour. Use small substitutions to begin with and gradually increase.

Soybeans have a high fat content. Unless you have a mill designed to grind soybeans, grinding them alone may clog your grinder. To prevent this from happening, grind your soybeans with wheat or other grains, or dry your soybeans in the oven before grinding.

Hints for Using Soybeans

1. Always soak soybeans overnight unless you are using them as fresh flour. Discard the soaking water and add fresh water to the beans before cooking them. This will help eliminate a strong bean flavor and gaseous properties.

2. If the soybeans have a strong bean flavor, they can be brought to a boil several times. Each time discard the water and start with fresh water. Skim off the foam.

3. Soybeans will at least triple in size after soaking and cooking.

4. Soybeans need to be flavored or seasoned before being eaten. They will take on the flavors of the foods with which they are combined. Vegetables, onions, garlic, and other seasonings enhance their flavor.

5. Because soybeans are high in protein, they become tough when cooked over high heat. Long soaking and slow cooking will prevent this from happening. Cooking in a pressure cooker will also give a tender bean. Cook at 15 pounds pressure for one hour. Do not fill cooker more than half full.

6. Add baking soda to the water in which the beans are soaked to reduce the strong bean flavor.

7. To avoid having dry, tough beans, add salt, seasonings, and other ingredients after the beans are cooked.

Soybean Products

From the soybeans, you can make soy flour, textured vegetable protein (TVP), soy milk, tofu (an unripened cheese made from soy milk), soy meat substitute (SMS), okara (soy pulp), tempeh, and soy purée. Each of these products is full of nutrition, and each can be made easily and inexpensively. The soy products blend well with other ingredients in breads, meat dishes, milk products, and desserts. They also extend such products as eggs and peanut butter so that those items go twice as far at a fraction of the supermarket price.

Soy Flour

Soak soybeans overnight. Bring to a boil and simmer 15 minutes. Drain. Grind drained beans with a hand grinder, electric food processor, or blender, using a coarse blade or crack. Place the grits on a cookie sheet, and bake them at 150° F. for 1 hour. Remove from oven and cool. Then grind into flour with a flour mill.

Textured Vegetable Protein (TVP)

Soak soybeans overnight. Bring to a boil and simmer 15 minutes. Drain. Grind with a hand grinder, electric meat grinder, or blender, using a coarse blade or crack. Place grits on a cookie sheet and bake in 150° F. oven for 1 hour, or dehydrate in food dryer.

For meat flavor, dissolve soup base or bouillon cubes in the water in which soybeans are soaked. Store TVP in an airtight container in a cool, dark place.

Soy Milk

1. Soak 1 pound soybeans for 8 to 12 hours or overnight. Keep beans covered with water during soaking.

2. Drain soybeans and add new water. Bring beans to a boil and drain. Repeat this step two or three times. This will remove the strong bean flavor.

3. Put 1 cup soybeans and 2 cups water in a blender and blend until smooth.

4. Put beans into a bag made from a loose-weave cloth. Squeeze out liquid into a bowl.

5. Add another cup of water to beans. Knead and squeeze until all liquid is gone. Repeat with rest of soybeans. You should have one gallon of soy milk; if not, add enough additional water to make one gallon.

6. Bring the milk to a boil over medium heat, stirring constantly. When milk begins to boil, stop stirring and cook 30 minutes. Add 2 tablespoons honey or sugar and ½ teaspoon salt. Refrigerate. Save the dry pulp for recipes calling for soy pulp or okara.

Medium-Rich Soy Milk: Follow the procedure for making soy milk, but on step 3 add only 1 cup water to 1 cup soybeans in the blender. This should make 2 quarts medium-rich soy milk. (If needed, add enough additional water to make the 2 quarts.) On step 6, cook milk in a double boiler.

Rich Soy Milk: Follow the procedure for making soy milk, but on step 3 add only ½ cup water to 1 cup soybeans in the blender. This should make 1 quart rich soy milk instead of 1 gallon. (If needed, add enough additional water to make 1 quart.) On step 6, cook milk in a double boiler.

Tofu (Soy Cheese)

Tofu, known in the Orient as "meat without bones," is an unripened cheese made from soy milk. The curdling takes place when acid or salt is added. The curds are removed from the whey and pressed into cakes similar to soft cheese made from animal milk.

About 75 percent of the original soy protein and 50 percent of the solids remain in the tofu. The whey is estimated to have 15 to 25 percent of the original nutrients.

Some of the natural soybean oils are dissolved in the whey in the curdling process. These oils contain lecithin, known for its ability to cut through oils; thus, soy whey is an excellent biodegradable soap. The tofu maker uses it to wash his tools. Some women use it as a shampoo and complexion soap. It makes an excellent soap for washing clothes, fine silks, and dishes, and can be used to polish wooden floors and woodwork. It can also be used as a plant nutrient. Some people use the whey in place of milk or water in breads and baked goods, or as a broth or soup stock. It certainly is "a soap you can drink."

To make tofu, bring 2 quarts soy milk to a boil. Remove from heat and add *one* of the following acids: 1 rounded tablespoon Epsom salts dissolved in ¼ cup water; or ¼ cup vinegar mixed with ½ cup water; or 3 tablespoons lemon juice mixed with ¼ cup water.

Let set until milk curdles (about 10 minutes). Lift the curds out with a slotted spoon and place in a cloth-lined cheese press. Fold the cloth over the curd and apply light pressure. Let drain for two hours.

Soy Meat Substitute (SMS)

Soy meat substitute (SMS) is similar to textured vegetable protein (TVP). TVP is made from the soybean and SMS is made from tofu or soybean curd. To make SMS:

1. Wrap tofu in a plastic bag and freeze.
2. Thaw tofu and squeeze out as much water as possible. Wrap in a clean cloth, put under a dinner plate, and press with a 10-pound weight for 10 to 20 minutes. Remove tofu and crumble it.
3. Dissolve 1 bouillon cube or 2 teaspoons soup base in 2 tablespoons of hot water. Add to one cup of crumbled tofu.

SMS can be used at this point or it can be dried. Wet SMS will keep 4 to 5 days in the refrigerator. Dry SMS will keep indefinitely if kept in an airtight container in a cool, dry place.

To Dry SMS: Spread SMS on a cookie sheet and put it in the oven at 250° F. Cook slowly, stirring often, until no moisture remains, but be careful not to brown it. SMS should be dry and crumbly, with the same color as when wet. SMS can also be dried in a dehydrator.

To Reconstitute SMS: Combine equal parts of boiling water and dry SMS. Let stand for 25 minutes, or until no water remains. Use as a meat extender. For example, use equal parts SMS and ground beef in meat loaf, hamburger patties, or other dishes made with ground beef.

Okara (Soy Pulp)

Okara, or soy pulp, is the name given to the ground soybeans left over after making soy milk. It may be added to meat loaf or casseroles or used as an extender in ground beef recipes. It may also be used in recipes that call for eggs: one teaspoon of okara may be used to replace 1 egg. Okara is a versatile addition for sweet breads, hotcakes, meat loaf, and pies.

Soy Purée

Put 1 cup okara in blender; add ½ cup water, and blend slowly until mixture is the consistency of smooth paste. Add more water, if necessary. Cook in a double boiler for 15 minutes. Store in an airtight container in the refrigerator.

Soy Milk Made with Soy Flour

2 cups soy flour
2 quarts water
3 tablespoons vegetable oil
3 tablespoons honey or sugar
Salt to taste

Mix soy flour and water in blender or mixer. Set aside for 1½ hours. Heat in a double boiler for 45 to 50 minutes. Add oil, honey or sugar, and salt. Return to blender and blend 1 to 2 minutes. This milk can be used to make tofu.

Soy Buttermilk

1 cup cultured buttermilk
4 cups soy milk

Combine soy milk and buttermilk. Set in a warm place overnight or until clabbered. Stir until smooth. Store in refrigerator. Save one cup starter for the next batch.

Soy Sour Cream

¼ cup soy milk
¼ cup vegetable oil
Few drops of lemon juice
Pinch of salt

Pour soy milk into a blender, Blend on slow speed, adding oil in a thin, steady stream. Add lemon juice and salt.

Variations: To make salad dressing, add your favorite salad dressing seasoning.

To make chip dip, add onion soup mix or dip mix.

To extend mayonnaise, combine 1 part mayonnaise and 3 parts soy sour cream.

Soy White Sauce

Substitute soy milk for milk in white sauce.

Soy Milk Gravy

Brown 4 tablespoons flour in 4 tablespoons oil or butter. Add 2 cups soy milk, stirring constantly until mixture thickens. Season with salt and pepper.

Tofu Mayonnaise

½ cup tofu, crumbled
1 teaspoon mustard
1½ tablespoons lemon juice
¼ cup salad oil
1 teaspoon sugar
¼ teaspoon onion salt
Pinch of garlic powder

Combine ingredients in a blender and blend until smooth. Store in refrigerator.

Tofu Salad Dressing

½ cup tofu, crumbled
1 teaspoon mustard
1 tablespoon lemon juice
¼ cup salad oil
2 teaspoons sugar
½ teaspoon parsley
½ cup milk
¼ teaspoon garlic powder
¼ teaspoon onion salt

Combine ingredients in blender and blend until smooth. Store in refrigerator.

Tofu Cottage Cheese

Mash tofu into bits the size of wheat. Salt to taste. Add cream or fruit. Store in refrigerator.

Soy Whipped Cream No. 1

¼ cup soy milk
1 teaspoon vanilla
Sugar or honey to taste
Pinch of salt
¼ cup vegetable oil

Mix soy milk, vanilla, sugar or honey, and salt in a blender. Blend on slow speed, adding oil in a thin, steady stream. If it is not thick enough, add a little lemon juice. Serve over desserts.

Soy Whipped Cream No. 2

½ cup soy milk
½ cup tofu
2 teaspoons sugar or honey
1 teaspoon vanilla

Whip soy milk, tofu, and sugar or honey in a blender until smooth. Add vanilla. Serve over desserts. Makes about 1¼ cups.

Soy Yogurt

Bring 1 quart fresh soy milk to a boil; cool to 110° F. Add ½ cup fresh cultured yogurt, stirring until smooth. Pour into containers. Follow instructions for setting yogurt (see index). Add fruit or honey if desired.

Frozen Soy Yogurt

2 cups fresh or frozen fruit
2 cups soy yogurt
¼ cup sugar
¼ cup corn syrup

Blend all ingredients in a blender. Pour into a shallow pan and place in freezer until slushy. Blend in blender again. Return to pan and freeze until firm. Break into chunks and blend again. Return to pan and freeze.

Frozen Soy Pops

1 cup soy milk
1½ cups sweetened frozen or fresh
    fruit
¼ cup sugar or honey

Blend all ingredients in a blender until smooth. Pour into molds and freeze.

Soy Ice Cream

10 cups medium-rich soy milk
2½ cups sugar

½ teaspoon salt

4 eggs, beaten

2½ teaspoons vanilla extract

Combine soy milk, sugar, and salt in a saucepan. Cook over low heat to boiling. Add small amount of hot milk mixture to eggs; mix well, and return to hot mixture. Cook and stir until thick. Add vanilla. Cool. Pour cooled mixture into ice-cream freezer. (Do not fill beyond ⅔ full.) Follow manufacturer's directions for freezing. Makes approximately one gallon.

Okara Pie Crust

1 cup okara

2 cups fine bread crumbs

1 cup sugar

½ teaspoon cinnamon

1 cup margarine or butter, melted

Place okara in a shallow pan and bake at 275° F. for one hour or until browned. Stir every 15 minutes. Combine remaining ingredients in a bowl. Add okara and mix well. Press into two 9-inch pie pans. Bake at 325° F. for 25 to 35 minutes. Cool. Fill with cream pudding or lemon pie filling.

Soy Pie Crust

½ cup soy flour

1½ cups white or wheat flour

½ teaspoon salt

⅔ cup shortening or ½ cup lard

⅓ cup soy milk

Sift the two flours together and add salt. Cut shortening or lard into flour until flour particles are the size of peas. Add soy milk, a little at a time, until moist. Press dough together into a ball. Roll out on floured board. Line a 9-inch pie plate. Double the recipe for a two-crust pie. To bake pie shell, line the shell with aluminum foil; spread over the foil ½ cup rice or dried beans. Bake at 450° F. for about 8 minutes. Remove foil and rice or beans, and return pie shell to oven for 3 to 4 minutes more, until it is well browned.

Soy Pumpkin Pie

2 cups cooked or canned pumpkin

2 cups soy purée

6 eggs

4 cups rich soy milk

2 cups sugar

2¼ teaspoons salt

Soy Pumpkin Pie made with Soy Pie Crust (above)

2 teaspoons cinnamon

1 teaspoon ginger

½ teaspoon cloves

Combine all ingredients; mix well. Pour into two 9-inch unbaked shells and bake at 425° F. for 15 minutes. Reduce heat to 350° F. and continue baking for 45 minutes. Cool. Serve with soy whipped cream.

Soy Rice Pudding

3 eggs, beaten

2 cups soy milk

1½ cups cooked rice

½ cup sugar

¼ cup raisins

1 teaspoon vanilla

½ teaspoon salt

1 teaspoon cinnamon

Combine all ingredients except cinnamon in a baking dish. Bake at 325° F. for 25 minutes. Remove from oven, stir, and sprinkle with cinnamon. Return to oven and continue baking for 25 to 30 minutes.

Tofu Cheesecake

1 cup Sweetened Condensed Milk (see index)

2 cups mashed tofu

⅓ cup lemon juice

1 teaspoon vanilla

Combine all ingredients in a blender. Blend until smooth. Pour into a graham cracker crust. Chill 2 to 3 hours. Top with cherry pie filling or strawberries.

Soy Whole-Wheat Bread

1 tablespoon dry yeast

¼ cup warm water

2 cups hot water or soy milk

¼ cup honey

1 tablespoon salt

3 tablespoons cooking oil

1 cup soy flour

4 to 5 cups whole-wheat flour

Dissolve yeast in ¼ cup warm water. Mix 2 cups hot water or soy milk, honey, salt, and oil in a large bowl. Cool. Add yeast mixture. Beat in soy and wheat flours to make a stiff dough. Mix and knead well until a smooth, elastic dough is formed. Place in a greased bowl, cover, and let rise until double in bulk. Divide into two parts and shape into loaves. Place loaves in greased loaf pans; let rise until double in bulk. Bake at 350° F. for 30 to 40 minutes.

Okara Corn Bread

1¼ cups flour

½ cup sugar (or ¼ cup, if less sugar is desired)

4 teaspoons baking powder

¾ teaspoon salt

½ cup yellow cornmeal

½ cup okara

1 cup soy milk

¼ cup shortening

2 eggs

Sift dry ingredients. Add okara, soy milk, shortening, and eggs. Mix until well combined. Pour into a greased 9-inch square pan or muffin tins. Bake at 400° F. for 20 minutes.

Soy Noodles

½ cup soy purée

1 egg

2 teaspoons cooking oil

Wheat flour

Combine purée with egg and oil. Add enough flour to make a stiff dough. Follow directions in Pasta section for making noodles (see index).

Okara Hamburger Patties

1 pound ground beef

1½ cups okara

1 egg

1 teaspoon salt

⅛ teaspoon pepper

½ cup chopped onion

Combine all ingredients and shape into patties. Brown on both sides in hot oil. Makes 6 to 8 patties.

Tofu Meat Loaf

1 pound ground beef

1 pound tofu, crumbled

¼ cup bread crumbs

2 eggs

2 tablespoons catsup, tomato soup, or tomato sauce

1½ teaspoons salt

½ teaspoon pepper

⅛ teaspoon garlic powder

½ medium onion, chopped

Combine all ingredients in a bowl and mix well. Shape mixture in a loaf pan or casserole dish. Bake at 350° F. for 45 to 60 minutes. Top with catsup, tomato soup, or tomato sauce. Return to oven for 10 minutes. Makes 8 servings.

Tuna Patties

½ cup dry SMS

1 cup warm water

2 eggs

½ cup chopped onions

1½ cups cracker crumbs

1 can (6½ ounces) tuna

½ teaspoon pepper

Salt to taste

Combine all ingredients and mix well. Set aside for 45 minutes. Form into patties and fry in oil until brown on both sides, or form into a loaf and bake at 350° F. for 20 to 25 minutes. Makes 4 servings.

Okara Meat Loaf No. 1

1½ pounds ground beef

2 cups okara

¼ cup chopped onions

½ cup chopped tomatoes

⅛ teaspoon pepper

1 teaspoon beef soup base

2 tablespoons soy sauce

1 egg

1 teaspoon dried parsley

Combine all ingredients in a large bowl and mix well. Shape and place in a greased loaf pan. Bake 1 hour at 350° F. Makes 6 to 8 servings.

Okara Meat Loaf No. 2

1 pound ground beef

1½ cups okara

1 small onion, chopped

2 eggs

1 teaspoon salt

2 tablespoons meat loaf spice (see index)

¼ cup catsup

1 cup oatmeal or cracker crumbs

Combine all ingredients. Shape and place in a greased loaf pan. Bake at 350° F. for one hour. Makes 6 to 8 servings.

Okara Meatballs

1 pound ground beef

1 cup okara

1 teaspoon salt

⅛ teaspoon pepper

1 egg

⅓ cup flour or cracker crumbs

3 tablespoons oil

Combine all ingredients except oil; mix well and shape into small balls. Brown in hot oil until meat is cooked. Makes 20 to 24 meatballs.

Okara Chicken

1 cup okara

1 cup bread crumbs

½ cup cornstarch

1 cup whole-wheat or white flour

1 teaspoon seasoning salt

⅛ teaspoon garlic

⅛ teaspoon pepper

1 fryer, cut in pieces

Combine ingredients. Coat chicken pieces; fry in oil or bake uncovered at 375° F. for 1 hour.

Soy Corn Dogs

1 cup flour

½ teaspoon baking powder

2 tablespoons sugar

1 teaspoon dry mustard

1 teaspoon salt

½ cup cornmeal

¼ cup okara

1 cup soy milk

1 egg

2 tablespoons melted shortening

12 hot dogs

In a large bowl combine dry ingredients. Add okara, soy milk, egg, and shortening, and mix until smooth. Dip hot dogs in batter and deep fry in oil at 375° F. until golden brown.

Variation: Roll cubes of cheese or ham in flour; dip in batter and fry.

Okara Pizza

2 tablespoons yeast

2 tablespoons sugar

⅓ cup warm water

¾ cup ground oat flour (see index)

2 cups wheat flour
1 teaspoon baking powder
1 teaspoon salt
¼ cup okara
¼ cup oil
⅓ cup soy milk
Pizza toppings (tomato sauce,
      mozzarella cheese, etc.), as
      desired

In a large bowl dissolve yeast and sugar in warm water. Combine remaining ingredients and add to yeast mixture. Knead until smooth and elastic, about 5 minutes. Press dough on a greased cookie sheet and top with desired toppings. Bake at 425° F. for 20 to 25 minutes.

Chop Suey

3 cups water
2 stalks celery, chopped
1 small onion, chopped
2 cups shredded cabbage
3 cups bean sprouts
2 tablespoons soup base (see index)
1 tablespoon soy sauce

¼ cup cornstarch
1 cup water
2 tablespoons oil
1 cup cubed tofu

Bring 3 cups water to a boil. Add celery, onion, and cabbage. Cook until tender. Add bean sprouts and cook for 5 minutes. Add soup base and soy sauce. Mix cornstarch with 1 cup water and add to cooked vegetables. Cook until thickened. Brown tofu in oil; add to vegetables. Makes 6 servings.

Tofu Casserole

2 cups cooked white or brown rice
Powdered soup base or bouillon
1½ cups chopped tofu
4 green onions with stems, chopped
Soy milk
Bread crumbs

Season rice with soup base or bouillon. Place half the rice in a casserole dish. Add a layer of tofu and a layer of half the onions. Add the remaining rice and pour enough soy milk over the rice to cover completely. Top with rest of onions and the bread crumbs. Bake at 350° F. for 30 minutes. Makes 4 servings.

Chop Suey (above) prepared in a wok

Egg Foo Yong

5 eggs
2 tablespoons chopped green onion
2 cups fresh bean sprouts
1 cup frozen green beans
1 teaspoon soy sauce
1 cup chopped tofu

Beat eggs. Add remaining ingredients. Drop mixture by heaping tablespoonfuls onto a hot oiled griddle. Brown on both sides. Serve with Egg Foo Yong Sauce. Makes 4 to 6 servings.

Egg Foo Yong Sauce: Combine in a saucepan ¾ cup chicken broth, ½ teaspoon salt, 1 tablespoon soy sauce, 2 teaspoons Worcestershire sauce, 3 tablespoons catsup, and ¼ teaspoon sugar. Bring to a boil. Mix 2 teaspoons cornstarch with 1½ tablespoons water and add to boiling broth. Cook until thick.

Guacamole

1 avocado, peeled and mashed
½ cup crumbled tofu
¼ teaspoon onion salt
2 tablespoons milk
2 tablespoons chopped onion
⅛ teaspoon garlic powder
Few drops lemon juice

Combine ingredients and mix well. Spread on bread, crackers, or crisp tortilla chips.

Soy Omelets

Omelet No. 1: Combine 1 cup soy purée with 4 beaten eggs, salt and pepper to taste, and grated cheese (optional). Mix well. Cook in a buttered skillet until eggs are set.

Omelet No. 2: Mash 1 cup tofu into small pieces. Put into a skillet and sauté in butter for 2 minutes. Add 4 beaten eggs; cook until eggs are set.

Soy Peanut Butter Extenders

With Soy Nuts: Blend roasted or deep-fried soy nuts in a powerful blender or food processor until fine and smooth. Add enough vegetable oil to make a paste. Combine equal amounts of peanut butter and soy mixture. Store in refrigerator, and stir before using.

With Soy Purée: Mix well 1 part soy purée with 2 parts peanut butter. Let set several hours in the refrigerator before using. Do not make up more peanut butter mixture than will be used in one week. Store in refrigerator, and stir before using.

With Soy Flour: Bake soy flour in a shallow pan at 300° F. until it is light tan (do not brown it). Add enough vegetable oil to make a medium-thick paste. Combine equal amounts of peanut butter and soy flour mixture. Store in refrigerator.

Fried Soy Nuts

Soak soybeans overnight. Rinse with water and drain. Heat fat or oil to 375° F. Add ½ to 1 cup soy beans at a time; bring temperature back up to 325° F. and cook to a golden brown. Drain on a kitchen towel. Use as nuts in candy and cookies, or sprinkle with salt and eat like peanuts.

Roasted Soy Nuts

Cover 1½ cups soybeans with water. Add 1 teaspoon salt. Soak overnight, adding more water if needed to keep the beans covered. Bring beans to a boil in the same water they were soaked in and cook 45 to 50 minutes. Add more water if needed to keep beans covered. Drain. Place beans in a shallow pan and roast at 350° F. for 35 to 40 minutes. Chop in a food blender or crack in a grinder.

Soy Nut Crisps

2 eggs
1 cup brown sugar
1 teaspoon vanilla
3 cups soy nuts, chopped in blender

Mix all ingredients to make a stiff dough. Drop walnut-size drops onto a cookie sheet. Press down with a wet fork. Bake at 350° F. for 8 to 10 minutes.

Okara Granola

4 cups okara
½ cup plus 2 tablespoons brown sugar
5 teaspoons oil or margarine
1 tablespoon vanilla
⅛ teaspoon salt
½ cup coconut
½ cup chopped nuts (optional)

Combine ingredients and mix well. Spread in a shallow pan and bake at 275° F. for one hour or until nicely browned. Stir every 15 minutes. Cool. Store in airtight jars.

Tempeh

The Oriental form of soybean meat is a delicious fermented soybean cake. This is made by introducing a fermenting microorganism (*rhizopus oligos-*

porus) to soybeans and then keeping them in a warm, moist atmosphere to develop.

The fermenting process increases the riboflavin, niacin, B_6, and pantothenic acid. Although the protein value of soybeans remains the same, it is partially broken down during fermenting. This makes tempeh an easily digested food, especially important for those who have digestive problems.

Scientists have learned that the microorganism used in fermenting soybeans produces an antibiotic against some disease-causing organisms. It has been said to inhibit the growth of a food-poisoning bacteria (*staphylococcus aureus*) and a pneumonia-producing bacteria (*klebsiella pneumoniae*).

Tempeh can be refrigerated for a couple of days before it is cooked. This will slow down the growth of the mold. All tempeh must be cooked before it is eaten. After cooking, tempeh may be stored in the refrigerator for a day or two. It may also be frozen for a few months. Slice it before freezing, because it tends to crumble after freezing. Tempeh can be kept indefinitely if dried in a food dryer or oven.

After making tempeh several times, try combining it with other grains, such as wheat, rye, barley, rice, and other beans. They all add their own flavor. You will find tempeh easy and fun to make, especially when you experiment with various flavorings.

Equipment Needed to Make Tempeh

1. A blender, food grinder, or hand grain mill
2. A dairy thermometer
3. A strainer or colander
4. Tempeh starter (*rhizopus oligosporus* mold). This is available at health-food stores or by writing to Gem Cultures, 30301 Sherwood Road, Fort Bragg, California 95437.
5. An incubator or container with a steady temperature between 80° and 90° F. This might be: (1) an oven with the pilot light or light bulb left on; (2) a styrofoam picnic cooler with a light bulb or heating pad inside; (3) a closet with a light; (4) any place where heat collects. Check the temperature with a thermometer.
6. Shallow aluminum foil baking pans perforated with small pinholes about 2 inches apart, or perforated plastic sandwich bags.

Process to Make Tempeh

1. Rinse whole soybeans and soak overnight. One cup dried soybeans will make one pound tempeh.
2. Remove hulls from beans by rubbing vigorously between hands. This will loosen the hulls and split the beans. Put the beans through a hand grain grinder, a meat grinder with a coarse blade, or a blender, cracking each soybean into four or five pieces.
3. Cover the beans with three to four times their volume in water. Add 1 tablespoon vinegar and bring to a boil. Cook 30 minutes. Skim off with a slotted spoon any hulls that float to the surface.
4. Drain beans through a strainer or colander. Spread the beans on a clean towel to drain off the moisture and cool them. Turn the beans occasionally to remove all surface moisture. When beans are cool and moisture is removed, they are ready for the starter.
5. Put the beans in a bowl and sprinkle with tempeh starter according to package directions. Use 1 teaspoon dry spore starter. Make sure all beans are well coated.
6. Fill the container with tightly packed beans, not more than ½-inch deep. Cover with aluminum foil or plastic wrap, and punch holes every inch or two. Plastic sandwich bags may be used, but do not pack more than ½-inch deep. Be sure to perforate the bags with a pin.
7. Set the containers in a warm, draft-free place with a constant temperature of 80° to 90° F. The ideal temperature is 86° F. Always check the temperature of your incubator first. Be sure the air moves freely and the temperature remains constant.
8. Leave for 20 to 24 hours. The beans should smell fresh and clean and be bound together in a compact mass with individual beans barely visible. The entire contents can be lifted out without crumbling. The presence of a strong, unpleasant odor indicates an unwanted bacterial growth, in which case it is best to throw the beans away. Your tempeh should have a fresh mushroom smell. Remove beans and cut into desired shapes.

Making Tempeh Starter

1. Place ¼ cup white rice in a clean canning jar. Add 2 tablespoons water and mix well. Cover jar with milk filter or with two layers of cheesecloth with a layer of gauze or cotton in between. Screw on lid.
2. Let jar stand at room temperature for 1 hour, shaking every 15 minutes.
3. Place jar on a rack in a pressure cooker and process for 20 minutes at 15 pounds pressure.
4. Remove jar and shake to break up any rice lumps. Cool; then add ⅛ teaspoon tempeh starter. Replace the filter and screw top on jar. Shake to mix well.
5. Place jar on its side in an incubator. Set the temperature at 86° to 88° F. Incubate for four days.
6. After four days the rice should be covered with black spores. Pulverize the rice in a blender for 2 minutes; it should become dark gray granules. To make tempeh, use ⅛ teaspoon of granules per pound of soybeans. Store the remaining starter in the freezer with the filter in place and lid screwed on tightly. Starter will keep for many months. Add frozen starter to soybeans. Do not thaw.

Tempeh Variations

Tempeh can be cut into slices, cubes, strips, or squares, and seasoned. Soak the pieces in any of the following solutions for a more flavorful tempeh. Score both surfaces before putting into flavoring solution. Soak the pieces 3 to 5 minutes, then drain.

1. *Beef-flavored Tempeh:* Soak in a solution of 1 cup water, 2 teaspoons beef soup base or bouillon, 1 teaspoon soy sauce, and ⅛ teaspoon onion powder.

2. *Chicken-flavored Tempeh:* Soak in a solution of 1 cup water, 2 teaspoons chicken soup base or bouillon, and ⅛ teaspoon onion powder.

3. *Pork- or Ham-flavored Tempeh:* Soak in a solution of 1 cup water, 1 teaspoon beef soup base or bouillon, 1 teaspoon chicken soup base or bouillon, and ⅛ teaspoon liquid smoke or smoked salt.

Additional flavor variations might include any one or combination of the following: soy sauce, salt, Worcestershire sauce, teriyaki sauce, onion powder, garlic powder, or salt and vinegar.

Cooking Tempeh

Pan-fried Tempeh: Heat oil, butter, or shortening in a skillet. Fry tempeh 1 to 2 minutes on each side, until well browned. Add ¼ cup water; cover and steam until water evaporates or tempeh is tender.

Deep-fried Tempeh: In a skillet or deep fryer heat 1 inch of oil or shortening to 350° F. Deep-fry tempeh 2 to 3 minutes on each side, until golden brown. Drain on paper towel.

Baked Tempeh: Brush tempeh with oil on both sides. Place in baking dish; bake at 350° F. for 20 to 30 minutes or until browned. You may also fry tempeh on both sides until barely browned and then bake in baking dish for 15 minutes at 350° F.

Tempeh Burgers

Cut tempeh into bun-sized squares ½-inch thick. Pan fry. Serve on buns with mustard, catsup, onion, pickles, lettuce, and tomatoes, or with tartar sauce.

Tempeh Croutons

Mix ½ cup butter and ¼ cup Parmesan cheese. Spread on both sides of a ½-inch-thick tempeh slice. Cut tempeh into cubes. Drop onto a hot oiled skillet and stir constantly until tempeh is browned on all sides and tender in the middle, approximately 5 minutes. Add to soups, stews, noodles, and salads.　　　*(Continued)*

Tempeh Burger (above) served on a whole-wheat hamburger bun (p. 28)

Tempeh Dippers: Cut tempeh in strips and pan or deep fry. Cool. Serve with a vegetable dip.

Barbecued Tempeh

Cut tempeh into desired shapes and fry in a hot oiled pan until browned on both sides. Place in a baking dish and cover with Basic Barbecue Sauce (see index). Bake at 350° F. for 15 to 20 minutes.

Tempeh Tacos

Break beef-flavored tempeh into chunks and pan fry. Season with Chili Spice (see index). Follow directions for making Mexican Tacos (see index).

Sweet and Sour Tempeh

1 can (20 ounces) pineapple tidbits
1½ tablespoons cornstarch
1½ tablespoons water
¼ cup vinegar
¼ cup brown sugar
2 teaspoons soy sauce
2 tablespoons butter
½ cup chopped green onions
½ cup green pepper strips
1 large tomato cut in wedges
1½ cups pan-fried or deep-fried
 tempeh chunks
Cooked rice
Toasted almonds

Drain pineapple and reserve juice. Mix cornstarch with water to form a paste. In a small saucepan, combine pineapple juice, vinegar, brown sugar, cornstarch paste, and soy sauce. Cook over medium heat until thickened. In a skillet, heat butter, and sauté onions and pepper until tender. Add pineapple, tomatoes, thickened juices, and tempeh. Cover and simmer 5 to 10 minutes. Serve over hot rice. Top with toasted almonds. Makes 4 to 6 servings.

Tempeh Curry

1 cup frozen peas
1 cup sliced carrots
1 cup peeled and diced potatoes
1 cup green beans
½ cup chopped green onion
1 tablespoon curry powder
1½ cups fried tempeh chunks
½ cup yogurt or sour cream

Cook vegetables in salted water until tender but still crisp. In a skillet or saucepan, combine vegetables, curry powder, and fried tempeh; add a little cooking liquid from the vegetables. Cover with yogurt or sour cream, and cook on medium heat for 10 minutes. Serve with rice. Makes 4 to 6 servings.

Tempeh Pizza

Okara Pizza Crust, or Pizza Dough (see
 index)
Spaghetti Sauce (see index)
Pan-fried tempeh cut into thin rounds
 or strips
1 medium onion, chopped
½ cup chopped green pepper (optional)
1 can drained mushrooms (optional)
½ cup chopped chives (optional)
1 cup grated cheese

Cover pizza crust or dough with sauce and top with remaining ingredients, as desired. Bake at 400° F. for 15 to 20 minutes.

Tempeh Pizza (p. 48) made with okara pizza crust (p. 43)

Corn and Mexican Dishes

Dried Corn

There are many varieties of corn. Dried whole yellow corn is what is called for in this chapter. It is the same field corn that is fed to livestock. The corn should be stored in whole kernels in tightly sealed containers; it will not keep long once the kernels have been broken down into flour.

Both the Mayan and the Aztec Indians cultivated a cuisine of corn, beans, and chilies. Because corn was a very important food to them, they built temples and held festivals in its honor. Corn is as important to the Mexican people as rice is to the Oriental—it is one of their main staples. For this reason, this chapter will include some famous Mexican food recipes.

There are three basic ways to prepare corn. You can grind it into cornmeal for cereal or breads, cook it whole for hominy, or make masa for tortillas and tamales. Cooking with corn can be fun, and many delicious dishes can be created by combining old and new ingredients and techniques.

Cornmeal

Corn may be ground in most hand or electric grain grinders. When the kernels are dry and hard, put them through on a coarse grind, then again on medium to fine grind, depending on your preference for cornmeal. The cornmeal is now ready to use for cereal or in cooking.

Corn Bread

1 cup cornmeal
1 cup flour
4 teaspoons baking powder
⅔ teaspoon salt
2 tablespoons sugar
1 cup milk
2 eggs, beaten
¼ cup melted butter or oil

Combine cornmeal, flour, baking powder, salt, and sugar in a mixing bowl. Make a well and add milk, eggs, and butter or oil, stirring just to moisten. Pour into a greased 8-inch square pan and bake at 400° F. for 20 minutes.

Corn Bread (below) with honey; Baked Hominy and Tomatoes (p. 52)

Corn Bread with Sour Milk

2 cups cornmeal
½ cup flour
2 cups sour milk
½ cup molasses or sugar
1 teaspoon salt
2 eggs, beaten
2 tablespoons melted butter
1 teaspoon baking soda

Combine cornmeal and flour. Gradually add milk. Mix in molasses or sugar, salt, eggs, and melted butter. Dissolve baking soda in a small amount of milk or water and stir into cornmeal mixture. Bake in a well-buttered 8-inch square pan at 400° F. for 20 to 30 minutes.

Eggless Cornmeal Muffins

1 cup flour
1 cup cornmeal
2 tablespoons sugar
Water or sour milk
2 tablespoons melted butter
1 teaspoon baking soda

In a mixing bowl stir together flour, cornmeal, sugar, and enough water or sour milk to make a thick batter. Refrigerate overnight. In the morning, add melted butter and baking soda. Bake in buttered muffin tins at 400° F. for 20 to 25 minutes. Makes 12 muffins.

Corn Bread Mix

5½ cups cornmeal
4 cups flour
½ cup sugar
4 teaspoons salt
8 teaspoons baking powder

Combine all ingredients and mix well. Store in jars, tins, or plastic bags in a cool place. Store in refrigerator or freezer if home-ground cornmeal is used.

Corn Bread or Muffins from Mix

2½ cups Corn Bread Mix (above)
2 eggs
1 cup milk
½ cup melted butter

Place mix in mixing bowl; add well-beaten eggs, milk, and butter. Stir until well moistened—don't overmix. Pour into a well-buttered pan or muffin tins and bake at 400° F. for 20 to 30 minutes or until golden brown. Makes 12 muffins.

Hominy

Hominy with Lime

2 quarts dry yellow corn

¾ cup hot builders lime (available at lumberyards or garden supply shops)

Soak corn 8 to 12 hours or overnight. Cover corn and lime with water to a depth of at least 2 inches. Bring to a boil, stirring often to prevent sticking; keep corn covered with water at all times. Boil 45 minutes or until water becomes thick and hulls slip off in your fingers. Drain corn in a colander and rinse 2 or 3 times to remove hulls. Return corn to pot, cover with water, and continue cooking 2 to 3 hours, until corn is soft.

Hominy with Lye

2 tablespoons lye

1 quart dry yellow corn

Dissolve lye in 1 gallon water. Add corn and boil 45 minutes. Remove from heat. Pour into a colander and rinse 2 or 3 minutes to remove hulls. Return corn to pot and cover with water. Bring to a boil, then pour off water. Repeat 4 times. In the fourth change of water, cook 2 to 3 hours, until hominy is tender.

Hominy with Wood Ashes

1 quart dry yellow corn

1 quart wet wood ashes

Combine ashes and 1 gallon water. Add corn and bring to a boil, stirring to prevent sticking; keep corn covered with water at all times. Boil until hulls slip off in your fingers. Pour into a colander and rinse thoroughly to remove hulls. Return corn to pot and cover with water. Bring to a boil, then pour off water. Repeat 4 times. In the fourth change of water, cook 2 to 3 hours, until hominy is tender.

Pork and Hominy (Posole)

1 pork roast (1½ to 2 pounds)

4 cups partially cooked hominy

1 medium onion, chopped

2 quarts water

¼ teaspoon dry parsley

Pinch of oregano

Salt and pepper to taste

Brown pork roast in a large pan. Add hominy, onion, and water. Cook until roast is tender. Remove bones and return meat to hominy. Add parsley, oregano, and salt and pepper. Cook a few minutes. Makes 6 to 8 servings.

Baked Hominy and Tomatoes

3 cups hominy

1 tablespoon butter

2 cups cooked tomatoes

3 green onions, chopped

¼ cup grated cheese

Salt and pepper to taste

Combine ingredients in a well-greased baking dish and bake at 400° F. for 45 minutes. Makes 4 or 5 servings.

Creamed Hominy

3 cups hominy

2 tablespoons butter

1 cup cream or top milk

½ teaspoon paprika

Salt and pepper to taste

Heat hominy in butter. Add cream, paprika, salt, and pepper. Continue to heat and stir until mixture boils. Makes 3 or 4 servings.

Mock Enchiladas

1 quart hominy

1 onion, chopped

1 pint Enchilada Sauce (see p. 53)

2 cups grated cheese

Heat hominy. Layer half the hominy, half the onion, and one-third of the cheese in a casserole dish. Repeat with the remaining hominy and onion, and half of the remaining cheese. Cover with sauce. Top with remaining cheese. Bake at 350° F. for 30 minutes. Makes 4 servings.

Hominy and Tamale Casserole

2 cups hominy

4 tamales

2 cups Enchilada Sauce (see index)

1 cup grated cheese

¼ cup finely chopped green onions

Place drained hominy in a greased casserole dish. Crumble tamales over hominy. Cover with enchilada sauce and top with cheese and onions. Bake at 350° F. for 20 minutes. Makes 6 servings.

Mexican Dishes

Mexican cuisine has three main ingredients: chilies, beans, and corn. Where we in the United States serve potatoes, refried beans (frijoles refritos) are served in Mexico. Refried beans are discussed in another chapter (see index). Chili is probably the one ingredient that draws so many people to Mexican food. There are many varieties. The chilies used in the following recipes are jalapeño peppers (dark green, 2½ inches long, and very hot) or California green chilies, sold in supermarkets as whole chilies, diced chilies, or green chilies, ranging from sweet to mild.

In Mexico, lard is used in doughs and for frying. It is preferable for authentic texture and flavor. Vegetable shortening may be substituted, but it will not give the same flavor as lard. The meat used for fillings is boiled, including the ground meat. The following recipes are some of the best-known and best-loved Mexican dishes.

Grinding Your Own Masa

Masa, used to make tortillas, is a moist dough made from ground dried corn that has been boiled in lime water. To residents of the United States, the most familiar masa is the instant, dehydrated masa. It has a different flavor from homemade masa. This chapter provides the procedure for making your own authentic masa from dry yellow corn.

The only equipment necessary for making masa is a corn grinder with metal blades. Because you will be putting wet corn through the grinder, grinders with stones will clog. Corona Hand Mills manufactures an inexpensive hand grinder with metal blades. A health food store may order one if they don't have it in stock, or write to Smithfield Implement Company, 97 North Main Street, Smithfield, Utah 84335 to order a grinder.

Masa

2 quarts dry yellow corn
¾ cup hot builders or hydrated lime

Cover corn and lime with water to a depth of 3 inches. Bring to a boil, stirring often to prevent sticking; keep corn covered with water at all times. Boil for 45 minutes or until hulls slip off in your fingers and water is thick. To test corn, pinch in half. If it has a dry, white streak down the middle, it is ready. Rinse corn in a colander 2 or 3 times to remove hulls. Grind corn in grinder with metal blades on fine grind. If corn is hard to grind, add a small amount of water while grinding.

Fresh masa will not keep well. Use it as soon as possible or freeze it for later use.

Corn Tortillas

Add a little water to masa to form a dough that holds together well and is pliable. Do not add salt. Shape into walnut-size balls.

To roll tortillas, place ball between two pieces of waxed paper or a damp cloth. Roll with a rolling pin until tortilla is about 6 inches in diameter and thin.

To press in a tortilla press, place waxed paper on top and bottom of press with tortilla dough in the middle. Press down firmly.

Cook tortillas on a hot cast-iron skillet or griddle. Do not grease unless tortillas stick. If they do, wipe the skillet with a cloth moistened with oil. Brown tortillas on both sides until flecked with brown spots. Store tortillas in a plastic bag or wrap in a dampened cloth.

Tamales

5 pounds masa
1½ pounds lard
1 to 2 tablespoons enchilada sauce
Salt to taste
1 to 1½ cups meat stock or poultry broth
Meat filling

Combine masa, lard, enchilada sauce, and salt. Mix well. Add enough stock or broth to make a dough that holds together well. It should be the consistency of thin cookie dough or thick mush.

Meat Filling: Use any of the following meats in making tamales: pork roast, beef roast, chicken, turkey, or a combination of any or all. (Chunky Wheat Meat may also be used, but do not boil.) Boil meat until tender (except wheat meat). Remove the meat and bones, saving the stock. Cool meat. Shred or cut into chunks. Add 1 cup enchilada sauce and 1 garlic clove, chopped fine, for every 2 cups of meat or wheat meat.

Procedure:
1. Soak corn husks in warm water until soft, at least 30 minutes. (Split husks can be used by overlapping to make one husk.)

2. Spread a 2½" x 2½" square of masa dough on each corn husk. Dough should be ¼" thick.

3. Spread 1 heaping tablespoon chilled meat mixture on each masa square.

4. Fold sides of husk to center and then fold in ends.

5. To steam: Place 1 inch water in a large saucepan. Place a rack in the bottom of the pan and stack tamales upright on the rack. Cover and steam for 45 to 60 minutes over low heat. When masa dough is firm, tamales are cooked.

For later use: Do not cook tamales immediately. Place raw tamales in cooking bags and freeze. When ready to use, remove from freezer and place bag in a steamer. Cut a small hole in top of bag for moisture to escape. Steam for 3 hours or until tamales are done.

Green Chili Stew

2 tablespoons fat
1½ pounds cubed steak
1 large onion, chopped
1 can chopped green chilies
Salt and pepper to taste

Melt fat in skillet. Add meat and cook until pink has entirely disappeared. Add onion and chopped chilies. Add salt and pepper. Cover with water and let simmer until tender. Do not let stew become dry; it should be soupy. Serve with corn tortillas or hot biscuits and butter. Makes 4 to 6 servings.

Chilaquiles

12 corn tortillas, ¼-inch thick (use
    homemade tortillas)
3 tablespoons lard
1 medium onion, chopped and browned
2 cloves garlic, minced
Pinch of oregano
Pinch of cumin
1 to 2 cups enchilada sauce
½ pound cheese, grated

Quarter tortillas and fry in lard until soft and limp. Stir in onion, garlic, oregano, and cumin. Cover with enchilada sauce and top with cheese. Simmer until cheese melts, or bake at 350° F. for 20 minutes. Makes 6 servings.

Chili Con Carne

1 large onion, chopped
1 tablespoon lard or shortening
3 cups pinto or red beans
2 cups tomato sauce
½ tablespoon chili powder

2 teaspoons salt
½ teaspoon pepper
2 cups Chunky Wheat Meat (see index)
    or 1 pound hamburger, browned

Sauté onion in shortening or lard until tender. Add beans, tomato sauce, chili powder, salt, and pepper. Cover and simmer for 1 hour. Add browned hamburger or wheat meat to bean mixture and continue cooking until heated through. Makes 6 to 8 servings.

Mexican Tacos

1 pound ground beef, boiled, or 2 cups
    Chunky Wheat Meat (see index)
1 small onion, chopped
3 hot peppers, chopped, or 1 tablespoon
    Chili Spice (see index)
1 clove garlic, minced
Salt and pepper to taste
1 dozen tortillas
1 pound grated cheese
2 or 3 tomatoes, chopped
Shredded lettuce

Mix meat, onion, peppers or chili spice, garlic, salt, and pepper. Place two tablespoonfuls in each tortilla. Fold tortillas in half and secure with a toothpick. Fry filled tortillas in hot lard until almost crisp. Remove toothpick and fill each taco with cheese, tomato, and lettuce.

Enchilada Sauce

6 to 8 whole red dried chilies, 5 to 8
    inches in length (California
    Sweet, Anaheim, or New
    Mexico)*
½ cup drippings or melted lard or
    shortening
½ cup flour
4 cups water
¼ teaspoon cumin
1 clove garlic, chopped
½ cup chopped onion
Salt to taste
Pinch of cinnamon (optional)

Remove seeds and stems from chilies. Cover with hot water and let stand for 30 minutes. Pour off water and place chilies in 1 cup water in blender. Blend until smooth. Remove purée from blender and put through a sieve or ricer to remove particles of skin. Melt drippings or lard in a saucepan over low heat. Blend in flour. Add 4 cups water and cook until thick. Remove from heat and add remaining ingredients and puréed chilies.

*Whole red chilies can be mild, medium hot, or hot. Use whichever one suits your taste, or mix them.

Procedure for Making Enchiladas

1. Dip each tortilla in medium-hot fat until soft and limp.

2. Pour ½ cup sauce in bottom of shallow pan, lay hot tortilla in pan, and sprinkle with cheese. Spoon 1 heaping tablespoon filling in the center.

3. Spoon 2 tablespoons sauce over filling and roll. Continue with each tortilla, placing enchiladas side by side.

4. Pour remaining sauce over enchiladas—enough to keep them from drying out in the oven. Top with remaining grated cheese. Bake at 350° F. for 20 to 30 minutes.

Beef and Pork Enchiladas

1 pound ground beef or pork
1 cup water
1 onion, chopped
1 clove garlic, chopped
Salt to taste
1 dozen corn tortillas
4 cups enchilada sauce
1 pound cheese, grated

Boil meat in water until cooked through. Add onion, garlic, and salt. Follow procedure for making enchiladas (above), adding 1 heaping tablespoon meat mixture to center of each tortilla.

Cheese Enchiladas

1 dozen corn tortillas
4 cups enchilada sauce
1 pound cheese, grated
1 onion, chopped
¼ cup green onions, chopped

Follow procedure for making enchiladas (above). Fill tortillas with cheese and onions. Top with green onions.

Chicken Enchiladas

1 medium chicken
4 cups enchilada sauce
1 medium onion, chopped
1 clove garlic, chopped
1 pound cheese, grated
1 dozen corn tortillas
¼ cup chopped green onions

Boil chicken until tender. Remove from heat and cool. Remove bones and chop meat, reserving broth. Make enchilada sauce, substituting chicken broth for water in the gravy. Add to chicken, onion, and garlic. Follow procedure for making enchiladas (above), adding 1 heaping tablespoon chicken mixture to center of each tortilla. Top with green onions.

Mexican Taco (p. 54); Chimichanga (p. 59) topped with Guacamole Sauce (p. 115)

Chili Rellenos

Drain 1 can (6 ounces) whole green chilies or use fresh chilies. To peel fresh chilies, put chilies on a broiler rack about 1 inch below broiling unit. Broil, turning a few times until chilies are blistered and lightly browned all over. As each chili is done, place it in a plastic bag; let stand until cool enough to handle. Peel with a sharp knife, catching the skin and gently pulling it away. Be careful not to tear the chili.

Slice chilies down the middle to remove seeds. Flour inside and out. Stuff chilies with one of the following fillings. Then coat with either Puffy Coating or Thin and Crispy Coating (recipes below). Fry in hot oil or grease. Top with Green Chili Gravy, if desired.

Cheese Filling: Stuff each chili with a piece of jack or cheddar cheese ½ inch shorter than the chili.

Beef Filling: Brown ½ pound lean ground beef. Stir in one tomato, chopped fine, or 3 tablespoons tomato sauce; 2 tablespoons finely chopped onion; ½ jalapeño pepper, chopped fine; and 1 clove garlic, minced. Cook until onion is tender. Use 1 or 2 tablespoons filling for each chili.

Tofu Filling: Combine 3 tablespoons grated tofu; 1 onion, minced; 1 tomato, minced. Use 1 to 2 tablespoons filling for each chili. Coat with Thin and Crispy Coating.

Puffy Coating: Beat 3 egg whites until stiff. Beat 3 yolks with 1 tablespoon water, 3 tablespoons flour, ¼ teaspoon salt, and ½ teaspoon baking powder. Fold into egg whites. Coat stuffed chilies.

Thin and Crispy Coating: Beat 3 egg whites until stiff. In a separate bowl, beat 3 yolks. Fold yolks into whites. Coat stuffed chilies.

Flour Tortillas

4 cups flour
1½ teaspoons salt
½ cup lard
Water

Mix flour and salt. Cut in lard. Mix in enough water to make a pliable dough. Knead dough until soft (it should be soft and pliable enough to stretch). Form dough in balls, cover with cloth, and let stand 30 minutes. Roll dough paper thin. Cook in a medium hot skillet or griddle until tortillas start to bubble. Turn and cook other side.

Green Chili Chicken Enchiladas

1 medium chicken
1 medium onion, chopped
1 clove garlic, chopped
4 cups chicken broth
¼ cup flour
½ teaspoon salt
1 can (3 ounces) chopped green chilies
1 jalapeño pepper, chopped (optional)
1 pound cheese, grated
1 dozen corn tortillas

Boil chicken until tender. Remove from heat and cool. Remove bones and chop chicken, reserving broth. Add onion and garlic to chopped chicken. Set aside. Add flour to broth and cook until thick. Add salt, chilies, and jalapeño pepper. Use this mixture in place of enchilada sauce in procedure for making enchiladas (p. 55). Place 1 heaping tablespoon chicken mixture in middle of each tortilla.

Chimichangas

2 pounds beef or pork roast, or a combination of both
Water
1 medium onion, chopped
1 can (3 ounces) chopped green chilies
¼ teaspoon cumin
1 clove garlic, chopped
½ cup broth
6 to 8 large soft flour tortillas
Green Chili Gravy (below)
Grated cheese
Sour cream

Cover roast with water and boil until tender. Cool and reserve broth. Remove bones and chop or shred meat. Simmer meat, onion, ½ can green chilies, cumin, and garlic in broth until onion is tender. Warm tortillas in oven or microwave. Spread approximately ½ cup meat mixture on tortilla, fold in ends, and roll. Secure with a toothpick. Fry in hot oil until brown and crisp. Top with Green Chili Gravy and garnish with grated cheese and sour cream.

Green Chili Gravy

2 tablespoons flour
2 tablespoons chopped green chilies
½ jalapeño pepper, chopped
2 cups water or broth
2 tablespoons finely chopped onions
⅛ teaspoon pepper
½ teaspoon salt

Combine flour with chilies and jalapeño pepper in a medium saucepan. Add water or broth and cook over medium heat, stirring constantly until thick. Add remaining ingredients. Serve over Chili Rellenos or Chimichangas (above).

Variety Grains

Rice

Rice is a versatile and economical food, is a good source of energy, and supplies carbohydrates, protein, vitamins, and minerals.

Rice should be stored in an airtight container and in a cool place. Brown rice will go rancid if it is not stored correctly. It will keep six months to a year in a cool, dry place, and for many years in the freezer. White rice will keep indefinitely in an airtight container.

Though there are many varieties of rice, there are basically only three different lengths:

Long grain rice has a length of four to five times its width. The grain is long and translucent and remains distinct and separate after cooking.

Medium grain rice is three times as long as it is wide, and is less expensive than long grain rice. It requires a shorter growing season and produces a higher yield. It is also easier to mill than long grain.

Short grain rice is one and one-half to two times longer than wide. It is the least expensive.

There are generally five different kinds of rice the consumer needs to be aware of and distinguish between:

Brown rice is the whole, unpolished rice with only the outer fiber (inedible hull) removed. It requires more water and longer cooking times. It has a nutty flavor and a chewy texture.

Regular white rice has the hulls, germ, and outer fiber (hull) removed. The grains are bland, fluffy, and distinct when cooked properly.

Parboiled, or converted, rice has been treated to keep some of the natural vitamins and minerals, and has been cooked by a special process before milling. Though it requires longer cooking than regular white rice, the grains are fluffy, plump, and separate after cooking.

Precooked rice is completely cooked. It needs only to stand in boiling water for several minutes.

Enriched rice has a coating of vitamins and minerals to fortify the nutritional content. The coating adheres to the rice and does not dissolve in cooking.

Wild rice is not truly rice, but the seed of a water grass found in the Great Lakes region. It is usually expensive, and the demand is usually greater than the supply.

Directions for Cooking Rice

Variety	Rice	Water	Salt	Cooking Time	Yield
Brown	1 cup	2½ cups	1 tsp.	45 minutes	4 cups
Regular	1 cup	2 cups	1 tsp.	14 minutes	3 cups
Parboiled	1 cup	2½ cups	1 tsp.	20 minutes	4 cups
Precooked	1 cup	1 cup	½ tsp.	5 minutes	2 cups

Hints for Cooking with Rice

1. Do not rinse rice before or after cooking. Nutrients on the surface of the rice are washed away if it is rinsed.

2. Too much water will result in soggy rice and wasted nutrients when the rice is drained. Too little water will result in dry rice.

3. Do not stir rice after it comes to a boil. Stirring will break the grains and produce gummy rice.

4. Keep lid tightly closed during cooking. Lifting the lid lets out the steam and lowers the temperature.

5. Remove from pan immediately after cooking. Rice left in the pan for over 10 minutes will lose its desirable fluffy consistency.

6. To test for doneness, press a kernel with a spoon. It should be soft throughout.

7. To reheat rice, place ½ inch water in a saucepan and bring to a boil. Add rice and simmer or steam 5 minutes.

Cooking Liquids for Rice

Chicken broth, beef broth, or consommé: Use 1 cup rice to 2 cups broth plus 1 teaspoon salt.

Beef or chicken soup base or bouillon: Dissolve 1 tablespoon soup base bouillon crystals in 2 cups water. Use 1 cup rice to 2 cups prepared bouillon plus 1 teaspoon salt.

Orange or apple juice: Use 1 cup rice to 2 cups juice plus 1 teaspoon salt.

Tomato or vegetable juice: Use 1 cup rice to 2 cups juice plus 1 teaspoon salt.

Carrot juice: Use 1 cup rice to 1½ cups water and ½ cup carrot juice plus 1 teaspoon salt.

For brown or parboiled rice, increase cooking liquid by ½ cup for every cup of rice.

Pan-Fried Rice

In a heavy skillet, melt ¼ cup oil or lard. Add 1 cup regular white rice and heat, stirring to prevent scorching. Fry 5 minutes. Stir in 2 cups cold water, 1 teaspoon salt, and ¼ teaspoon pepper. Cover and simmer 30 minutes or until all liquid is absorbed and rice is cooked.

Steamed Brown Rice

1 cup brown rice
2½ cups water
1 teaspoon salt

Combine rice, water, and salt in the top of a double boiler. Bring to a boil and cook, covered, 2 minutes. Bring water to boil in bottom of double boiler, and place rice over boiling water. Steam for 45 minutes, or until rice is tender and liquid is absorbed.

Brown Rice Pilaf

1 cup brown rice
2½ cups water
2 teaspoons chicken soup base or bouillon
1 cup sliced celery
½ cup chopped onion
2 tablespoons butter or margarine
½ cup toasted, chopped almonds (optional)

Cook brown rice with water and soup base or bouillon. In a small skillet, cook celery and onion in butter until tender. Stir into hot cooked rice; add almonds, and mix well. Makes 4 servings.

Herbed Rice

⅓ cup chopped onion
⅓ cup chopped celery
⅓ cup fresh sliced mushrooms
¼ cup butter or margarine
2 tablespoons chopped parsley
½ teaspoon marjoram
½ teaspoon thyme
1 cup cooked green peas
2 cups rice cooked in chicken broth

Sauté onion, celery, and mushrooms in butter or margarine until tender. Add herbs and peas. Stir into hot rice, and mix well. Makes 6 servings.

Spanish Rice

¼ cup cooking oil or lard

1 cup rice

2 cups water or broth

1 teaspoon salt

½ teaspoon chili powder (optional)

2 cloves garlic, minced

1 small onion, chopped

¼ teaspoon pepper

2 tomatoes, chopped, or ¼ cup tomato
 sauce

In a heavy skillet, melt oil or lard. Add rice and heat, stirring to prevent scorching. Fry 5 minutes. Stir in remaining ingredients. Cover, and simmer 30 minutes, or until all liquid is absorbed and rice is cooked. Makes 4 servings.

Guatemalan Rice

¼ cup cooking oil or lard

1 cup rice

2 cups water

1 teaspoon salt

¼ teaspoon pepper

2 cloves garlic, minced

1 small onion, chopped

1 raw carrot, chopped

½ cup frozen peas

2 fresh tomatoes, chopped, or 1 cup
 canned tomatoes

In a heavy skillet, melt oil or lard. Add rice and heat, stirring to prevent scorching. Fry 5 minutes. Stir in remaining ingredients. Cover, and simmer 30 minutes, or until all liquid is absorbed and rice is cooked. Makes 4 servings.

Spanish Skillet Dinner

1 cup rice

2½ cups tomato juice

¼ cup vinegar

1 medium onion, chopped

1 clove garlic, minced

2 teaspoons salt

¼ teaspoon pepper

¼ teaspoon Tabasco sauce

1 medium tomato, chopped

1 small green pepper, chopped

1 pound browned ground beef or 2 cups
 Chunky Wheat Meat (see index)

Cook rice in tomato juice, to which vinegar, onion, garlic, salt, pepper, and Tabasco have been added. When rice is tender, add tomato, green pepper, and ground beef or wheat meat. Cook 5 minutes. Makes 6 servings.

Curry Rice

¼ cup butter or margarine

1 cup rice

2 cups water

1 teaspoon salt

1 teaspoon chicken soup base or bouillon

½ teaspoon curry powder

¼ teaspoon paprika

In a heavy skillet, melt butter. Add rice and heat, stirring to prevent scorching. Cook 5 minutes. Stir in remaining ingredients and cook 30 minutes, or until rice is tender. Makes 4 servings.

Curry Casserole

1 pound ground beef or 2 cups Chunky
 Wheat Meat (see index)

½ cup chopped onion

1 cup chopped celery

1 can (10½ ounces) mushroom soup

½ cup milk or soy milk

2 cups cooked rice

½ teaspoon garlic salt

½ teaspoon salt

Brown ground beef. Add onion and celery; sauté until tender. Add milk to mushroom soup. Mix all ingredients and pour into casserole dish. Bake at 350° F. for 30 minutes.

If you use wheat meat, omit browning and sauté onion and celery in 2 tablespoons butter or margarine. Makes 6 servings.

Tuna and Rice

1 tablespoon margarine

½ cup chopped onion

2 cups cooked rice

1 can (10½ ounces) mushroom soup

1 can (7 ounces) tuna, drained

1 cup cooked peas

¼ cup chopped pimiento (optional)

Sauté onions in margarine until tender. Combine with remaining ingredients in a casserole dish. Bake uncovered at 350° F. for 20 to 30 minutes. Makes 6 servings.

Rice Fruit Salad (below)

Rice Fruit Salad

2 cups cooked rice, chilled
1 can mandarin oranges, drained
1 cup pineapple chunks, drained
1 cup melon balls or mixed fruit
½ cup strawberries
1 pint cream, whipped, or Soy Whipped
    Cream (optional)

Combine rice and fruit. Fold in whipped cream if desired. Refrigerate. Makes 8 to 10 servings.

Rice Pastry Shell

1 cup white rice flour
1 tablespoon potato flakes
½ teaspoon salt
¼ cup margarine or butter
4 tablespoons ice water

Combine rice flour, potato flakes, and salt. Cut in margarine or butter until mixture is in even bits about the size of small peas. Add water and mix thoroughly. Pat dough into a 9-inch pie plate. Bake at 425° F. for 15 to 20 minutes.

Oats

The Scots have used oats for centuries and are probably responsible for introducing them to America. Oats contain seven B vitamins, vitamin E, and nine minerals. They are 10 to 12 percent protein and are cholesterol free. Oats are found in five main forms:

Rolled oats are the whole grain with the hull removed and the oats rolled.

Oat groats are the whole grain with only the hull removed.

Steel-cut oats are oats that have been broken into several pieces for quick cooking.

Quick-cooking oats are small-grain oats that have been rolled and steamed to precook them, then flattened very thin.

Oat flour is finely ground flour used primarily for baking.

Oats, which have a bland flavor, are very versatile. They may be used in cereals, cookies, desserts, breads, and main dishes. They may also be used to thicken soups, gravies, sauces, stews, and puddings.

Oat Flour

Place rolled oats in a blender or food processor. Blend 1 minute. Use as you would white flour. For thickening, use same amount of oat flour as white flour. For baking, substitute no more than ⅓ cup oat flour for regular flour.

Toasted Oats

Spread rolled oats on a cookie sheet and bake at 375° F. for 15 to 20 minutes, or until oats are golden brown. Store in a cool, dry place. Use in place of bread crumbs or nuts. Add to meat loaf, salads, or cereals for a delightful new flavor.

Cinnamon Apple Oats

2 cups water
⅔ cup rolled oats
½ cup dried apple bits or fresh chopped
    apples
3 tablespoons brown sugar
1 teaspoon cinnamon
½ cup raisins or dates
¼ teaspoon salt

Bring water to a boil in a saucepan. Add remaining ingredients. Cook on low heat 10 to 15 minutes, stirring occasionally. Makes 3 or 4 servings.

Granola

3 cups rolled oats
¼ cup wheat germ
¼ cup sesame seeds
1 cup sunflower seeds
½ cup coconut
1 cup chopped nuts
1 cup raisins
⅓ cup margarine or oil
½ cup brown sugar
¼ teaspoon salt
¼ cup water
¼ cup honey
1 teaspoon cinnamon

In a large mixing bowl, combine rolled oats, wheat germ, sesame seeds, sunflower seeds, coconut, nuts, and raisins. In a small skillet or saucepan, melt margarine; add brown sugar, salt, water, honey, and cinnamon. Cool slightly and pour over rolled-oats mixture. Mix well and spread in a 13″ x 9″ baking pan. Bake at 350° F. for 15 to 20 minutes, stirring occasionally. Cool. Store in an airtight container in a cool place.

Peanut Butter Granola

5 cups rolled oats
½ cup wheat germ
¼ cup honey
1 cup chopped peanuts
1 cup creamy or chunky peanut butter
1 cup coarsely chopped dried bananas
    or apples
1 cup raisins

Mix all ingredients well in a large bowl. Let stand for 1 hour. Pour onto a greased cookie sheet and bake at 300° F. for 1 hour, stirring every 15 minutes. Makes about 8 cups.

Honey Oat Muffins

1 cup flour
1½ cups rolled oats
¼ cup brown sugar
1 teaspoon salt
1 teaspoon baking powder
1 cup milk
⅓ cup cooking oil or melted butter
1 egg, beaten
¼ cup honey

Combine dry ingredients; make a well, and add remaining ingredients. Stir just until moistened. Fill muffin cups and bake at 400° F. for 15 to 20 minutes. Makes 12 muffins.

Honey Oat Bread

2 tablespoons dry yeast
½ cup warm water
¼ cup shortening or cooking oil
⅓ cup honey
1 tablespoon salt
2 cups boiling water

6 to 6½ cups flour
2 cups rolled oats
½ cup instant nonfat dry milk

Dissolve yeast in ½ cup warm water. In 2 cups boiling water, melt shortening; add honey and salt. Cool to lukewarm. Combine 2 cups flour, the oats, and the dry milk. Stir into cooled shortening and honey liquid. Add yeast, and beat with electric mixer at high speed for 3 to 4 minutes. Add remaining flour and knead to make a smooth, elastic dough. Cover and let rise until double in bulk. Divide dough and shape into loaves. Place in greased bread pans and bake at 350° F. for 50 minutes.

Oat Stuffing

¼ cup butter or margarine
¼ cup chopped celery
¼ cup chopped onion
1½ cups rolled oats
1 egg, beaten
¾ cup chicken or beef broth
¼ teaspoon salt
⅛ teaspoon pepper

Melt butter in skillet; add celery and onions. Sauté until tender. Mix oats and egg; add to onion mixture and cook over medium heat, stirring constantly until oats are dry and light brown, 3 to 5 minutes. Add remaining ingredients and continue stirring until liquid evaporates, 2 to 3 minutes. Serve in place of rice or pasta. Makes 4 servings.

Variations:
Add 1 medium tomato and ¼ cup chopped green pepper in place of celery.
Add 2 tablespoons soy sauce and 1 can drained water chestnuts.
Add 1 small can drained mushrooms.
Add ¼ teaspoon sage, ½ teaspoon oregano, ¼ teaspoon basil, and 2 tablespoons parsley flakes.
Add ¼ teaspoon cinnamon and ¼ cup chopped apple.

Tuna Oat Salad

½ cup Toasted Oats
1 can (6½ ounces) tuna, drained
¼ cup chopped green onions
¼ cup chopped green pepper
¼ cup chopped celery
¼ cup milk
½ cup salad dressing
2 tablespoons pickle relish
½ teaspoon celery seed
½ teaspoon chopped parsley

Combine all ingredients and mix well. Serve as salad or as sandwich filling.

Variations:
Add 4 chopped hard-boiled eggs in place of tuna.
Add 1 cup chopped or ground meat in place of tuna.

Juicy Hamburgers

1½ pounds ground beef
¾ cup rolled oats
½ cup chopped onion
⅓ cup catsup
1 egg
1 teaspoon salt
¼ teaspoon pepper

Combine all ingredients and mix well. Shape into patties and fry or broil to desired doneness.

Meat Loaf

1½ pounds ground beef
1 cup tomato sauce or catsup
¾ cup rolled oats
¼ cup chopped green pepper
½ cup chopped onion
1 egg
1 teaspoon salt
⅛ teaspoon pepper
¼ teaspoon sage
¼ teaspoon Italian Seasoning (see index)

Combine all ingredients and mix well. Place in baking dish and bake at 350° F. for 1 hour. Makes 6 to 8 servings.

Variations:
Substitute Meat Loaf Spice (see index) for onion and spices.
Add ½ cup cheese cut into chunks.
Add 1 small can green chilies, drained, and 1 tablespoon Chili Spice (see index) in place of green peppers.

Meatballs

1½ pounds ground beef
¾ cup rolled oats
¼ cup chopped onion
¼ cup chopped green pepper
⅓ cup tomato sauce
1 egg
1 teaspoon salt
¼ teaspoon pepper
½ teaspoon Italian Seasoning (see index)

Combine all ingredients and mix well. Shape into balls and brown in hot oil. Makes 14 to 16 meatballs.

Serve meatballs with Spaghetti Sauce or Sweet and Sour Sauce (see index). Serve over noodles, spaghetti, or rice.

Oat Pastry Shell

1 cup rolled oats
⅓ cup finely chopped nuts
⅓ cup brown sugar
½ teaspoon cinnamon
½ cup coconut
¼ cup melted butter or margarine

Combine all ingredients and mix well. Press into bottom and sides of lightly greased pie plate. Bake at 375° F. for 8 to 10 minutes. Makes one 9-inch pie shell.

Ice Cream Pie

9-inch Oat Pastry Shell
1 quart ice cream or frozen yogurt

Spoon softened ice cream or frozen yogurt into pie crust. Top with oat topping (below). Freeze until ready to serve. If desired, top with sweetened strawberries or other fruit.

Oat Topping

1½ cups rolled oats (quick or old-fashioned)
⅓ cup brown sugar
⅓ cup butter or margarine
¼ cup finely chopped nuts
¼ cup coconut
½ teaspoon cinnamon

Combine all ingredients, mixing well. Cook in a skillet over medium heat, stirring constantly, for 5 minutes or until golden brown. Serve over desserts, fruit salads, yogurt, ice cream, or pudding.

Frozen Banana Pops

4 bananas
8 wooden sticks
1 package (6 ounces) chocolate or butterscotch chips
2 tablespoons butter or margarine
1 cup oat topping

Cut bananas in half and insert stick in each half. Freeze until firm. Melt chocolate or butterscotch chips in butter. Pour into tall glass. Dip bananas in butter mixture and roll in topping. Freeze until ready to use.

Crunchy Banana Cake

½ cup butter or margarine
1 cup brown sugar
2 large bananas, mashed
1 teaspoon baking soda
1 egg
1 teaspoon vanilla
1 cup oat flour
1 cup flour
1 teaspoon salt
2 cups oat topping (above)

Cream butter and sugar until light and fluffy. Mash banana; add baking soda and let stand. Add egg and vanilla to sugar-butter mixture and beat. Add oat flour, flour, and salt, mixing well. Add bananas and baking soda. Pour into greased 13″ x 9″ pan and sprinkle with oat topping. Bake at 350° F. for 45 minutes.

Pudding Parfaits

Make any variety of pudding. In dessert dishes, alternate layers of pudding with oat topping. Chill and serve.
Variations:
Add drained fruit in layers with pudding and topping.
Sweeten yogurt with honey or sugar and layer with fruit and topping.

Crunchy Crisp

Spoon any sweetened and thickened fruit into a baking dish. Top with oat topping. Bake at 350° F. for 30 minutes.

Oatmeal Cookies

1 cup butter or margarine
1¼ cups brown sugar
2 eggs
1 teaspoon vanilla
1½ cups flour
2½ cups rolled oats
1 teaspoon baking powder
½ teaspoon salt
1 teaspoon baking soda
1 teaspoon cinnamon
½ teaspoon nutmeg
½ teaspoon ginger

Cream butter and sugar until light and fluffy. Add eggs and vanilla and mix well. Combine dry ingredients; add to sugar mixture and mix well. Drop by teaspoonfuls on a greased cookie sheet and bake at 350° F. for 10 to 12 minutes or until golden brown. Makes 5 to 6 dozen cookies.

Variations:

Add 1 cup raisins.

Add 1 cup chopped nuts.

Add 1 cup chocolate, carob, butterscotch, or peanut butter chips.

Add 1 cup shredded or flaked coconut.

Add 1 cup dried or candied fruit.

Add 1 cup cornflakes.

Granola Bars

4 cups toasted oats

½ cup raisins

½ cup nuts

½ cup coconut

⅔ cup butter or margarine, melted

½ cup brown sugar

⅓ cup honey or molasses

1 egg, beaten

½ teaspoon vanilla

½ teaspoon salt

Combine all ingredients and press into a well-greased cookie sheet or jelly-roll pan. Bake at 350° F. for 20 minutes. Cool and cut into bars.

Millet

Millet is an alkaline grain rather than an acid grain like most others. An ancient grain, it is used in place of rice in northern China, parts of Russia, and parts of Africa and India. It is easily digested, and high in vitamin B_2, potassium, iron, magnesium, and calcium.

Millet may be cooked whole as a cereal or ground into flour for baking. A bland grain, it may be used with a wide variety of seasonings or combined with other grains. Ground millet can replace half of the cornmeal in corn bread or tamale pie. It can also be substituted for rice in most dishes.

Millet Cereal

2 cups boiling water

½ cup millet

½ teaspoon salt

Bring water to boil. Add millet and salt. Cook 30 minutes. Serve hot with milk and with butter or sweetened with sugar or honey.

Millet and Lentil Soup

¼ cup chopped onion

2 tablespoons butter

½ cup lentils

½ cup millet

3 cups water

1 teaspoon salt

¼ teaspoon pepper

1 clove garlic, minced

¼ cup chopped celery

2 carrots, chopped

¼ teaspoon cumin

¼ teaspoon oregano

Sauté onion in butter until tender. Combine with rest of ingredients and simmer for 30 to 60 minutes.

Millet Pilaf

¼ cup chopped onion

½ cup cup chopped celery

2 tablespoons butter or margarine

2 cups beef or chicken broth

⅔ cup millet

¼ cup toasted slivered almonds

1 teaspoon salt

Sauté onion and celery in butter, Add broth and bring to a boil. Add millet, and simmer 20 minutes. Add almonds and salt, and cook until vegetables are tender.

Barley

Barley is a grain that originated in ancient China. It is a food staple in Eastern Europe and North Africa. Barley is excellent in casseroles and soups and as a substitute for rice. It can also be ground into flour. Nutritious and easy to digest, it has a sweet, nutlike flavor.

Barley Water

Stir 1 tablespoon barley into 3 cups boiling water. Turn heat down and simmer, stirring occasionally, until barley is soft. Strain. Salt to taste.

Barley Cereal

Add ¾ cup barley and ½ teaspoon salt to 3 cups boiling water. Simmer until barley is tender.

Barley Soup

½ cup barley
1 medium onion, chopped
2 stalks celery, chopped
2 large carrots, sliced
2 large potatoes, cubed

Cook barley with onion, celery, carrots, and potatoes in 2 quarts water. Simmer until vegetables are tender, about 30 minutes. Add salt to taste.

Rye

Rye is the principal cereal in the Soviet Union and is used widely in the Scandinavian countries. It is an excellent grain supplement in recipes using wheat or corn. Add 2 parts of rye to 5 parts of flour. Rye is mainly used in breads.

Rye Bread

1 tablespoon yeast
1¾ cups water
¼ cup molasses
1 egg
½ cup cooking oil
1 tablespoon salt
4 to 4½ cups white or whole-wheat
    flour
1 cup rye flour, unsifted
2 tablespoons caraway seeds

Dissolve yeast in ¾ cup water. Combine 1 cup water, molasses, egg, and oil. Add salt and 2 cups flour, and beat 2 minutes with mixer. Add yeast mixture and 1 cup flour, and beat 2 more minutes. Stir in remaining flour, rye flour, and caraway seeds. Knead 8 to 10 minutes, or until smooth and elastic. Cover and let rise 1 hour. Punch down and form into long loaves. Place on a greased cookie sheet sprinkled with cornmeal. Bake at 350° F. for 30 minutes.

Pumpernickel Bread

1 package yeast
2¾ cups warm water
¼ cup molasses
1 tablespoon margarine, melted
1½ cups rye flour
4½ cups whole-wheat flour
⅓ cup yellow cornmeal
1 tablespoon salt
1 cup mashed potatoes (room
    temperature)
1 teaspoon caraway seeds

Dissolve yeast in ¾ cup warm water. Combine flours. Combine 2 cups water, molasses, margarine, and yeast mixture. Add 2 cups flour mixture, cornmeal, and salt. Beat 2 minutes at medium speed. Add potatoes and beat 2 minutes more. Stir in caraway seeds and enough additional flour to make a soft dough. Turn onto a floured board and let rest 15 minutes. Knead until smooth and elastic. Place in greased bowl, cover, and let rise in warm place until double in bulk. Punch down; let rise again. Turn out on a lightly floured board and shape into round loaves. Place in greased 8- or 9-inch cake pans or on a greased cookie sheet. Let rise until double in bulk, about 45 minutes. Bake at 350° F. for 50 minutes. Makes one large or two small loaves.

Dried Beans and Legumes

Dried Beans and Legumes

Dried Beans and Legumes

Dried beans, one of the oldest foods still in use today, are truly an international food. Beans are an important staple for millions of people. They are generally within the range of most budgets.

Dried beans are an incomplete protein, so they should be served with cheese, milk, meat, eggs, or grains. They are a rich source of B-complex vitamins, iron, and other minerals. There is no cholesterol in the beans themselves; dishes made with them have cholesterol only if other ingredients contain it. For a longer storage life, keep beans in an airtight container in a cool, dry place.

Varieties Available

Black beans (black turtle beans) are popular in Latin American, Oriental, and Mediterranean dishes.

Garbanzo beans (chick peas) have a nutty flavor and are commonly used in salads.

Great Northern beans are large, white beans used in baked beans and soups.

Red kidney beans are popular for chili.

Lima beans (large or baby) are used in soups and casseroles. They cook in 1 hour.

Mung beans are used for sprouting. The sprouts are used in Oriental cooking.

Navy beans are small, white beans used in baked beans and bean pots.

Pinto beans are pink and speckled and are used mainly in Mexican cooking.

Pink beans are used in Mexican cooking. They can also be used as a substitute for pinto beans.

Split peas are yellow or green peas used mainly in soups. They do not need to be soaked, and they cook in 30 to 45 minutes.

Lentils are disc-shaped legumes used in soups. They do not need to be soaked, and they cook in 30 minutes.

Cooking Dried Beans

1. Sort beans and rinse.
2. Put beans in a pan and cover with warm water (room temperature). Soak 8 to 12 hours or

overnight. Keep beans covered with water during soaking. For a quick soak, bring water to a boil, add beans, and simmer 2 minutes. Soak 1 hour in heated cooking water.

3. Remove soaking water and add new water if desired. (Beans can be cooked in the soaking water.) Cover beans with water and bring to a boil. (Those not covered will be dry and hard.) Reduce heat, cover, and simmer until beans are tender—1 to 3 hours.

Hints for Cooking Dried Beans

1. If you do not have meat or salt pork, add 2 tablespoons butter or shortening to beans during cooking to enhance the flavor.

2. Beans do not have to be soaked before cooking, but cooking times will be longer if they are not.

3. Cooking beans in hard water lengthens the cooking time.

4. Acidic ingredients will retard the softening of the beans. Add ingredients such as tomatoes, chili sauce, vinegar, and catsup after beans have been softened.

5. Beans will more than double their volume during cooking. Be sure to use a large enough pan and ample water.

6. Salt is a necessary ingredient for flavoring beans. Add it after beans have softened. Because it is a mineral, it tends to lengthen the cooking time.

7. Older beans will take longer to cook.

8. You can give beans a ham flavor without using ham by adding ½ teaspoon liquid smoke 15 minutes before beans are done. You can also add Chunky Wheat Meat Sausage (see index).

Sprouting Mung Beans

Mung beans are the bean sprouts used in Chinese cooking. In order for mung beans to look and taste like the Chinese sprouts, they have to be sprouted under pressure. Here is the secret to sprouting mung beans.

1. Put beans in a pan and run warm water over them. Swish to clean thoroughly. Remove those that float to the top. Soak beans in water (room temperature) for 18 to 24 hours. Change water if beans begin to smell sour.

2. Drain beans and place in a colander or a container with holes in the bottom, such as a gallon can with holes punched in the bottom. One inch of beans will expand 25 times. Place a piece of burlap

or cheesecloth, doubled, on top of the beans. On top of the cloth, place a weight, such as a brick, a gallon jug full of water, or a bag of rocks. The weight will move as the bean sprouts grow.

3. Rinse beans three times a day by pouring water over them and letting them drain. Do not disturb beans. Keep at room temperature.

4. After 5 to 7 days the roots should be about 4 inches long. Put the beans in cold water and rinse well. Remove the hulls that float to the top.

Cooked White Beans

1 pound navy or Great Northern beans
Water
Salt pork or ham bone (optional)
2 stalks celery, chopped
1 medium onion, chopped
2 tablespoons butter or margarine
1 tomato, chopped
1 teaspoon salt
½ teaspoon pepper
⅛ teaspoon ginger

Sort beans and soak 8 to 12 hours. Drain, then cover with water or vegetable water. Add pork and simmer until beans are tender. Sauté celery and onions in butter or margarine. Add to beans with tomato and seasonings. Simmer 30 minutes.

Baked Beans

1 pound dried white beans
Water
½ cup brown sugar or molasses
½ cup catsup or tomato sauce
Salt pork, ham bone, or ham pieces
1 medium onion, chopped
½ teaspoon dry mustard
2 teaspoons salt
½ teaspoon pepper

Sort and soak beans 8 to 12 hours. Drain, then cover with fresh water. Bring beans to a boil and cook until tender. Remove from heat and drain, reserving liquid. In a baking dish, combine remaining ingredients and beans. Add enough cooking liquid to cover. Bake uncovered at 325° F. for 2 to 3 hours.

Chili Beans

1 pound red, pink, or pinto beans
Water
1 medium onion, chopped
2 cloves garlic, minced

1 teaspoon salt

Chili spice to taste (see index)

1 pound ground beef, browned, or 2
    cups Chunky Wheat Meat (see
    index)

Sort and soak beans 8 to 12 hours. Drain, then cover with fresh water. Add onion and garlic; cook beans until tender. Add salt, chili spice, and ground beef. Simmer 30 minutes. If using wheat meat, add just before serving.

Pork and Beans

2 pounds navy beans

Water

1 large onion, chopped

Salt pork, ham bone, or ham pieces

1 quart tomato juice

¼ cup sugar

2 teaspoons salt

¼ teaspoon cloves

¼ teaspoon allspice

Sort beans and soak them 8 to 12 hours. Drain, then cover with fresh water. Bring to a boil and add onion and salt pork or ham. Cook until beans are tender. Add remaining ingredients and simmer 30 minutes longer.

To can pork and beans, bring soaked beans to a boil and cook 5 minutes. Remove from heat and let set 20 minutes. Drain. Fill hot jars about ¾ full with beans. Add a piece of salt pork or ham to each jar. Combine tomato juice, sugar, salt, onion, cloves, and allspice, and bring to a boil. Pour over beans, leaving 1 inch head space. Adjust cap and process pints for 1 hour and 5 minutes or quarts for 1 hour and 15 minutes at 10 pounds pressure. (At high altitudes, consult your local county extension agent for recommended processing time.)

Baked Lima Beans and Ham

⅓ cup chopped onion

1 can (8 ounces) tomato sauce

¼ cup catsup

4 cups cooked lima beans

Ham pieces or bacon

2 tablespoons sugar or honey

2 tablespoons vinegar

1 teaspoon Worcestershire sauce

1 teaspoon dry mustard

1 cup grated cheese

Combine onion, tomato sauce, and catsup. Simmer until onion is tender. Add remaining ingredients, topping with grated cheese. Bake at 375° F. for 30 minutes.

Refried Beans

1 pound pinto or black beans

Water

Salt pork, ham hock, bacon, or sausage

1 teaspoon salt

1 medium onion, chopped

¼ cup fat

Sort beans and soak them 8 to 12 hours. Drain and cover with fresh water. Cook beans with meat until tender. Add salt. Mash, blend, or put beans through a ricer. Sauté onion in fat until tender. Add beans and cook until thick. Serve.

To extend refried beans, cook beans until soupy and add cornstarch or flour to thicken.

Black Beans and Rice

2 cups black refried beans (above)

2 cups Guatemalan Rice (see index)

Serve beans over rice. Top with sour cream or cheese.

Bean Dip

2 cups refried beans

1 clove garlic, minced

¼ cup finely chopped onion

1 jalapeño pepper, chopped

2 tablespoons Chili Salsa (see index)

Combine all ingredients and mix well.

Split Pea Soup

1 pound split peas

2 quarts water

1 ham bone

½ cup finely chopped celery

½ cup finely chopped carrot

1 medium onion, chopped

1 teaspoon salt or smoked salt

¼ teaspoon pepper

¼ teaspoon rosemary

1 teaspoon parsley

Combine all ingredients and bring to a boil. Reduce heat and simmer gently 2 to 3 hours or until peas are soft. Remove ham bone; trim meat, cube, and return to soup. If a thick soup is desired, continue cooking until desired consistency is reached.

Split Pea Soup (p. 68); Four-Bean Salad (p. 70); Black Beans and Rice, made with Guatemalan Rice (p. 59) and Refried Beans (p. 68) topped with cheese and sour cream

Lentil Soup

1½ cups lentils
1 medium onion, chopped
2 stalks celery with leaves, chopped
2 carrots, sliced
4 tablespoons butter
1 tablespoon chopped parsley
1 teaspoon turmeric
Pinch of cayenne pepper
1 teaspoon salt
¼ teaspoon pepper
6 cups water or vegetable water

Combine all ingredients in a pot and cook 30 to 45 minutes or until tender.

Minestrone

4 slices bacon
1 cup sliced carrots
1 cup chopped onions
2 cups shredded cabbage
1 cup diced potatoes
2 quarts water
3 cups cooked kidney beans
2 teaspoons salt

½ teaspoon pepper

1½ cups dry macaroni

3 tablespoons fresh parsley, minced

½ teaspoon basil

2 cloves garlic, minced

Parmesan cheese (optional)

Cook bacon and remove from grease. Cook carrots, onions, cabbage, and potatoes in bacon grease 5 minutes. Add water, beans, salt, and pepper. Bring to a boil and cook over low heat 1 hour. Add bacon, macaroni, and remaining ingredients and cook 20 minutes or until macaroni is tender. Serve with grated Parmesan cheese.

Kidney Bean Salad

2 cans (15 ounces each) or 3 cups kidney beans

½ cup chopped celery

2 large carrots, sliced

½ cup chopped green pepper

1 large onion, chopped

¾ cup Hickory Barbecue Sauce (see index)

1 tablespoon brown sugar

¼ cup cooking oil

1 teaspoon salt

Drain beans and add celery, carrots, green pepper, and onion. Combine remaining ingredients and pour over beans. Refrigerate for 4 hours before serving.

Four-Bean Salad

1 can (16 ounces) green beans

1 can (16 ounces) red kidney beans

1 can (16 ounces) wax beans

1 can (16 ounces) garbanzo beans

1 medium onion, chopped or sliced

½ cup green pepper, sliced

½ cup salad oil

¾ cup apple cider vinegar

½ cup sugar

½ teaspoon salt

½ teaspoon pepper

Drain the four cans of beans. Add onion and green pepper. Combine oil, vinegar, sugar, salt, and pepper. Pour over beans. Mix well and chill overnight.

Pinto Bean Cake

½ cup cooking oil or melted shortening

1½ cups sugar

1½ cups pinto beans, mashed

2 eggs, beaten

¾ cup grated apples

½ cup milk

1 teaspoon lemon juice

2 cups flour

2 teaspoons baking powder

½ teaspoon salt

½ teaspoon nutmeg

½ teaspoon cinnamon

¼ cup raisins

Combine shortening, sugar, and beans. Beat in eggs, apples, milk, and lemon juice. Add dry ingredients and beat well. Add raisins. Pour into a greased and floured baking pan. Bake at 350° F. for 40 to 50 minutes. Glaze while warm with orange or lemon frosting.

Pasta
and Crackers

Pasta

Creating your own pasta can be a rewarding experience, and homemade pasta costs less than the store-bought kind. Pasta is basically flour and water mixed together and cooked; other ingredients are added for flavor, color, or texture. Flavor and color can be varied by experimenting with grain and vegetable combinations. Select a vegetable from your garden and add it to your pasta. You can create your own exotic noodles with a little experimenting.

Making pasta takes little time and equipment. You will need a rolling pin and knife or a pasta machine. Even though a pasta machine may be a bit expensive, if you use large amounts of pasta, it will save you money at the supermarket, and in time it will pay for itself.

Pasta can be frozen before or after cutting. Make a big batch at a time and put some in the freezer. If it is going to be frozen after cutting, be careful not to compact it. Place it gently in a container or layer it with waxed paper between layers. Store in sealed plastic bags. You can add pasta to boiling water while still frozen, but the cooking time must be doubled.

To dry pasta, dust with flour and spread on floured trays, or hang from a string or clothes hanger. Place papers beneath to catch the little pieces that break off. When removing the dried pasta, break at the point it curves over hanger. The pasta will then be half the size of the original.

To cut your own noodles by hand, dust both sides of flattened dough and roll up like a jelly roll. Slice in desired widths with a serrated knife. Separate the noodles by hand.

Using a pasta machine makes the job easier and less messy. You just knead, then roll the dough through a set of rollers, adjusting the rollers closer until you have a very thin dough. Next you feed it through a selected set of holes to cut it into spaghetti or noodles. The end result is noodles all the same size. Experiment with your pasta machine. You will find it can be used for making many other foods as well—for example, crackers, pastry, and tortillas.

Cooking Pasta

1. Cook 1 pound pasta in 8 quarts water and 2 tablespoons salt. Fresh pasta will cook in 1 to 2 minutes, depending on thickness.

2. Use a deep pan to cook pasta. This will allow pasta to move freely and keep it from sticking together.

3. Add 2 tablespoons olive oil or butter to cooking water. This will keep pasta from sticking to the sides of the pan and prevent water from boiling over.

4. When pasta is done, it should be firm but tender. Remove from water with a wooden fork or tongs. Place in a warm bowl lightly coated with butter or olive oil. This will keep the pasta from sticking together and also add flavor.

5. Use a slotted spoon to remove small pasta, such as shell macaroni. If you must use a colander, quickly return pasta to the same pan it was cooked in. *Do not rinse* unless the pasta is going to be used in a salad or salad mold.

Egg Pasta

1½ cups flour
2 eggs
1 tablespoon cooking oil
2 tablespoons water, if needed

Place flour in a mixing bowl. Make a well in the flour. Put eggs and oil in the center of the well. With fingers or a fork, carefully mix the eggs and oil into the flour. Add more flour or water, if needed, to make a stiff dough. Knead and set aside for 10 minutes. Cover dough to prevent drying out. Roll out the dough with rolling pin, or put through pasta machine. Cut into desired shapes. Cook according to directions.

Variations:

Use any of the following flours in the pasta: wheat, buckwheat, barley, soy, oatmeal, cornmeal.

For herbed pasta, mix herbs of your choice with the flour before making regular egg pasta.

For vegetable pasta, use any of the following vegetables (cooked or fresh) to create your pasta: spinach, beets, carrots, garlic, onions, zucchini, tomatoes, green beans, broccoli. Purée vegetables in food chopper or blender. Add about ¼ cup purée with eggs and oil to ½ cup flour to make a stiff dough. Increase amount of vegetable purée to taste. Adjust amount of flour to make stiff dough.

Pastapia

Follow directions for Egg Pasta. Roll out and cut into 4-inch squares. In fat heated to 350° F., deep fry squares until golden brown. Drain on paper towel and sprinkle with powdered sugar or drizzle with honey.

Eggless Pasta

2 cups flour
½ cup hot water
1 tablespoon cooking oil

Place flour in a mixing bowl. Make a well in the flour and add water and oil. With fingers or a fork, carefully mix all ingredients. Add more flour, if needed, to make a stiff dough. Knead and set aside for 10 minutes. Roll out dough. Cut into desired shapes. Cook according to directions.

Spinach Noodles

2 cups flour
2 beaten eggs
¼ cup puréed spinach
2 tablespoons melted butter or oil

Place flour in a mixing bowl. Make a well. Combine spinach, eggs, and melted butter or oil. Add to flour and mix well. Add additional flour, if needed, to make a stiff dough. Knead and set aside for 10 minutes. Roll and cut into noodles. Cook in 8 quarts of boiling water and 2 tablespoons salt.

Whole-Wheat Noodles

1 cup whole-wheat pastry flour, sifted
½ cup all-purpose flour
3 eggs
1 tablespoon cooking oil or melted
    butter

Combine flours in a mixing bowl. Make a well. Add eggs and oil or butter in center of the well. With a fork or fingers, carefully mix the eggs and oil into the flour. Add water or flour, if needed, to make a stiff dough. Knead and set aside for 10 minutes. Roll out dough and cut into desired shapes. Cook in 8 quarts of boiling water and 2 tablespoons salt.

Potato Pasta

1½ cups flour
1½ cups mashed potatoes
1 teaspoon salt
3 tablespoons hot water
3 eggs

Place flour in a mixing bowl. Make a well. Combine mashed potatoes, salt, water, and eggs. Add to flour and mix well. Add more water or flour, if needed, to make a stiff dough. Knead and set aside for 10 minutes. Roll out dough and cut into desired shapes. Cook in 8 quarts of boiling water and 2 tablespoons salt.

Eggless Potato Pasta

2 cups flour
2 cups mashed potatoes
1½ cups hot water

Place flour in a mixing bowl. Make a well. Combine mashed potatoes and water. Add to flour and mix well. Add more flour, if needed, to make a stiff dough. Knead and set aside for 10 minutes. Roll out dough and cut into desired shapes. Cook in 8 quarts of boiling water and 2 tablespoons salt.

Chocolate Pasta

2 cups flour
2 cups powdered sugar
1 cup unsweetened cocoa powder
3 eggs
Pinch of salt

Combine ingredients. Follow directions for making Egg Pasta. Roll dough to ⅛-inch thick and cut into desired shapes.

Wafers: Cut dough with cookie cutters and bake 3 to 4 minutes at 350° F. Cool.

Ice Cream Sandwiches: Cut ice cream in the same shape as wafers. Place ice cream between two wafers.

Ice Cream Cones: Cut dough in 4-inch squares. Roll each square into a cone with no opening at one end and a wide opening at the other. Place aluminum foil in the middle of the cone to hold the shape. Bake 3 to 4 minutes at 350° F. Cool. Fill with ice cream, pudding, or whipped cream.

Soup Pasta

Make a stiff Egg Pasta, roll into a ball, and freeze approximately 30 minutes. Remove pasta from freezer and grate on coarse grater. Sprinkle with a small amount of flour to prevent sticking together. Add grated pasta to boiling stews, soups, and gravies.

Meat Pasta Sauce No. 1

2 carrots, chopped fine
1 medium onion, chopped
3 tablespoons olive oil or cooking oil
½ pound ground beef
1 can (6 ounces) tomato paste
1 cup water
1 can (4 ounces) mushrooms or
    ¼ pound fresh mushrooms
1 clove garlic, minced
1 tablespoon dried parsley
½ teaspoon sweet basil
½ teaspoon oregano
½ teaspoon salt
1 tablespoon brown sugar
½ teaspoon lemon peel
2 tomatoes, skinned and chopped

Sauté carrots and onions in oil. Cook until tender. Add ground beef and cook until meat is browned. Add remaining ingredients and simmer uncovered until thick.

Meat Pasta Sauce No. 2

¾ pound ground beef
¼ pound pork sausage
½ cup chopped onion
¼ cup chopped celery
1 clove garlic, minced
2 cans (6 ounces each) tomato paste
2 cans (16 ounces each) or 4 cups
    tomatoes
3 tablespoons Parmesan cheese
2 tablespoons parsley flakes
1½ teaspoons salt
1 teaspoon oregano
½ teaspoon sweet basil

Brown ground beef and sausage. Add onion and celery and cook until tender. Add remaining ingredients and simmer 1½ hours. Serve over noodles or spaghetti.

Tomato Pasta Sauce No. 1

1 large onion, chopped
3 teaspoons olive oil or cooking oil
2 cans (8 ounces each) tomato sauce
1 teaspoon sugar
½ teaspoon oregano
Salt and pepper to taste
½ cup Parmesan cheese

Sauté onion in oil. Add remaining ingredients, except cheese, and simmer 20 to 30 minutes. Serve with spaghetti or noodles and sprinkle with cheese.

Tomato Pasta Sauce No. 2

1 medium onion, chopped
2 cloves garlic, minced
3 tablespoons olive oil
2 cans (16 ounces each) or 4 cups
    tomatoes, puréed
2 bay leaves
1 teaspoon sugar
½ teaspoon oregano

Homemade pastas (pp. 72-73); Beef Ravioli (p. 75)

Salt and pepper to taste
¼ cup grated Parmesan cheese

Sauté onion and garlic in oil until tender. Add remaining ingredients, except cheese. Simmer 20 minutes. Serve with spaghetti or noodles and sprinkle with cheese.

Tomato Pasta Sauce No. 3

2 tablespoons olive oil or cooking oil
2 cloves garlic, minced
½ large onion, chopped
1 can (16 ounces) or 2 cups tomatoes, mashed
2 cans (6 ounces each) tomato paste
1½ cups water
1½ teaspoons Italian Seasoning (see index)
Salt and pepper to taste

Sauté garlic and onions in oil until tender. Add remaining ingredients. Simmer 25 to 30 minutes. Serve with spaghetti or noodles.

Tomato Pasta Sauce No. 4

½ medium onion, chopped
2 tablespoons cooking oil

1 large clove garlic, minced
1 pound ripe tomatoes, peeled and chopped
⅛ teaspoon oregano
¼ teaspoon dried parsley
¼ teaspoon sweet basil
1 teaspoon sugar
Salt to taste

Sauté onion in oil. Add remaining ingredients and cook until onion and garlic are transparent. Serve with spaghetti or noodles.

Parmesan Pasta Sauce

1 cup (½ pound) butter, melted
1 teaspoon onion salt
1 teaspoon garlic salt
¼ cup Parmesan cheese
¼ teaspoon parsley
½ cup warm milk or cream

Combine all ingredients. Serve over pasta. Makes 4 to 6 servings.
Variation: Omit parsley and add ½ teaspoon dry green onions and ¼ teaspoon pepper.

Pasta Sauce for Potato Noodles

½ teaspoon parsley

¾ cup warm milk

¼ cup Parmesan cheese

½ teaspoon onion salt

½ teaspoon garlic salt

Salt to taste

Combine ingredients. Serve with potato noodles.

Pasta Fritters

1¼ cups flour

¼ teaspoon salt

3 egg yolks

¼ cup olive oil

1¼ cups milk, or half-and-half, or
water

1½ cups parboiled spaghetti, chopped

1 cup chopped onions

3 egg whites, whipped

Combine flour and salt in a mixing bowl. Add remaining ingredients, except egg whites, and mix well. Fold in egg whites. Drop a few teaspoonfuls at a time into hot fat (375° F.). Cook 25 to 30 seconds or until golden brown. Drain on paper towel.

Batter Noodles

2 cups flour

⅛ teaspoon salt

1 tablespoon olive oil

5 eggs

In a mixing bowl combine flour and salt. Gradually whisk in oil and eggs. Batter should look like cake batter. Squeeze batter out of a paper cone into salted, simmering water. Bring water to a boil, cover, and poach noodles 30 to 40 seconds or until tender. Drain carefully. Serve with butter or pasta sauce.

Sour Cream Noodles

1 recipe egg noodles

½ teaspoon sweet basil

1 tablespoon chopped green onion

2 tablespoons chopped parsley

Pepper to taste

1 cup sour cream or heavy sweet cream

Parmesan cheese

Add noodles to 8 quarts boiling salted water. Cook 3 to 4 minutes; drain. Add basil, onion, parsley, and pepper. Toss gently, adding cream a little at a time. Sprinkle with cheese to taste.

Cannelloni

2 cups ricotta or creamed cottage
cheese

½ pound ground pork, browned, or
1 cup Chunky Wheat Meat
Sausage (see index)

2 eggs

Egg Pasta rolled and cut into 4″ x 6″
rectangles

8 quarts water

Tomato pasta sauce

Parmesan cheese

Combine cheese, pork or wheat meat sausage, and eggs. Place 1½ teaspoons filling in center of each dough rectangle and fold over. Press edges together. Bring water to a boil. Add pasta rolls and boil 10 minutes. Remove with slotted spoon and drain.

Place cannelloni rolls in a buttered casserole dish; top with a tomato pasta sauce and sprinkle with Parmesan cheese. Bake at 375° F. for 15 minutes. Makes 6 servings.

Procedure for Making Ravioli

Method 1: Roll egg pasta, in thin strips, through a pasta machine. Put strips in ravioli attachment. Place filling in pasta and roll. Cut into squares with ravioli or pizza cutter.

Method 2: With a rolling pin or pasta machine, roll dough out thinly into two strips, each 4 to 6 inches wide. Place 1 teaspoon filling on one strip of dough every 1½ to 2 inches. Place the other dough strip on top, and press between each mound of filling. Cut with ravioli or pizza cutter and seal edges with fork or fingers.

Method 3: Roll out pasta dough. Cut dough into 2-inch squares. Place 1 teaspoon filling in each square and fold over. Press edges together with fork or fingers.

Drop ravioli into boiling water and cook 20 to 30 minutes. Remove with a slotted spoon. Keep warm until served. Serve with a tomato pasta sauce and Parmesan cheese.

Beef Ravioli

½ pound ground beef

¼ cup chopped onion

1 tablespoon butter or margarine

⅛ teaspoon thyme

½ cup spinach, parboiled and drained

1 egg

Salt and pepper to taste

In a skillet, brown meat with onion. Chop meat into fine pieces and stir in remaining ingredients. Mix well and continue cooking 2 to 3 minutes. Place filling in prepared dough, following procedure for making ravioli (above).

Chicken Ravioli

1 cup chicken meat, cooked and
    chopped
¼ cup chopped onion
1 garlic clove, minced
2 tablespoons olive oil or cooking oil
¼ cup bread crumbs
¼ cup heavy cream
½ cup spinach, drained
1 tablespoon chopped parsley
Salt and pepper to taste

    In a skillet combine chicken, onion, garlic, and oil.
Cook 2 to 3 minutes. Add remaining ingredients, mix
well, and continue cooking 2 to 3 minutes. Place filling in
prepared dough, following procedure for making ravioli
(p. 75).

Cheese and Spinach Ravioli

1 cup grated cheese
1 cup spinach, parboiled and drained
1 teaspoon salt

    Combine all ingredients and follow procedure for
making ravioli.

Sausage Ravioli

½ pound pork sausage
2 tablespoons chopped onion
½ cup ground cooked spinach
1 egg
2 tablespoons Parmesan cheese
Salt and pepper to taste

    Brown meat and onion in skillet. Combine remain-
ing ingredients and mix well. Follow procedure for making ravioli.

Cheese Ravioli

2 cups cottage cheese
¼ cup Parmesan cheese
2 tablespoons dried parsley
1 egg
1 teaspoon salt
1 teaspoon sugar
½ teaspoon cinnamon
½ teaspoon grated lemon peel

    Combine all ingredients and mix well. Follow proce-
dure for making ravioli.

Wheat Meat Ravioli

    Fill with Sloppy Chunky Wheat Meat (see index),
following procedure for making ravioli (above).

Wonton Wrappers or Egg-Roll Skins

2¼ cups flour
1 teaspoon salt
2 eggs
2 to 4 tablespoons hot water

    In a mixing bowl, combine flour and salt. Make a
well, and add eggs and water. Mix well, then knead until
smooth. Cover with damp cloth and refrigerate 30 minutes. Roll out paper thin and cut into 3-inch squares for
wonton or 7- to 8-inch squares for egg rolls.

Egg Rolls

½ cup water
2 cups shredded cabbage
½ cup chopped celery
½ pound ground beef or pork
½ cup chopped green onions
1 teaspoon salt
2 tablespoons soy sauce
2 tablespoons cooking oil
1 tablespoon cornstarch, dissolved in
    2 tablespoons water
2½ cups bean sprouts
Egg-roll skins

    Bring water to a boil. Add cabbage and celery and
cook 5 minutes, stirring to prevent sticking. In a large
skillet, brown meat. Add remaining ingredients, except
bean sprouts, and cook 3 to 4 minutes. Remove from heat
and add bean sprouts. Spoon 2 tablespoons of mixture
diagonally across each egg-roll skin; fold in ends, and roll
skin around filling. Seal edges. (See illustration.) Set a
wok or skillet over high heat and pour in 3 cups oil. Heat
to 375° F. and deep fry egg rolls 3 to 4 minutes or until
crisp and golden. Drain on paper towel. Serve with sweet
and sour sauce (see index).

Meat-filled Wontons

2 tablespoons cooking oil

1 pound ground beef

½ pound ground pork

2 tablespoons soy sauce

1 tablespoon Worcestershire sauce

½ cup chopped green onions

1 teaspoon cornstarch, dissolved in
   cold water

Wonton wrappers

In skillet, lightly brown beef and pork in oil. Add remaining ingredients. Cook until liquid thickens. Cool.

To assemble wontons: Place 1 heaping teaspoon filling in center of each wonton wrapper. Bring one corner over the filling to the opposite corner, folding the wrapper at an angle so that two overlapping triangles are formed with their points side by side and about ½ inch apart. Pull the two bottom corners of the folded triangle forward and below the folded edge so they meet one another and slightly overlap (creating a frame around the mound of filling). Pinch the two ends firmly together. (See illustration.)

To cook: Set wok or skillet over high heat; pour in 3 cups oil, and heat to 375° F. Deep fry 8 to 10 wontons at a time for 2 to 3 minutes, or until crisp and golden. Drain on paper towel. Serve plain or with sweet and sour sauce (see index).

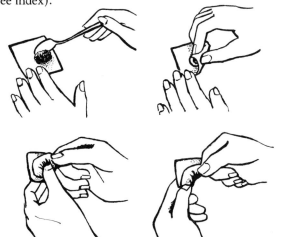

Wheat Meat Wontons

3 cups Chunky Wheat Meat Sausage
   (see index)

2 tablespoons vegetable oil

2 tablespoons soy sauce

1 tablespoon Worcestershire sauce

½ cup chopped green onions

1 teaspoon cornstarch, dissolved in
   water

Wonton wrappers

Combine all ingredients except wonton wrappers and cook over low heat until liquid thickens. To assemble and cook wontons, follow instructions under Meat-filled Wontons.

Spinach Lasagna

8 to 12 lasagna noodles

1½ pounds ground beef

1 can (6 ounces) tomato paste

1 can (8 ounces) tomato sauce

1 can (16 ounces) or 2 cups tomatoes

1 teaspoon garlic salt

1 teaspoon salt

1 teaspoon sugar

1 teaspoon basil

1 teaspoon Italian Seasoning (see
   index)

2 cups chopped cooked spinach

2 cups creamed cottage cheese

1 egg

¼ cup Parmesan cheese

1 pound mozzarella cheese, sliced

Cook lasagna noodles according to directions. Brown ground beef. Add tomato paste, tomato sauce, tomatoes, and seasonings. Mix spinach with cottage cheese, egg, and Parmesan cheese. In a 13″ x 9″ pan, alternate layers of noodles, cottage cheese, meat sauce, and mozzarella cheese. Top with mozzarella cheese. Bake at 350° F. for 30 minutes. Makes 10 servings.

Noodle Tuna Casserole

1 recipe Egg Pasta, cut in noodles

1 cup diced celery

1 medium onion, chopped

2 tablespoons butter or margarine

1 cup milk

1 can (10 ounces) cream of mushroom
   soup

1 can (6½ ounces) tuna, drained

1 cup grated cheese

Potato chips (optional)

Cook noodles according to directions. Sauté celery and onion in butter or margarine until tender. Combine noodles, celery and onion, milk, soup, and tuna. Pour into a buttered casserole dish. Top with cheese and crushed potato chips. Bake at 350° F. for 15 minutes or until hot and bubbly. Makes 4 to 6 servings.

Pasta Dumplings

1½ cups flour
1¾ teaspoons baking powder
¾ teaspoon salt
3 tablespoons shortening
½ cup milk
2 eggs
2 tablespoons fresh parsley, chopped

Mix flour, baking powder, and salt. Cut in shortening. Add milk, eggs, and parsley, mixing well. Add to stew, soup, or casserole. Cover and let simmer 10 to 15 minutes.

Noodle Cheese Ring

1 recipe Egg Pasta, cut in noodles
6 tablespoons margarine
6 tablespoons flour
3 cups milk
1 teaspoon salt
1 teaspoon paprika
3 cups grated cheese
3 eggs, well beaten
3 to 4 cups hot cooked vegetables

Cook noodles according to directions. Drain and place in a greased ring mold. In a saucepan, melt margarine over medium heat and blend in flour. Stir in milk and cook, stirring constantly, until thick. Add salt, paprika, and cheese, and cook until cheese melts. To half of the sauce add beaten eggs; pour over noodles. Set mold in a pan of hot water and bake at 350° F. for 45 minutes. Unmold on a large platter, and pour remaining sauce over ring. Fill center with vegetables. Makes 6 to 8 servings.

Beef Stroganoff

3 tablespoons butter or margarine
1 can (4 ounces) or ½ pound fresh
    mushrooms
1 large onion, sliced
1½ pounds round steak sliced in 1-inch
    strips, or 1½ pounds ground beef
1 cup water
2 teaspoons Worcestershire sauce
1¼ teaspoons salt
⅛ teaspoon pepper
1 cup sour cream
1 recipe Egg Pasta, cut into noodles
    and cooked

Melt butter or margarine in large skillet. Sauté fresh mushrooms and onions until tender. Remove from pan. Add meat and brown. Add mushrooms, onions, water,

Worcestershire sauce, salt, and pepper. Cook over low heat for 2 hours for round steak or 30 minutes for ground beef. Just before serving, add sour cream. Thicken sauce, if desired. Serve over noodles. Makes 6 servings.

Crackers

Making crackers can be fun, and their taste will surpass that of crackers purchased in a store. Homemade crackers will not have all the additives and preservatives of the commercially packaged crackers. If you do not have a pasta maker, roll your crackers paper thin with a rolling pin. Try experimenting with different flavors and seasonings to create your own unique cracker. Try cutting crackers into different shapes. With a little practice, you can have a better-looking and better-tasting cracker than you can buy.

Hand Method: Roll dough to ⅛-inch thickness with a rolling pin.

Machine Method: Roll dough on pasta machine, rolling from number 1 to number 4.

Soda Crackers

2¼ cups flour
¼ cup lard
¼ teaspoon baking soda
¼ teaspoon salt
Cold water

Mix ingredients with enough cold water to make a stiff dough. Roll very thin and cut into squares. Place on a lightly greased cookie sheet, and bake at 350° F. until lightly browned.

Oatmeal Crackers

2 cups rolled oats
1 cup flour
½ cup sugar
½ cup lard or shortening
1 egg
½ teaspoon salt
½ teaspoon baking soda
Milk

In a medium-size bowl, combine rolled oats, flour, and sugar. Cut in lard. Add egg, salt, baking soda, and enough milk to make a stiff dough. Roll out thin, and cut into squares or desired shapes. Place on a greased cookie sheet, and bake at 325° F. until lightly browned.

Cheese Crackers

5 tablespoons butter
¼ cup sharp Cheddar cheese
2 cups flour
¼ cup water
½ cup rolled oats

In a medium-size bowl, combine all ingredients, mixing to form a soft dough. Roll out thin and cut into desired shapes. Place on a greased cookie sheet, and bake at 350° F. until lightly browned.

Cheddar Cheese Crackers

½ cup rolled oats
1 cup white flour
½ teaspoon salt
½ cup water
¼ cup butter or margarine
5 tablespoons Cheddar cheese powder
¼ cup grated cheese

In a medium-size bowl, combine all ingredients to form a soft dough. Roll thin and cut into desired shapes. Bake at 350° F. until slightly browned.

Sourdough Crackers

4 tablespoons butter
½ teaspoon salt
¼ cup sugar
3 cups flour
¼ cup barley flour
¼ teaspoon baking soda
½ cup Sourdough Starter (see index)
1 cup water

In a medium-size bowl, combine butter, salt, sugar, flour, and barley flour. Add baking soda, sourdough, and water. Knead into a soft dough. Roll out thin and cut into desired shapes. Place on a greased cookie sheet, and bake at 375° F. until lightly browned.

Sesame Seed Crackers

2 cups flour
½ teaspoon salt
1 teaspoon baking powder
7 to 8 tablespoons water
⅓ cup cooking oil or shortening
4 tablespoons sesame seeds

In a medium-size bowl, combine dry ingredients with water and oil. Add sesame seeds, and knead until a smooth dough is formed. Roll dough to ⅛-inch thick. Cut into desired shapes. Place on a greased cookie sheet, and bake at 375° F. until lightly browned.

Onion-Rye Crackers

1½ cups flour
½ cup rye flour
2 tablespoons dehydrated onions
1½ teaspoons baking powder
1 teaspoon salt
¼ cup cooking oil or shortening
7 to 8 tablespoons water

Combine dry ingredients. Mix in oil and water. Knead until a smooth dough is formed. Roll out thin and cut into desired shapes. Place on a lightly greased cookie sheet, and bake at 375° F. until golden brown.

Chicken-Vegetable Crackers

2 cups all-purpose flour
1½ teaspoons granulated dry onion
1 teaspoon vegetable seasoning salt
1 teaspoon baking powder
¼ cup butter or shortening
1 teaspoon chicken soup base
7 to 8 tablespoons water

Combine dry ingredients in a bowl. Cut in butter or shortening. Dissolve soup base in water and add to flour mixture. Make a stiff dough. Roll thin and cut in desired shapes. Place on a lightly greased cookie sheet, and bake at 350° F. for 8 to 10 minutes or until lightly browned.

Bacon Crackers

¾ teaspoon salt
2 cups flour
¼ cup butter or margarine
2 tablespoons crumbled bacon
½ teaspoon liquid smoke
6 to 7 tablespoons water

Combine salt and flour in a bowl. Cut in butter or margarine. Add bacon, liquid smoke, and water. Make a stiff dough. Roll thin and cut in desired shapes. Place on a greased cookie sheet, and bake at 350° F. for 8 to 10 minutes or until lightly browned.

Nacho Cheese Crackers

1¼ cups all-purpose flour
¾ cup cornmeal
½ teaspoon salt
1 teaspoon baking powder
4 tablespoons Cheddar cheese powder
  or ¼ cup grated sharp cheese
¼ cup butter or margarine
7 to 8 tablespoons water

Combine dry ingredients and cheese and cut in butter or margarine. Add water to make a stiff dough. Roll thin and cut in desired shapes. Place on a greased cookie sheet, and bake at 350° F. for 8 to 10 minutes or until lightly browned.

Variation: Add 1 teaspoon chopped dried red chilies.

Wheat Sesame Crackers

1½ cups whole-wheat flour
1½ cups all-purpose flour
¼ cup wheat germ
1½ teaspoons salt
2 cups rolled oats
4 tablespoons sugar
½ cup cooking oil or shortening
1½ cups milk or water
¼ cup sesame seeds

Mix dry ingredients with oil and milk or water. Add sesame seeds and knead until a smooth dough is formed. Roll out thin, and cut into desired shapes. Place on a lightly greased cookie sheet and bake at 375° F. until golden brown.

Graham Crackers

¾ cup whole wheat or graham flour
1½ cups flour
½ teaspoon salt
1 teaspoon baking soda
⅓ cup brown sugar
⅓ cup shortening or margarine
¼ cup honey, warmed
3 tablespoons water

In a medium-size bowl, combine flours, salt, baking soda, and brown sugar, and cut in shortening or margarine. Combine water and honey, and add to dry ingredients. Blend well. Roll out half the dough on an ungreased cookie sheet to ¼-inch thickness. Prick dough with a fork. Repeat with remaining dough. Bake at 375° F. for 8 to 10 minutes or until golden brown. Remove from oven and cut into squares. Cool.

Dairy Products and Eggs

Milk and Cream

For centuries man has been trying to find ways to preserve milk. Milk contains most of the essential minerals, vitamins, protein, and carbohydrates necessary for general good health. Because it will not keep long in its natural state, it is converted into by-products to preserve the nutritional value for longer periods of time.

If you have cows or goats, there will probably be days when you will have extra milk on hand. You will want to preserve the extra milk for times when you do not have a surplus.

Raw milk tastes different from pasteurized milk. Powdered milk and canned milk also have a different flavor. When changing from one type of milk to another, do it gradually by mixing the new milk with equal parts of the familiar-tasting milk. This will allow family members to become accustomed to the new taste. You may also serve the new milk in egg-nogs and other drinks.

If you buy milk from the grocery store, you can save money by mixing it with powdered milk or soy milk.

Reconstituted powdered milk and pasteurized milk may be used in making most dairy products, with the exception of butter and cream. To make top-quality dairy products, raw milk is best.

Preserving Milk and Cream

Freezing: Whole or skimmed milk and cream may be frozen. Pour the milk or cream into sterilized glass containers. leaving a 2-inch headspace. Frozen milk may keep for 4 to 6 months, and cream will keep for 2 to 3 months.

Since the butterfat tends to separate during freezing, thawed milk has a different texture, even though the taste remains the same. Thawed cream will not whip successfully, but may be used in frozen desserts or for cooking. When using thawed cream in cooking, beat slightly before adding to your food.

Canning: Sterilize canning jars. Heat milk to just below boiling and pour into hot jars. Fill within ½ to 1 inch of top. Process in a pressure cooker for 10 minutes at 10 pounds of pressure or 1 hour in a water bath, keeping jars covered with 2 inches of water at all times.

Nonfat Dry Milk

Dry milk is made from fresh milk with the cream and water removed. The calcium and other vitamins and minerals of liquid milk are retained. It will keep at room temperature for several months; for long-term storage, it must be kept in an airtight container in a cool, dry place.

Dry milk may be used in almost any recipe calling for milk. Add the dry milk solids to other dry ingredients and increase the amount of liquid by the amount needed to reconstitute the dry milk.

If recipe calls for	Use
1 quart milk	1 cup dry milk and 4 cups water
1 cup milk	¼ cup dry milk and 1 cup water
½ cup milk	2 tablespoons dry milk and ½ cup water

Whipped Topping

½ cup instant nonfat dry milk

½ cup ice water

2 tablespoons lemon juice

¼ cup sugar

1 teaspoon vanilla

Mix dry milk and ice water. Beat until stiff peaks form. Add lemon juice and beat 3 to 4 minutes. Add sugar and vanilla, and beat until well blended.

Pudding Mix

3 cups sugar

5 cups instant nonfat dry milk

1 teaspoon salt

2½ cups flour or 2 cups cornstarch

Combine all ingredients and mix well. Store in an airtight container in a cool place.

Vanilla Pudding

1¼ cups Pudding Mix (above)

2½ cups warm water

1 egg, beaten

1 tablespoon butter

¾ teaspoon vanilla

In a saucepan combine pudding mix and water. Cook over medium heat until thickened, stirring constantly. Add half the hot mixture to beaten egg; stir to mix thoroughly. Return egg mixture to saucepan and cook 1 minute. Add butter and vanilla. Chill. Makes 6 servings.

Chocolate Pudding: Add ¾ cup cocoa and ¼ cup additional sugar to 1¼ cups pudding mix.

Caramel Pudding: Use brown sugar in place of granulated sugar in pudding mix.

Coconut Pudding: Add 1 cup coconut to vanilla pudding.

Sweetened Condensed Milk

1⅓ cups instant nonfat dry milk

½ cup warm water

1 cup powdered sugar

¼ cup softened butter or margarine

Add dry milk to warm water. Stir in remaining ingredients and beat until smooth. Refrigerate. Makes 2 cups.

Honey-sweetened Condensed Milk

4 tablespoons butter or margarine

⅔ cup boiling water

1⅓ cups instant nonfat dry milk

½ cup honey

Pinch of salt

Melt butter in water. Blend in blender with dry milk until smooth. Add honey and salt, and blend again. Makes 2 to 2½ cups.

Buttermilk

Buttermilk can be obtained from making butter or from a culture. To make cultured buttermilk, add ¼ cup commercial cultured buttermilk to 1 quart milk. Leave in a warm place, or incubate at 70° F. until thick. The organisms in the buttermilk increase and produce an acid that will keep other organisms from growing. Because of this ability, buttermilk is used to temporarily preserve milk in warm weather when other means are not available. If buttermilk develops an off flavor or odor, contamination has probably occurred in the milk or the container. Sterilizing jars and pasteurizing the milk will help prevent this from happening.

Buttermilk Using Powdered Milk

Reconstitute 1 quart powdered milk in a clean jar, making certain all lumps are out. Add ½ cup buttermilk and let stand until it clabbers, about 10 hours. Save ½ cup to mix buttermilk for the next batch. Occasionally buy a commercial fresh start.

Sweet-Cream Butter (p. 86); Spanish Omelet (pp. 97-98)

Buttermilk Dressing for Cole Slaw

½ cup buttermilk

½ cup salad dressing

1½ teaspoons lemon juice

½ teaspoon dill seed

½ teaspoon dry mustard

1 teaspoon salt

¼ teaspoon pepper

Combine all ingredients and mix well. Pour over chopped cabbage and other slaw ingredients in your favorite recipe.

Yogurt

Yogurt is a fermented milk produced by the action of bacterial microorganisms that change the lactose of the milk into lactic acid, causing an acid curd. Yogurt was first used as a means of preserving milk. The lactic acid acts as a preservative and keeps the milk palatable. Yogurt may be made from a number of milks, including cow's milk and goat's milk, either skimmed, whole, or reconstituted. Even cow's milk yogurt will vary according to the milk solids present. Whole milk will give a smooth, creamy taste, and skim milk will make the yogurt lower in calories.

Incubation Methods for Making Yogurt

Vacuum Bottle: Pour hot water into a vacuum bottle (thermos) to warm. Remove water and pour in yogurt mixture. Set in a warm, draft-free place overnight.

Oven: Pour yogurt mixture in a casserole dish or covered glass dish. Heat oven on warm setting. Turn oven off and place yogurt dish in warm oven. Let set overnight.

Water Bath: Set yogurt containers in 105° F. to 115° F. water. Replace water periodically.

Heating Pad: Test the temperature of a heating pad by placing a bowl of warm water on the pad for several hours. Check the temperature of the water. Turn the switch to the setting that registers 100° F. to 110° F. and put the pad in a box. Place the containers of yogurt mixture on the heating pad and wrap towels around them. Place the lid on the box and let set for 5 to 6 hours.

Stove Top: Place yogurt mixture in a covered container and set over the pilot light of a gas range or on the back of a wood-burning stove. Check in about 5 hours.

Commercial Yogurt Maker: In a yogurt maker, the yogurt is maintained at the proper temperature. Yogurt makers are available at most health food and department stores.

Hints for Making Yogurt

1. Do not disturb yogurt mixture during incubation. Moving it will cause the whey to separate, and the yogurt will be lumpy and watery rather than thick and smooth.

2. Incubate yogurt mixture between 105° F. and 110° F., if possible. Heat in excess of 115° F. will kill the bacteria. If the mixture is too cool, the bacteria will not grow.

3. Use a fresh yogurt start. The older the yogurt start, the longer it will take the yogurt to incubate.

4. Check the carton on store-bought yogurt to see if it has live cultures. If the label says "With active yogurt cultures," the yogurt contains yogurt bacteria. If it says "Heat treated after culturing," the product was made with live bacteria but received heat treatment after culturing, which completely kills the live bacteria.

5. You can use a pure yogurt culture instead of prepared yogurt. This takes longer to thicken your mixture. Follow directions on the cultures for incubation time.

6. Save enough yogurt to start the next batch. Bacteria will eventually become dormant, and a new start will be needed. When the yogurt becomes watery or has a tart flavor, use a new start.

7. The longer yogurt is incubated, the more acidic it will be and the stronger the taste.

8. It is natural for water or whey to accumulate on top of the yogurt after refrigerating. Mix it in or pour it off.

Yogurt from Whole Milk

1 quart whole milk
¼ cup instant nonfat dry milk
3 tablespoons yogurt

Combine milk and dry milk. Mix well to remove any lumps. Heat milk on low heat until mixture reaches 180° F. Allow milk to cool to between 105° F. and 115° F. Mix a little warm milk with the yogurt, then stir yogurt into milk mixture. Incubate at between 105° F. and 115° F. until clabbered. Be careful not to disturb it. Refrigerate and use within one week.

Powdered Milk Yogurt

2⅔ cups warm water (100° F.)
1 cup *noninstant* powdered milk
2 tablespoons yogurt

Mix water with powdered milk in a blender or mix by hand until all lumps are out. Combine yogurt and milk and mix for a few seconds. Pour into containers and incubate.

Uses for Yogurt

1. Add jams and fruits (canned or fresh), honey, or syrup to yogurt.

2. Use in salad dressings with herbs and spices.

3. Use in place of sour cream in dips, dressings, and most other recipes calling for sour cream.

4. Use as buttermilk with equal parts water and yogurt.

5. Serve on baked potatoes—plain or with bacon bits, chives, or onions.

6. Use in toppings or sauces for vegetables such as asparagus, string beans, cauliflower, or broccoli.

Yogurt Dressing

½ cup yogurt
½ cup salad dressing
1 tablespoon lemon juice
¼ teaspoon onion powder
1 tablespoon parsley
Pinch of paprika
1 tablespoon chili sauce

Combine all ingredients and refrigerate.

Yogurt-Avocado Dip

½ cup yogurt
½ cup salad dressing
1 avocado, mashed
½ clove garlic, minced
¼ teaspoon onion powder
1 teaspoon lemon juice

Combine all ingredients, mix well, and refrigerate. Use as dip for fresh vegetables.

Yogurt Dressing for Fruit Salad

1 cup yogurt
½ cup powdered sugar
1 teaspoon vanilla

Combine all ingredients and fold into fruit salad.

Frozen Yogurt

1 envelope unflavored gelatin
¼ cup water
¼ cup sugar
⅓ cup corn syrup or honey
2 cups whole-milk plain yogurt
2 cups fresh or frozen unsweetened
   fruit, mashed or blended
½ cup cream
2 teaspoons vanilla

Dissolve gelatin in water. Add sugar and corn syrup or honey; stir until dissolved. Add yogurt, fruit, cream, and vanilla. Chill until thick; then freeze in shallow container until soft and mushy. Remove from container, whip, and return to freezer.

Frosty Yogurt Pops

1 package (3 ounces) flavored gelatin
1 cup boiling water
¼ cup sugar
1 cup whole-milk plain yogurt
1 teaspoon vanilla

Dissolve gelatin in boiling water. Add sugar and cool. Mix in yogurt and vanilla. Place in containers and freeze.

Sour Cream

Use pasteurized cream to make sour cream. To pasteurize raw cream, warm it in the top of a double boiler to between 155° F. and 160° F. Hold at this temperature for 30 minutes. Remove from heat and cool rapidly by placing pan in cold water and changing the water often to keep it cold. Stop cooling when cream reaches 85° F. Pour into bottles. Add 5 teaspoons buttermilk for each pint of cream. Shake bottle until contents are thoroughly mixed. Set the cream in a warm place (70° F. to 85° F.) for 24 hours. At the end of 24 hours the cream may be used, but the flavor will be improved if it is stored in the refrigerator until cool. The cream may be made smoother and stiffer by whipping, but be careful not to overwhip.

Dried Beef in Sour Cream Gravy

2 tablespoons butter
½ cup chipped dried beef
½ cup onion
2 tablespoons flour
1½ cups sour cream
2 cups cooked peas
2 tablespoons chopped parsley

Melt butter in a frying pan; add dried beef and onion. Cook until onion is tender. Sprinkle with flour and add sour cream. Stir and cook slowly over low heat until thickened. Add peas and parsley. Serve over toast.

Sauerkraut and Sausage with Sour Cream

4 cups sauerkraut
2 whole cloves
1 bay leaf
1 cup water
1 cup sour cream
Salt to taste
2 cups Chunky Wheat Meat Sausage
   (see index) or ½ pound ground
   sausage, browned

In a saucepan cook sauerkraut, cloves, and bay leaf in water until most of the liquid has evaporated. Remove cloves and bay leaf. Add sour cream, salt, and sausage. Continue cooking over low heat until heated through. Serve.

Sour Cream Dressing

1 cup sour cream
2 garlic cloves, crushed
½ teaspoon salt
¼ teaspoon pepper

¼ cup chopped green onions
2 teaspoons lemon juice
1 teaspoon sugar

Combine all ingredients and mix well. Serve on cabbage, cucumbers, or lettuce.

Butter

Butter can be made from either sweet or sour cream. It can be made from cow's or goat's milk. An electric mixer, a blender, a churn, or even a glass jar with a lid can be used to make butter.

The first step in making butter is to separate the cream from the milk. A cream separator removes all the butterfat from the milk very quickly; the skim milk that is left can be used in making cottage cheese or for drinking. Another method is to allow the cream to rise to the top of the milk and then skim it off with a dipper.

Cream from goat's milk is harder to remove. Because the fat globules are small and well emulsified, the cream takes much longer to separate from the milk. Goat's milk may be strong or "goaty" while waiting for the cream to separate, so it is best to use a cream separator. Milk should be between 80° F. and 90° F. when poured into a cream separator.

Sweet Cream Butter

1. Pour cream into instrument you have chosen to use to make butter. Cream should be between 50° F. and 65° F. If you wish to color your butter, it should be done now with a few drops of special butter color.

2. Beat or churn the cream through three stages: whipped cream, stiff whipped cream, and, finally, butter and buttermilk. If you use a blender and the mixture reaches a point at which it will no longer blend because the cream is too thick, you may add a little cold water to get the cream moving again. It will take 2 to 3 minutes of mixing in the blender or 20 to 30 minutes by hand to make butter.

3. When the butter is in grains the size of wheat, pour off the remaining milk from the butter. Pour butter grains into a sieve or colander and rinse with cool water until the water is clear. (Any milk left in the butter will cause it to spoil.)

4. When water runs clear, place butter in a bowl and work out all remaining liquid by kneading the butter with a wooden spoon or paddle against the sides and bottom of the bowl. Add 2 to 3 teaspoons salt per pound of butter and work in with paddle. If butter is too salty, some of the salt can be washed out with cool water.

Sour Cream Butter

Ripen the cream by adding ¼ cup buttermilk to each quart cream. Let set at room temperature for 24 hours or until clabbered. Chill before churning. Follow directions for making Sweet Cream Butter. The leftover buttermilk can be used to drink or in any buttermilk recipe. It will not be as thick as commercial buttermilk.

Storing Butter

Method 1: Mix 1 part sugar, 1 part saltpeter, and 2 parts salt. Use 2 tablespoons mixture to 1 pound butter. Mix into butter. This will keep butter sweet for 2 years.

Method 2: In a large crock or container, place 15 pounds butter. Combine 3 ounces saltpeter and ¼ pound sugar; dissolve in enough water to cover butter to a depth of 2 inches. Pour solution over butter; cover with a clean white cloth. Butter will keep for 2 years.

Canned Butter or Margarine

Melt butter or margarine slowly over low heat until it bubbles. Let simmer 5 minutes. Pour into sterilized jars, leaving ⅛-inch headspace. Seal jars. When jars have cooled, place in refrigerator and turn several times until butter hardens. Butter should keep 2 years.

Stretching Butter

1. Whip 1 can evaporated milk into 1 pound butter. Refrigerate.

2. Beat 1 pound butter into 1 pound margarine until fluffy. Slowly beat in 1 cup milk and 1 cup warm water. Refrigerate.

3. Whip 1 pound butter into 1 cup cooking oil to make a soft butter.

Whipped Butter

Whip together ½ cup butter and ½ cup cream or milk. Use as is or try one of the following variations.

Garlic Butter: Add 2 cloves crushed garlic, 1 teaspoon salt, pepper to taste, and ½ teaspoon Worcestershire sauce. Or use 2 teaspoons garlic salt in place of garlic cloves and salt.

Honey Butter: Add ½ cup honey.

Maple Butter: Add ½ cup maple syrup.

Chive Butter: Add 4 tablespoons chopped chives.

Parsley Butter: Add 4 tablespoons chopped parsley.

Nut Butter: Add 4 tablespoons finely chopped nuts.

Herbed Butter Sauce

½ cup butter
2 tablespoons chopped onion
2 tablespoons chopped parsley
⅛ teaspoon marjoram
⅛ teaspoon thyme
¼ teaspoon salt
1 tablespoon Parmesan cheese

Melt butter in saucepan. Add remaining ingredients and cook until onion is tender. Makes ¾ cup.

Hard and Semi-hard Cheeses

Cheese making is an ancient art, going back to early civilizations. It is mentioned in the Bible; in the book of Samuel, David is told to carry it to his brethren who were fighting the Philistines (2 Sam. 17:18). The Romans introduced cheese to England. Trappist monks guarded its secrets and developed new processes during the Dark Ages. Cheese was included among the provisions on the *Mayflower*.

Legend tells us that the first cheese using rennet was discovered by accident. A traveler put some milk in a leather pouch made from the stomach of a calf. As he started on his way, several things began to happen. The bacteria in the milk ripened it, and the rennet in the calf's stomach caused it to curdle. When the traveler stopped for a meal, he found the milk had become cheese.

The first cheese factory in the United States was started in Rome, New York, in 1851. Today cheese production around the world is largely a factory industry.

There are hundreds of varieties of cheese. The differences in cheeses depend mainly on how and to what extent various cheese-making steps are carried out. Some of the best cheeses came about through someone's apparent failures.

You now have a chance to bring cheese making back to the home without all the additives used in commercial cheese making. Turning milk into cheese takes only a few hours of your time. You can create your own varieties with a little imagination and experience, and we have included tips on various ingredients and flavorings. The final thrill will come when you taste your cheese and share it with family and friends. This section gives you step-by-step instructions for making a few of the popular cheeses.

Making cheese is an excellent way to use up surplus milk. Cheese is made by first increasing the milk's lactic acid level in order to curdle it. The milk is then heated, and rennet (which solidifies most of the milk's protein and butterfat) is added. The solid part of the milk is called curd; the watery part that separates from the solid curd is whey. The milk solids in the curd contain about 80 percent of the protein and most of the calcium and vitamins of the original milk. In addition, the vitamin-B content is increased in the curing process. The kind of milk used, the degree of acidity, the temperature and length of heating, the amount of rennet, and the way the curd is cut, dried, pressed, and aged will all affect the final result.

Ingredients in Cheese

Milk: Cheese can be made from goat's milk or cow's milk, raw or pasteurized. Whole milk will make a richer cheese than skimmed or partially skimmed milk. Not more than half the milk should be fresh from the cow. A good cheese is made from half evening milk and half morning milk. If you use raw milk, it should not be more than two days old. One gallon milk will make approximately one pound of cheese.

Starter: A starter is needed to develop the proper amount of acid to coagulate the milk. You can use buttermilk, yogurt, or a commercial culture. Raw milk already contains the bacteria necessary for clabbering milk, but the starter will speed up the process. If you do not use a starter with raw milk, let one gallon fresh milk set at room temperature overnight. Use the next day with other milk.

Rennet: Rennet is a proteolytic enzyme or any number of substances used in coagulating milk. The enzyme is found in the stomach of a calf, lamb, or kid. Some plant sources of the same substance are lemon or lime juice. Calcium chloride and lactic acid will also coagulate milk.

Cheese rennet tablets are available at drug stores, health food stores, or from American Supply House, P.O. Box 1114, Columbia, Missouri 65201.

You can make your own rennet from the stomach of a suckling lamb, calf, or kid—one that has not eaten grass or other solid food. An animal

Assortment of homemade cheeses, cheese balls, and cheese spreads

with little value would be the best to use. The fourth stomach of a calf will be the biggest. Remove the stomach and roll it in ashes (the lye in the ashes protects the stomach from flies and bacteria). Hang the stomach to dry in a warm, dry, airy place away from animals or anything that would contaminate it. When the stomach is dry, cut it open and remove the brownish powder (the milk inside the stomach has turned to powder). Store it in a cool, dry place. (The rennet will break down if exposed to high heat.) To use, mix ⅛ teaspoon powder with a few drops water. Add enough water, a drop at a time, to make a thick paste. Then add enough cool water to dissolve it, just as you would use a rennet tablet. This will coagulate 8 to 12 gallons of milk.

Cheese Color: If you want orange cheese, you will have to add cheese color, which can be obtained at health food stores, drugstores, or from the American Supply House at the address mentioned above.

Equipment Needed

1. Cheesecloth, muslin, linen, or other clean cloth.

2. Dairy thermometer or other thermometer that registers as low as 86° F.

3. Double-boiler arrangement for cooking the cheese. Do not use aluminum. A plastic pail or bucket inside a canner with a rack on the bottom works well.

4. Long knife or spatula with a blade the depth of the kettle.

5. Paraffin—1 to 2 pounds.

6. Cheese press (see p. 92).

The following recipes can be doubled or tripled.

Colby Cheese

Colby is an American cheese similar to Cheddar, but it has a more open texture and contains more moisture, and the curd is not matted or milled. A sharper cheese, it does not keep as long but ripens faster because of the increased moisture content.

1. *Prepare milk.* Heat milk in a double-boiler arrangement to 86° F. Add 1 cup starter to 2 gallons whole milk. Cover and let stand at room temperature for 1 to 2 hours.

2. *Add color.* This step is optional. Heat milk to 86° F. and pour in color solution according to manufacturer's directions. Stir thoroughly with a wooden spoon. Do not add color and rennet at the same time.

3. *Add rennet.* Dissolve ¼ rennet tablet (Hansen's Cheese Rennet) in a little cold water. Heat milk to 86° F.

Add rennet solution. Stir for one minute. Cover with a lid or towel and let stand undisturbed for 30 to 45 minutes.

4. *Test the curd.* Put a finger into the curd at an angle and remove. The curd is ready when it breaks clean over your finger.

5. *Cut the curd.* With a long knife or spatula, cut all the way through the curd in parallel lines about ½ inch apart. Turn the pan and cut another set of lines to make ½-inch squares. Following the lines already made, cut diagonally through the curd both ways at a 45-degree angle to break the curd into pieces.

6. *Cook the curd.* Very slowly raise the temperature to 102° F. Gently stir with a spoon every few minutes to keep the curd from sticking together. This step should take 30 to 45 minutes.

7. *Firm the curd.* When the temperature reaches 102° F., remove from heat and let the curd and whey stand for 20 to 30 minutes, stirring occasionally. The curd will become firm enough so that a handful of pieces pressed together will easily shake apart. The curd should be the size of marbles.

8. *Drain off whey.* Pour or scoop off the whey, leaving the curds in the pot.

9. *Salt the curd.* Sprinkle the curds with 2 tablespoons salt. Work in gently with hands.

10. *Press the curd.* Place the curd in cheesecloth and squeeze out as much whey as possible. Place the curds in the plastic pipe or cheese press. Place the wooden follow on top of the curd and lower the jack to apply pressure. Tighten further or increase pressure every 30 to 60 minutes for 3 to 4 hours. Remove cheese from press and rewrap with a new cloth. Turn upside down and return to press. Press for 12 to 16 hours.

11. *Form a rind.* Remove cheese from press and remove cheesecloth. Let cheese dry until it forms a rind—4 to 5 days. Turn several times each day.

12. *Paraffin the cheese.* Heat paraffin in a container big enough to dip the cheese in. Dip cheese in paraffin, one-half at a time. Be sure entire cheese is covered.

13. *Ripen cheese.* Store cheese at between 40° F. and 50° F. The vegetable drawer of the refrigerator is a good place. Ripen for 30 to 60 days.

To make the following cheeses, follow the instructions for making Colby cheese, omitting some steps and adding others where indicated.

Cheddar Cheese

Cheddar is the most popular American cheese, ranging in color from nearly white to yellow. It has a mild to sharp flavor and is aged for 3 to 6 months or longer. Cheddar cheese was first made in the village of Cheddar in Somersetshire, England, in the 1500s.

1. Prepare milk.
2. Add color.
3. Add rennet.
4. Test curd.
5. Cut curd.
6. Cook curd.
7. *Omit* "Firm the curd."
8. Drain off whey.
9. Cheddar the curd: Place warm water in the bottom of a broiler pan. Cover the rack with a double layer of cheesecloth, and spread the curd on the cloth to a thickness of one inch. Place thermometer in the curd. Heat in the pan on the top of range or in oven to between 98° F. and 100° F. *Exact temperature is critical.* Too much heat will ruin the cheese. Cover pan if necessary to maintain this temperature for about 20 minutes, until the curd turns into a solid mass. Slice with knife into 1-inch-wide strips and turn strips every 15 minutes for 1 hour. Make certain the temperature does not exceed 100° F. Remove from heat, and cut into 1-inch cubes.
10. Salt the curd. Place cubes in a bowl and work in 2 tablespoons salt. Let cubes stand 10 to 15 minutes.
11. Press curd.
12. Form rind.
13. Paraffin cheese.
14. Ripen cheese 1 to 3 months.

Monterey Jack Cheese

Monterey or jack cheese was first made about 1892 on farms in Monterey, California. It is semisoft when made from whole milk, but can be hard for grating when made from skim milk.

1. Prepare milk.
2. *Omit* "add color."
3. Add rennet.
4. Test curd.
5. Cut curd into ¼-inch cubes.
6. Cook curd: Heat the curd to 100° F., stirring frequently. Keep at this temperature for one hour.
7. *Omit* "Firm curd."
8. Cool curd: After one hour at 100° F., add enough cold water to the curd to bring the temperature down to 86° F.
9. Drain whey.
10. Add salt.
11. Press curd.
12. Form rind.
13. Paraffin cheese.
14. Ripen cheese 6 to 8 weeks at between 55° F. and 60° F. and at 70 percent humidity.

Mozzarella Cheese

Mozzarella is from Southern Italy. Originally it was made from buffalo milk; now it is made from cow's milk. It is a creamy white, semisoft cheese with a mild flavor. It contains no salt, so it is elastic and bland. Its primary use is in making pizza and other Italian foods.

1. Prepare milk.
2. *Omit* "add color."
3. Add rennet.
4. Test curd.
5. Break up curd: After the curd develops, break it up with your hands rather than cutting with a knife.
6. Cook curd: Heat the curd and whey until they are as hot as your hands can stand. With your hands mat the curd (press into block shape) until it is firm. Save the whey.
7. Drain curd.
8. Salt curd, if desired.
9. Press curd.
10. Cook cheese: Put the cheese back into the whey that has been reserved; heat to just below boiling. *Do not boil.* With cheese still in the whey, remove the pan from heat and let stand until cool.
11. Drain cheese: When the cheese is cool, remove it from whey and let drain for 24 hours. Cheese should be soft and pliable. It may be eaten now or aged for 30 to 60 days. It will melt better if it is aged a few weeks.

Smoked Cheese

Smoking cheese will increase the age of the cheese by coating it with bacteria-inhibiting compounds. The hickory or hardwood smoke will also add a delicious flavor. Almost any hard or semihard cheese is good for smoking. To smoke cheese, low heat is required. Too much heat will sweat the butterfat. Smoking should not cook the cheese, only flavor and slightly dry it. Smoke for 4 to 6 hours, turning every hour. See Drying, Curing, Smoking section for smokehouses.

Bleu Cheese

Bleu cheese began as an attempt to copy Roquefort, making it from cow's milk rather than sheep's milk. It failed as a copy but became a success as a new cheese. More whey remains in the cheese, resulting in a sour taste. The bleu cheese mold thrives in a sour environment. The mold culture not only gives the cheese flavor but it also imparts a buttery, soft consistency.

Only Roquefort cheese, aged and manufactured in Roquefort, France, is allowed to bear the Roquefort name. After the cheese is made, it is stored to maturity in the Roquefort caves, which have many crevices where rainwater collects. This is the secret of Roquefort cheese—proper temperature and high humidity while ripening.

Equipment Needed: cheese rennet, colander, cheese press for soft cheese, cheesecloth, mold or culture—bleu or Roquefort.

You can make your own mold culture by spreading bleu or Roquefort cheese on a damp slice of bread. Place the bread in a jar with holes in the lid. Cover jar with a cloth and set aside in a warm place. When bread is covered with mold, remove from jar and dry at room temperature. (Drying the bread in the oven will kill the mold.) When the bread is dry, crumble it into a powder and use as mold powder. You can also purchase a commercial brand.

Day one: Follow Colby Cheese procedure.
1. Prepare milk.
2. *Omit* "add color."
3. Add rennet: Heat milk to 85° F. Dissolve ¼ rennet tablet in cold water. Pour slowly into milk and stir. Set aside for 2 hours.
4. *Omit* "cook curd."
5. Drain curd: Carefully ladle cheese into a large colander lined with cheesecloth. Do not break into curds. Let set for 2 hours or more.
6. Press curd: Remove curd from colander into a soft-cheese press lined with cheesecloth. Alternate layers of bleu cheese powder or crumpled bleu cheese. Apply light pressure.

Day two: Slowly unwrap cheese, being careful not to break it. Wrap in a new cloth, turn upside down, and return to press.

Day three: Remove cheese from press. If cheese begins to collapse, return it to press until firm. Keep cheese at high humidity and 65° F. Turn frequently.

One week: Rub the outside of the cheese with salt. Prick with a nail to make holes approximately one inch apart. This will supply air for mold to grow. Salt every week or two to control mold. Ripen for 4 to 12 months.

Bleu cheese has a sour taste because it contains a large amount of whey and does not go through the process of post-heating. Mold thrives in a sour environment. If you need to control the mold, scrape or wipe off with a cloth soaked in vinegar. Do not paraffin bleu cheese.

Cheese Variations

1. *Milk:* The most basic way to vary your cheese is to vary the milk base. The flavor of cheese made from pasteurized milk will not be the same as that of cheese made from raw milk. Since most of the fat in milk is retained in cheese, you can increase or decrease the richness by using more or less cream. The more cream in your milk, the richer and softer your cheese will be.

2. *Starter:* The starter increases the milk's lactic acid content, enabling the milk solids to form curds. Increasing the starter will increase the acid level of the cheese, resulting in a tart flavor.

3. *Rennet:* The rennet coagulates the milk solids into

curd. The speed with which the rennet acts is influenced by both the acidity and the temperature of the milk. The faster the curdling takes place, the more liquid is expelled from the curd and the harder the cheese will be. The warmer the milk and the higher the acid content, the faster the curdling will take place. The higher the acidity of the milk, the less rennet is needed. A proper balance between temperature, acidity, and rennet is needed to create a firm but not leathery cheese.

4. *Cooking the curd:* The size of the curd and the way it is heated and drained affect the ultimate quality of the cheese. For a harder cheese, cut the curd into smaller pieces. Cooking the curd at a slightly higher temperature or firming it longer will also produce a harder cheese. For softer cheese, cut the curd into larger pieces, cook at a lower temperature, or firm it for a shorter time.

5. *Seasoning:* In addition to or in place of salting the curd, you can use a variety of seasonings to give your cheese unique flavors not available in commercial cheeses. Try seasoned salt, garlic salt, onion salt, hickory seasoning, or other herbs and spices. Just before pressing, try adding one of the following: bits of onion, bacon, hot peppers, garlic, pimientos, or olives.

6. *Pressing:* The harder and longer the curd is pressed, the harder the cheese will be. The firmer and less moist the cheese, the longer its life.

7. *Ripening:* Another word for ripening is *curing* or *aging.* Two changes take place during the ripening process. First, enzymes change the cheese from a tough, rubbery mass to a soft, mellow product. Second, microorganisms present in the cheese act on substances to develop the flavor. This ripening takes place under controlled conditions of temperature and humidity for various lengths of time.

8. *Temperature:* Ripening should take place at temperatures between 40° F. and 60° F. The lower the temperature, the slower will be the ripening. The vegetable drawer of a refrigerator is an ideal place to ripen your cheese. How long it should ripen depends on your individual taste. The longer the ripening period, the firmer, drier, and sharper the cheese becomes.

9. *Melting:* During ripening, hydrolysis of the proteins in cheese occurs. This improves the melting quality. A new cheese will not melt properly.

Special Helps for Making Cheese

1. Off flavors in cheese may be caused by the milk itself or by microbial contamination. What the animal has eaten will affect the flavor of the cheese. Be sure to sterilize your equipment.

2. If numerous holes (large or small) appear, the curd is gassy. (Swiss cheese is made by a special process. The holes found in that cheese are not those that we are referring to here.) The cheese will be misshapen and have a bloated appearance. This is caused by unwanted bacteria.

To prevent bloating, make sure all utensils and containers are well sterilized. If the milk is not pasteurized, make sure it is not more than 2 days old. Bloating can also be caused by old starter that is not active enough and allows undesirable bacteria to grow. Use fresh starter.

3. Too much acid in the cheese will cause it to be sour. This condition can be caused by adding too much starter or leaving the starter in too long. The cheese will also become sour if it is left in a warm place to ripen, or if all the whey is not removed during pressing.

4. If the surface of the cheese cracks, it has either been allowed to dry out or has not been pressed long enough. Keep it in a humid place, if possible, and wipe with a damp cloth moistened with salt water or paraffin. One way to assure a firm cheese without cracks is to press in a warm (not hot) location. This softens the curd enough to allow it to form a solid body free from openings.

5. If mold develops on the cheese, it can be removed by rubbing with a cloth soaked in vinegar. The vinegar will not harm the cheese.

6. To freeze cheese, cut into small sections or slices, or grate and place in plastic bags. Defrost in refrigerator to prevent crumbling.

Avocado Cheese Dip

⅔ cup Cheddar cheese, finely grated
½ cup cream cheese
2 avocados, peeled and mashed
½ teaspoon Worcestershire sauce
1 tablespoon grated onion
½ teaspoon salt
1 clove garlic, minced
¼ teaspoon Tabasco

Combine all ingredients, mix well, and chill.

Pimiento Cheese Spread

1 cup Cheddar or Colby cheese, finely grated
¼ cup salad dressing
1 tablespoon lemon juice
1 small can chopped pimientos, drained
2 tablespoons chopped chives
1 tablespoon Worcestershire sauce
1 tablespoon grated onion
1 tablespoon mustard

Combine all ingredients, mix well, and chill.

Bleu Cheese Dressing

⅓ cup bleu cheese
1 cup salad dressing
2 tablespoons lemon juice

1½ cups yogurt or sour cream
1 teaspoon chopped green onions
    or chives
1 clove garlic, minced
¼ teaspoon onion powder

Combine all ingredients, mix well, and refrigerate.

Bleu Cheese Dip

1 cup cream cheese
½ cup crumbled bleu cheese
1 tablespoon horseradish
½ cup salad dressing
1 clove garlic, minced
¼ teaspoon onion powder

Combine all ingredients, mix well, and refrigerate.

Soft Cheese

Soft cheeses are characterized by their small size and high moisture content. The moisture is caused by draining the curd slowly without pressure. The curd is put in bags or colanders and allowed to drain for several hours or several days. The high moisture content causes an acid flavor. These cheeses are generally eaten unripened.

Cottage Cheese

Cottage cheese is easy to make, tastes good, and is low in calories and high in nutrition. Cottage cheese is made basically the same way today as it was a hundred years ago. It can be made from fresh raw milk, skim milk, pasteurized milk, or reconstituted milk. Raw milk already contains the beneficial bac-

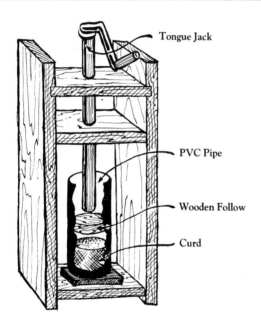

Tongue Jack

PVC Pipe

Wooden Follow

Curd

How To Build a Hard-Cheese Press

The purpose of a hard-cheese press is to apply enough pressure to the curd to remove the whey. An excellent press can be made from a tongue jack (the kind used to jack up mobile homes and trailers) fitted into a wooden frame. Here is how to make such a press.

Parts

A tongue jack (obtained from a trailer supply store or a salvage yard)
A 10-foot length of 2″ x 8″ lumber
An 8-inch piece of PVC sewer pipe 6 inches in diameter
Twelve sixteen-penny nails

Instructions

1. From the 10-foot length of 2″ x 8″ lumber, cut two boards 32 inches long, three boards 13 inches long, and one board 8 inches long. From the remaining piece of lumber cut a circle 5¾ inches in diameter.
2. In the center of two of the 13-inch boards, drill a hole just big enough for the body of the tongue jack to pass through.
3. All the way across each of the 32-inch boards, cut three grooves ½ inch deep and 1⁹⁄₁₆ inches wide. These grooves should be 2 inches, 13 inches, and 29 inches from the top of each board.
4. Insert the 13-inch boards into the grooves in the 32-inch boards. The two drilled boards fit into the grooves 2 inches and 13 inches from the top of the 32-inch boards. The undrilled 13-inch board fits into the groove 29 inches from the top, forming the bottom of the frame. Nail all the boards into place.
5. Insert the body of the tongue jack through the holes in the two top 13-inch boards and anchor the tongue-jack collar to the top board. Your hard-cheese press is now completed. The use of the PVC pipe, the 8-inch board, and the wooden circle (referred to in the recipes as the *wooden follow*) is explained below.

How To Use Your Hard-Cheese Press

1. Turn the handle of the tongue jack until the jack is as high as it will go.
2. Place the 8-inch board on the bottom board of the press. (This board will keep the pressed curd from falling out of the PVC pipe when you want to remove the curd from the press.)
3. Stand the PVC pipe on top of the 8-inch board.
4. Put the curd that needs to be pressed into the PVC pipe.
5. Place the circle of wood (the wooden follow) into the PVC pipe so that it sits flat on top of the curd.
6. To press the curd, lower the tongue jack by turning the tongue-jack handle. Press the curd according to the instructions in the recipe you are using.

A simpler but harder-to-use press can be made without a tongue jack and wooden frame. Just place the PVC pipe on a board, put the curd into the pipe, and set the wooden follow on top of the curd. You can regulate the pressure in this simple press by placing weights of various sizes on top of the wooden follow.

teria that cause the milk to clabber. Pasteurized or reconstituted skim milk will not clabber by itself no matter how long it sets. Therefore, you must add a starter that contains the necessary bacteria. Rennet tablets may also be used to set the curd.

If you are freezing cottage cheese, drain it in a colander before you rinse it and pack it in containers.

Equipment Needed

1. Glass, stainless steel, or enamel pan or crock. *Do not* use aluminum.
2. Starter—either buttermilk or yogurt.
3. Colander.

Cottage Cheese Using Raw Milk

1. *Prepare milk.* Heat 1 gallon whole or skim milk to between 70° F. and 80° F. Add ¼ cup to ½ cup buttermilk. If fresh milk is used, do not heat before adding starter. Cover loosely and set in warm place (room temperature) until clabbered—18 to 24 hours, depending on the temperature and the bacteria count. The milk is clabbered when it has the consistency of jelly.
2. *Cut curd.* When clabber is firm, cut into ½-inch squares with a long knife, first lengthwise, then crosswise.
3. *Cook curd.* Heat the curd slowly to 110° F., stirring gently every five minutes to keep it from sticking together. Avoid breaking curd into smaller pieces. Maintain temperature until curd is firm and doesn't break easily—20 to 30 minutes.
4. *Drain curd.* Pour the curd into a colander and drain. Gently pour cold water over curd until cooled. The longer the curd is rinsed, the less sour the cheese will be. Let drain in colander 2 to 3 hours.
5. *Salt and cream.* Salt to taste and add cream to your liking. Chill thoroughly before serving.

Cottage Cheese with Rennet

1 gallon milk
½ to 1 cup buttermilk or yogurt
⅛ junket tablet (rennet)

Heat milk to 70° F. Dissolve junket tablet in ½ cup cold water. Stir the starter and the junket solution into milk. Remove milk from heat and let stand at room temperature 12 to 18 hours. Follow steps 2 to 5 in recipe for Cottage Cheese Using Raw Milk. Different varieties of milk will make different amounts of cottage cheese. One gallon milk should make between 1 and 1½ pounds.

Processed American Cheese

1 gallon fresh raw milk
3 tablespoons butter
½ teaspoon baking soda
½ cup sour cream
1½ teaspoons salt
Orange food coloring (optional)

Follow directions for Cottage Cheese Using Raw Milk.

1. *Prepare milk.* Skim off cream when it has risen, and set it aside to sour.
2. *Cut curd.* When the curd is thick and soured (clabbered), it is ready to be cut. Cut into ½-inch squares with a long knife.
3. *Cook curd.* Heat the curd until it is too hot to touch. *Do not boil.*
4. *Drain curd.* When curd becomes rubbery, place in colander and drain off whey. Remove as much as possible by pressing lightly. Place curd in a cloth and squeeze out the remaining liquid, or let drain in colander. The curd should be very dry. The drier the curd, the harder the cheese will be.
5. *Recook.* Place dry curd in a bowl and cut in 3 tablespoons butter and ½ teaspoon baking soda. Let stand for at least 2 hours, or overnight. Place in double boiler and add 1 teaspoon salt, ½ cup sour cream, and food coloring, if desired. Cook until all curds are melted and smooth, stirring occasionally to mix ingredients.
6. *Add flavoring.* When the cheese is smooth, add any of the variations listed below if desired. Pour into a well-buttered mold or container. Cover with a lid or plastic wrap. Refrigerate. When cheese is cold and firm, it is ready to eat. Keep covered with a lid or plastic wrap.

Variations:
Omit food coloring and add 1 jalapeño pepper, chopped.
Add ¼ cup fresh or canned pimiento.
Add ¼ teaspoon smoke flavoring and bacon bits.
Add ¼ cup chopped chives.
Add 1 tablespoon Parmesan cheese for an aged flavor.

Cottage Cheese Dip

1 cup cottage cheese
½ cup yogurt or sour cream
1 tablespoon Worcestershire sauce
½ teaspoon garlic salt
1 tablespoon chives
½ teaspoon vegetable seasoning

Combine all ingredients; mix well, or blend in blender.

Cottage Cheese Vegetable Dip

1 cup salad dressing
1 cup cottage cheese
1 teaspoon monosodium glutamate
   (optional)
1 teaspoon onion salt
1 teaspoon garlic salt
1 teaspoon vegetable salt
½ teaspoon dried lemon peel

Combine all ingredients; mix well, or blend in blender.

Cheese Spread

4 cups dry cottage cheese curd
1 teaspoon baking soda
⅓ cup butter or margarine
1½ teaspoons salt
1 cup warm milk
Orange food coloring (optional)
½ cup sour cream

To 4 cups dry curd, add 1 teaspoon baking soda. Cut in ⅓ cup butter or margarine. Let stand 30 minutes or more. Place in a double boiler and add salt and warm milk; add coloring, if desired. When cheese has melted, add sour cream. Cook until smooth. Add any of the variations for Processed American Cheese, if desired. Pour into a bowl and stir occasionally until cool. Refrigerate. Makes 1 to 1½ quarts.

You can vary the consistency of the cheese by the amount of milk or cream added. More milk will give a softer spread. Less milk makes a harder cheese.

Cottage Cheese Cookies

2 cups flour
1 teaspoon baking powder
¼ teaspoon salt
¼ cup butter, softened
¼ cup shortening
¾ cup brown sugar
⅓ cup granulated sugar
2 eggs
1 cup cottage cheese
3 tablespoons frozen orange or pineapple juice concentrate, thawed

In a mixing bowl combine the flour, baking powder, and salt. Set aside. In a large bowl beat the butter, shortening, and both sugars until creamy; beat in the eggs one at a time. Add cottage cheese and juice concentrate, and blend until smooth and creamy. Using a large spoon, fold in flour mixture a little at a time, stirring until smooth.

Drop dough by rounded teaspoonfuls onto a lightly greased cookie sheet. Bake at 350° F. for 12 to 15 minutes, until lightly browned. Remove from cookie sheet immediately and let cool on a wire rack

Jalapeño Cheese

4 cups cottage cheese curd
1 teaspoon baking soda
¼ cup margarine
1½ teaspoons salt
½ cup sour cream
1 or 2 jalapeño peppers, chopped

To cottage cheese curd, add baking soda. Cut in margarine, and let stand 30 minutes or more. Place in a double boiler and add salt. When cheese has melted, add sour cream. Cook until smooth; stir in jalapeño peppers. Pour into a loaf pan and cool. Store in refrigerator. If a softer cheese is desired, add a little sweet milk while heating.

Cream Cheese with Rennet

1 quart milk
1 quart cream
¼ cup buttermilk
⅛ junket tablet (rennet)

This cream cheese may be made with either cream or milk or a combination of both. It may be either raw or pasteurized. Heat milk and cream to 85° F.; add ¼ cup buttermilk. Remove from heat. Dissolve junket in a small amount of cold water, add to milk, and stir well. Cover and keep at room temperature until the milk has formed a soft, solid mass. Line a colander with cheesecloth. Cut curds into 1-inch cubes and pour into colander. Let drain 1 hour. Pick up the four corners of the cheesecloth to form a bag. Suspend the bag over a bowl and let drain at least 12 hours, until all the whey has drained off and a solid mass remains. Salt to taste. If you want a firmer cream cheese, line a small cheese press with cheesecloth. Place curds in press and apply light pressure. When the consistency of the cheese is to your liking, remove from press, place in container, and refrigerate. Cream cheese will keep well in the refrigerator for 1 week. It can also be frozen, but do not keep longer than 4 months.

Cream Cheese from Raw Milk

1 cup buttermilk
2½ quarts fresh raw milk

Add buttermilk to ½ quart milk in a gallon container and let stand 24 hours. Add remaining 2 quarts fresh raw milk and let stand another 24 hours. Put the container of clabbered milk in hot water and let stand 30 minutes. Pour clabbered milk into a loose-weave cloth bag or a colander lined with cheesecloth. Drain for 2 to 6 hours. Put cheese into a bowl, and salt to taste.

For a firmer cream cheese, place in a cloth-lined cheese press. Apply light pressure. When cheese reaches desired firmness, remove from press and refrigerate.

Yogurt Cream Cheese

Place yogurt in several layers of cheesecloth or any fine piece of cloth. Tie the four corners together to form a bag. Hang above sink or bowl to drain. Drain at least 12 hours. When it is consistency you desire, remove and refrigerate. For a sharper cream cheese, use yogurt that is several days old. Season to taste with salt and sugar.

Cream Cheese Spreads or Dips

For spreads, dips, or sandwich fillings, add any of the following to cream cheese: minced green onion, chives, caraway seeds, pimiento, olives, chilies, bacon bits, nuts, or crushed pineapple.

Whipped Cream Cheese

1 cup cream cheese
2 tablespoons sour cream or yogurt
1 tablespoon milk
2 tablespoons sugar or honey

Whip ingredients together until fluffy. Store in an airtight container in the refrigerator.

Cream Cheese Ball

2 cups cream cheese
1 cup Cheddar cheese, finely grated
1/3 cup green onion, chopped
1 tablespoon green pepper, finely chopped
1 clove garlic, finely chopped
1/2 teaspoon Worcestershire sauce
1 tablespoon parsley flakes
1 tablespoon paprika
1/4 teaspoon salt

Combine all ingredients; mix well, and form a ball. Roll in nuts, parsley, or paprika.
Variations:
Add 3 tablespoons chopped pimiento.
Add bacon bits or crumbled bacon and 1/2 teaspoon smoke flavoring.
Add a jalapeño pepper, chopped, and a few drops of Tabasco.
Add a can of chopped green chilies, drained, and a few drops of Tabasco.

Cream Cheese Salad

2 packages (3 ounces each) lime-flavored gelatin
Water, as directed on gelatin package
2 cups cream cheese
1 cup crushed pineapple
1 cup chopped pecans or walnuts
1/4 cup diced maraschino cherries

Prepare gelatin, following directions on package. When gelatin is slightly thickened (about the consistency of egg whites), stir in cream cheese, pineapple, nuts, and cherries. Pour into mold and set until firm. Makes 8 to 10 servings.

No-Bake Orange Cheesecake

1 package (3 ounces) orange-flavored gelatin
1/2 cup hot water
1 cup orange juice
1 cup cream cheese
1 cup cream
1 tablespoon orange peel

Dissolve gelatin in hot water and add orange juice. Beat in cream cheese. Whip cream until stiff; fold into gelatin mixture. Fold in orange peel. Pour into graham cracker crust. Refrigerate.
Graham Cracker Crust: Mix together 1 cup graham cracker crumbs, 1/4 cup brown sugar, and 1/4 cup melted butter or margarine. Press into a 9-inch pie tin.

Cream Cheesecake

2 cups sour cream or yogurt
1 1/2 cups cream cheese
2 eggs
1 cup powdered sugar
1 tablespoon lemon juice
1 tablespoon vanilla
2 cups whipped cream or whipped topping

Combine all ingredients except whipped cream and mix well with mixer or in a blender. Fold in whipped cream. Pour into graham cracker crust. Refrigerate.

Cream Cheese Fudge

1/2 cup cream cheese
3 tablespoons cream
2 cups powdered sugar
2 squares unsweetened chocolate, melted
1 teaspoon vanilla

½ **cup nuts, chopped**
½ **cup maraschino cherries, chopped**

Combine all ingredients except nuts and cherries. Blend until smooth. Fold in nuts and cherries. Press into a buttered 8-inch square pan. Chill.

Whey

Whey is the clear liquid that separates from the casein during cheese making. It contains about half the total milk solids. Although casein and fat are removed, whey contains other proteins, lactose, water soluble vitamins, and some minerals. Most of the milk sugar or lactose remains.

Because of the high nutritive value of whey, there has been an attempt by the cheese industry to find various uses for it. They have come up with a dried milk product similar to nonfat dry milk. Dried whey has proven to be very desirable in making cakes and other bakery items. It improves the flavor, tenderness, and browning properties in baked goods, and produces a soft, moist, light cake.

Liquid whey can be substituted in place of water or milk in baking. It can also be used in sauces, soups, and beverages. When whey is substituted for milk in a recipe, the fat content of the recipe is reduced. The amount of sugar can also be reduced.

Whey Cheese

Whey cheese is made by boiling whey until most of the water evaporates. The sweeter the whey, the sweeter the final product will be. If sourness does occur, it can be overcome by adding a small amount of baking soda.

Heat whey over low heat, stirring occasionally until it comes to a full boil. Simmer 8 to 12 hours. The more whey used, the longer it will take to cook down. When whey becomes the consistency of porridge, stir to prevent burning. Cook to desired consistency. Remove from heat and put kettle in a pan of cold water. Stir with a spoon until cheese is cool. Store in refrigerator.

Variation: Add a little cream before cooking begins for a more mellow product.

Ricotta Cheese

As whey begins to heat over low heat, add 1 pint whole milk for each gallon of whey. (For dry Ricotta cheese, use skim milk.) When the temperature reaches 200° F., stir in ½ cup vinegar or lemon juice. Remove whey from heat and cool. Place curds in a cloth-lined colander or cloth bag, and drain 8 to 12 hours. Remove curds and add salt to taste. Refrigerate.

For dry cheese, add just enough buttermilk to moisten curds. Place in a cloth-lined cheese press. Press 24 hours under medium heavy pressure. Remove and dry in a warm place or in a food dryer at 90 to 100° F. When cheese is dry, it can be grated.

Whey Lemonade

Strain the whey left over after making cottage cheese. To 1 quart whey, add ⅓ cup sugar or honey and the juice of 2 lemons. Chill and serve.

Whey Sherbet

2 quarts liquid whey
1 package (6 ounces) fruit-flavored
     gelatin (use your favorite flavor)
2 cups sugar
1 cup corn syrup or honey
¼ **cup cream or milk**
1 cup sweetened fresh fruit,
     mashed or blended

Heat whey to 150° F. Add gelatin, sugar, and corn syrup or honey. Stir until dissolved. Add cream or milk. Heat mixture to 150° F. and hold at that temperature for 20 minutes. Remove from heat and cool. Place in ice-cube tray or similar container and freeze until slushy. Remove from freezer and beat 5 minutes. Fold in fruit and return to freezer until completely frozen. If you prefer, use a commercial ice-cream freezer and freeze according to manufacturer's instructions.

Eggs

If you have your own hens, you will notice there are times when they lay more eggs than at other times. You may also have other opportunities to obtain a large quantity of eggs at a good price. There are methods of preserving eggs over a long period of time.

Freezing Eggs

To freeze egg yolks or whole eggs, add ¼ teaspoon salt and ¼ teaspoon sugar or honey to ½ cup yolks or eggs. Freeze in ice-cube trays. One and one-half tablespoons frozen yolk equals one fresh egg yolk. Three tablespoons frozen egg equals 1 fresh whole egg.

Whites may be frozen without any additional ingredients. Freeze in ice-cube trays. One cube (2 tablespoons) frozen egg white equals 1 fresh white. After thawing, the whites are satisfactory for cooking. The freezer life of eggs is up to 8 months. Thaw completely at room temperature before using.

Storing Eggs

The following methods will keep eggs well from 6 months to a year, depending on where they are stored. The cooler the temperature, the longer the eggs will last. Brush the egg to clean. Do not wash eggs to be stored; the eggshell is covered by a gelatinous film that helps protect the egg from bacteria and evaporation, and washing removes this film.

Mineral Oil Method: Dip egg into light mineral oil. Drain off excess oil. The thick film remaining partially closes the pores, reduces the loss of moisture, and prevents air from getting to the eggs. Pack in clean boxes and store in a cool place.

Boiling Method: Dip eggs briefly in hot water. This stabilizes the albumen and pasteurizes the egg. Pack eggs in sawdust, straw, or oatmeal, and store in a cool place.

Salt Method: Place eggs, large end down, in jars or other containers with layers of salt between them. Add a thick layer of salt at the top; cover tightly and store in a cool place.

Lard or Shortening Method: Dip eggs in melted lard or shortening. Pack in sawdust, straw, oatmeal, or powdered charcoal. Store in a cool place.

Water-Glass Method: Obtain water glass (sodium silicate) at your drugstore. Use 1 part water glass to 9 parts water. Bring water and water glass to a boil. Cool. Place eggs in a crock or plastic bucket and pour cooled liquid over them. Make sure all eggs are covered, and allow 2 inches for evaporation. Store in a cool place. Wash eggs before cracking them.

How to Tell If Eggs Are Good

1. Float eggs in water. If the large end turns up, they are *not* fresh. This is an infallible rule.

2. Hold the egg up to the light. A good egg is translucent, while a bad egg is perfectly opaque. The difference is as easily perceived as that between a blue egg and a white egg.

Substitutes for Eggs

Snow can be used as an excellent substitute for eggs in puddings, pancakes, and so forth. Two heaping tablespoons snow will take the place of 1 egg, and the recipe will turn out equally well. Use fresh-fallen snow or the under layers of older snow. The ammonia in snow imparts to it rising properties, and the exposed surface of snow loses ammonia by evaporation very soon after it has fallen.

Gelatin may also be used as an egg substitute. For one egg, mix 1 teaspoon unflavored gelatin and 3 tablespoons cold water; add 2 tablespoons boiling water, and stir to dissolve. This mixture can be substituted for up to half the eggs called for in a recipe requiring 4 eggs.

Egg Yolk Substitute: Mix 2 cups water and 1 cup flour in a blender until thick. Cook in a double boiler 45 to 60 minutes. With a mixer, whip in 2 tablespoons cooking oil and ¼ teaspoon salt. Use 2 or 3 tablespoons for binder in hamburgers or meat loaf.

Egg White Extender: Add 1 teaspoon cold water to 2 egg whites. Makes 3 egg whites.

Egg Extender: For each egg omitted from your recipe, add ½ teaspoon baking powder. For thickening purposes, 1 teaspoon cornstarch equals 1 egg.

Quick Eggnog

4 eggs
1 quart milk
½ cup apple juice
¼ teaspoon almond extract
½ cup honey or sugar
1 teaspoon cinnamon
¼ teaspoon salt
Dash of nutmeg

Combine all ingredients in a blender. Blend until smooth. Cool.

Fluffy Omelet

6 eggs
¼ cup water
¼ teaspoon salt
⅛ teaspoon pepper
1 tablespoon margarine

Beat eggs and water. Add salt and pepper. Heat margarine in a skillet. Pour in egg mixture and cook slowly. Lift edge with spatula, allowing a portion of uncooked omelet to flow underneath. Remove from heat. Top with filling and fold in half. Serve immediately. Makes 3 or 4 servings.

Omelet Fillings: Use one or a combination of any of the following: mushrooms, green peppers, green onions, pimientos, cheese, tomatoes, crumbled bacon.

Spanish Omelet: Combine 2 tablespoons green chilies, ½ cup cottage cheese, ½ cup sour cream, crumbled bacon, and cheese. Fill omelet; fold and garnish with Chili Salsa.

Jelly Omelet: Before folding omelet, garnish with your favorite jelly.

Blender Mayonnaise

1 egg
¼ teaspoon dry mustard
2 tablespoons lemon juice
½ teaspoon salt
Dash of paprika
1 cup cooking oil

Combine egg, mustard, lemon juice, salt, and paprika in blender. With the blender running, slowly add oil in a steady stream. Blend until thick. Refrigerate.

Drying, Curing, and Smoking

Drying Fruits and Vegetables

Successful drying of fruits and vegetables depends on the removal of enough moisture to prevent spoilage. The best results are obtained from a food dehydrator. Both fruits and vegetables to be dried should be free from blemishes. Overripe fruit is better used in fruit leathers.

Pretreating Vegetables

Gather vegetables early in the morning, if possible. Prepare the vegetables for drying as soon as you can. Vegetables should be blanched or precooked before drying. This sets the color and prevents undesirable changes during drying. Vegetables that are blanched before drying require less rehydration time.

Steam blanching is preferred to boiling because fewer nutrients are lost in the water. To steam blanch:

1. Put 2 inches of water in a large cooker or pot. Set a rack above the water, and bring water to a boil.

2. Place vegetables not more than 2½ inches deep in a wire basket or enamel colander.

3. Set the basket on the rack above the water. Cover and boil until each piece of vegetable is heated through. Vegetables should feel tender but not completely cooked.

If you cannot steam blanch, place the vegetables in a wire basket and immerse in boiling water, cooking according to directions for steam blanching.

Pretreating Fruits

Fruits are pretreated for the sake of appearance. Pretreating helps to retain color and vitamins, but it is not necessary. Following are a few suggestions for pretreating fruit. You can experiment to see which works best for you.

Natural solutions: Dip fruit in full-strength lemon, orange, or pineapple juice. Drain on paper towels to absorb excess moisture.

Ascorbic acid: Use 1 teaspoon per quart of water. Allow fruit to soak 2 minutes. Drain on paper towels to absorb excess moisture.

Sodium bisulfite (obtain from druggist): Use 1 teaspoon for every 2 quarts of water. Dip fruit for just 2 minutes. Drain on paper towels to absorb excess moisture.

Salt solution: (This is the least desirable treatment.) Soak fruit for 10 minutes in a solution of 4 to 6 tablespoons salt for every gallon of water. Rinse fruit thoroughly and drain on paper towels to absorb excess moisture.

Sulfuring

Sulfuring is recommended to preserve color and to decrease loss of vitamins A and C in apples, apricots, nectarines, peaches, pears, and plums. Before sulfuring, dip cut-up fresh fruit in a solution of 1 cup sugar, corn syrup, or honey dissolved in 1 quart water. Drain the fruit in a colander and arrange on trays. (Note: We recommend that you do the sulfuring outdoors.)

1. Place fruit on trays, not over one layer deep.

2. Stack the trays about 1½ inches apart to permit sulfur fumes to circulate.

3. Prepare a tight wooden box or heavy carton to cover the trays. It should be slightly larger than the stacked trays. Cut an opening 1" x 6" at the bottom of the box or carton for ventilation. Close the opening after the sulfur has burned up.

4. Place sulfur in a clean metal container that is shallow, but deep enough to prevent overflow. (A tin can or lid works well.) Use 2 teaspoons sulfur for each 1 pound of fruit.

5. Set the can beside the stacked trays, or below the trays if a dehydrator is being used. Set fire to the sulfur, taking care to keep the flame away from the trays. (Do not leave the match in the can; it may keep the sulfur from burning up completely.) Cover the trays with the box or carton and process according to the following times:

> Apples—½ hour
> Apricots—1 hour
> Nectarines—1½ hours
> Peaches—1½ hours
> Pears—2 hours
> Plums—1 to 2 hours

Methods of Drying Fruits and Vegetables

A temperature of 110° F. to 120° F. is best for drying fruits and vegetables.

Drying in a dehydrator:

1. Rub trays with oil. Place the food to be dried on trays in layers no more than ½-inch deep. Examine the food from time to time to be sure there is uniform drying. If needed, rotate the trays every hour or two.

2. Dry until food is leathery to brittle and is free of moisture.

Drying in the sun:

1. Place trays in direct sunlight and cover with net or screen to keep insects out. Turn occasionally.

2. After a few days, remove trays to the shade and continue drying. This prevents sunburn and scorching. Dry until food is leathery to brittle and is free of moisture.

Drying in the oven:

1. Dry no more than 4 to 6 pounds of fresh fruit or vegetables in the oven at a time. Place the produce on trays at least 2 inches smaller than the width and depth of the oven.

2. Have trays at least 2½ inches apart. Allow 3 inches of space at top and bottom. Set oven between 110° and 140° F.

3. Turn the produce from time to time for even drying. Dry until food is leathery to brittle and is free of moisture.

Storing Dried Foods

Store all dried foods in a cool, dry place (60° F. or below) to maintain maximum color, flavor, texture, and aroma. Place dry foods in airtight containers. Label and date each container. Since dried foods absorb moisture and odors, do not place containers on a basement floor.

For maximum flavor and nutrition, use within the following times: fruits and vegetables, 1 year; leathers, 6 months; meats and jerky, 1 to 3 months. Meat may become rancid after 3 months unless it is kept in the freezer.

Do not store vegetables and fruits together in the same container.

Reconstituting Dried Foods

The basic rule to follow in reconstituting dried foods is to combine equal amounts of boiling water and food and let stand 5 minutes. Simmer in unabsorbed liquid and add more water, if necessary. Cook until no more liquid can be absorbed.

Never add salt or sugar when reconstituting. They hamper absorption.

Dried vegetables and fruits, home-canned pickles, and homemade sausages and jerky

When reconstituting meats, fruits, and vegetables for pies and casseroles, cover with boiling water and let stand for 5 to 20 minutes.

Pasteurization

Dried food, shelled nuts, raisins, or coconut can be pasteurized in glass jars. This preserves freshness and prevents rancidity.

Place food in clean glass jars on oven rack so they do not touch. Bake at 165° to 175° F. for 30 to 60 minutes, depending on size of jars. Remove from oven and screw lids on tightly (don't worry if bottles do not seal). Store in a cool, dark place.

Hints and Uses for Dried Fruits

To reconstitute fruit, cover with boiling water (use equal amounts fruit and water) and let stand for five minutes.

To soften fruit for snacks, place fruit in a plastic bag with 3 drops of water and place in the refrigerator overnight.

To make fruit cobblers and pies, pour 2 cups boiling water over 2 cups dried fruit and let stand 5 minutes. Add your favorite topping or crust and bake.

To soften fruit for use in cookies, candy, and cakes, place fruit in steamer and steam 2 to 3 minutes.

Dry melons for snacks.

Make your own dried fruit mix.

Add dried fruit to oatmeal just before serving.

Add dried fruit to drinks and whir in blender.

Grind dried berries into powder and use to flavor or color desserts, salads, and syrups.

For variety, sprinkle fruit with flavored gelatin before drying.

Season dried fruit with grated orange or lemon peel.

Sprinkle apples with cinnamon before drying.

Drain old bottled fruit and dry. Use to make holiday gift boxes.

Add dried fruits to cooked cereal, granola, or gelatin salads or desserts.

Hints and Uses for Leather

Use honey or corn syrup if extra sweetener is needed.

Spread blended fruit or vegetables ⅛- to ¼-inch thick on plastic wrap. Remove wrap while leather is still warm, and roll in a new sheet of plastic wrap.

Use old bottled fruit to make leather. Just drain and purée.

Use overripe fruit in leather. Wash, stem, and pit fruit. Blend in blender, using small amounts at a time. Add spices or flavorings for variety. Add sweetening if necessary.

Make tomato leather. Reconstitute and use in soups and sauces.

Hints and Uses for Dried Vegetables

Powder dried tomatoes and add to sauces, casseroles, soups, and stews.

Sprinkle powdered dried vegetables over salads. (Onions, garlic, cucumbers, tomatoes, and celery are good.)

Grind dried corn for cornmeal.

Dry mushrooms and add to soup mixes, spices, and casseroles.

Sprinkle zucchini, cucumber, and potato slices with seasoning salt before drying. Serve with vegetable dips.

Dry grated carrots and zucchini. To reconstitute, add ½ cup boiling water to 1 cup dried grated carrots or zucchini. Let stand 20 to 30 minutes. Use in favorite cookie or cake recipes.

Dry leftover vegetables and add to soups, stews, and casseroles.

Parboil potatoes before drying them.

The more the fruits or vegetables are cooked before drying, the faster they can be reconstituted.

Dry pumpkin, pulverize, and use in pie or pudding recipes.

To reconstitute vegetables for casseroles, add an equal amount of boiling water and let stand 5 minutes.

Hints and Uses for Dried Meats

All meats except jerky should be cooked before drying. Meat will be tough if not cooked.

Never add salt to liquid when reconstituting.

Add reconstituted meat to casseroles, stews, or soups.

Powder dried meat in a blender and use in stocks, casseroles, soups, and stews.

Dry leftover meat and add to soups, stews, and sauces.

Meat should be dried to brittle stage, with no soft spots.

Miscellaneous Uses for Food Dehydrator

Dry cheese and pulverize or grate. Add to foods without reconstituting.

Dry bread crumbs or cubes for croutons.

Make your own baby foods with any dried fruit, vegetables, or meat. Place food in blender with water and blend.

Make your own backpacking foods. Dehydrate canned soup by placing it on plastic wrap as you would leather. Dry and store in plastic bags. Just add boiling water for a nice bowl of hot soup.

When crackers, cereals, or chips become soft or soggy, place them in dryer for an hour to make them crisp.

Use dryer to dry dough ornaments and cake decorations.

Use dryer to dry homemade noodles.

Instant Soup

1 cup water
**2 tablespoons powdered dried
    vegetables**
1 bouillon cube

Bring water to boil, and add powdered dried vegetables and bouillon. Stir until dissolved. Makes 1 serving.

Vegetable Soup Mix

**1 package (16 ounces) dry green split
    peas**
1 package (16 ounces) lentils
2 cups brown rice
4 cups dry minced onion
1 package (12 ounces) pearl barley
**4 to 6 cups dehydrated vegetables
    (peas, carrots, corn, potatoes,
    cabbage, green beans, celery,
    zucchini)**

Combine ingredients and store in an airtight container in a cool, dry place.

Vegetable Soup: In a kettle bring to boil two quarts of water. Add 1 cup vegetable soup mix and simmer 1 to 1½ hours. Add 3 teaspoons salt and 1 can (8 ounces) tomato sauce. Makes 4 to 6 servings.

Tomato Sauce

1 cup dehydrated tomatoes

1 cup hot water

½ teaspoon salt

Dash of pepper

½ teaspoon onion powder

1 tablespoon sugar

Combine tomatoes and hot water in blender. Let stand 5 minutes. Blend until smooth. Add remaining ingredients and blend unto smooth.

Creamy Cucumber Dressing

6 to 8 tablespoons dried cucumbers, coarsely pulverized

½ cup mayonnaise

½ cup buttermilk or yogurt

1 teaspoon instant minced onion

¼ teaspoon salt

⅛ teaspoon garlic salt

½ teaspoon onion salt

Combine ingredients in a glass jar and stir until blended. Chill before serving. Makes about 1 cup dressing.

Corn Chips

1 cup dried corn

1 cup water

¼ teaspoon dried onion powder

¼ teaspoon dried garlic powder

½ to 1 cup grated sharp cheese (optional)

Salt

Bring water to a boil in a saucepan and add corn. Let stand 5 minutes. Simmer 20 to 30 minutes or until water is absorbed. Pour corn into blender and add seasonings and cheese. Blend until smooth. Spread a thin layer on a well-buttered cookie sheet and sprinkle with salt. Bake at 225° to 250° F. until partially dried. Score with a pizza cutter. Return to oven and bake until dry. Remove from oven and cool. You can also dry in dryer by spreading a thin layer on plastic wrap as you would with leather. Dry until crispy. Break into chips. Serve plain or with dip.

Variation: Use 2 cups fresh, canned, or frozen corn. Omit cooking, and blend until smooth.

Potatoes Au Gratin

2 cups dried potatoes, sliced

2 cups water

3 tablespoons margarine

3 tablespoons finely chopped onion

3 tablespoons flour

½ teaspoon dry mustard

½ teaspoon salt

⅛ teaspoon pepper

2 cups milk

2 cups grated cheese

Bring water to a boil, and pour over potatoes. Let stand 1 hour. Melt margarine and sauté onion. Blend in flour, dry mustard, salt, and pepper. Add milk. Cook until mixture thickens. Add 1½ cups cheese and stir until melted. Grease a 1-quart casserole dish, and add potatoes and sauce in layers. Sprinkle with remaining cheese. Bake at 350° F. for 1 hour. Makes 4 to 6 servings.

Fruit Frosty

1 cup dehydrated fruit (bananas, strawberries, peaches, apples, cranberries, or papaya)

1 cup yogurt

¾ cup milk

1 teaspoon cinnamon (optional)

½ teaspoon vanilla

¼ cup honey

2 cups cracked ice

Place fruit, yogurt, milk, cinnamon, and vanilla in blender. Blend until smooth. Add honey and blend again. Add ice and blend until desired consistency is obtained. Makes 4 to 6 servings.

Energy Snack

2 cups raw sunflower seeds

1 cup soy nuts (see index)

2 cups nuts (cashews, pecans, walnuts, Brazil nuts, peanuts)

1 cup raisins

½ cup coconut flakes

2 cups dried fruit (bananas, dates, apricots, apples)

1 cup carob chips

Combine ingredients. Store in an airtight container in a cool, dry place.

Brine-Curing Vegetables

Almost any vegetable can be brine-cured. The brine produces lactic acid, which grows or ferments until it has killed any bacteria present. This gives the vegetables a slightly acid or vinegary taste.

To brine-cure vegetables:

1. Use only fresh vegetables that are free from blemishes. Wash and drain.

2. Place vegetables in a crock, glass jar, wooden barrel, or plastic container. *Do not use metal.* Cover with a brine solution of 1 cup salt dissolved in 2 quarts of water.

3. Cover vegetables with a plate or heavy object to weight them down. Keep at room temperature.

4. The next day add 1 cup salt for every 5 pounds of vegetables. This will maintain a 10 percent brine solution. Remove scum as it forms on top of brine.

5. Each week add ¼ cup salt for every 5 pounds vegetables. Fermentation should continue for 3 to 4 weeks. If no bubbles rise to the surface when the pot is shaken, fermentation has stopped and vegetables are ready.

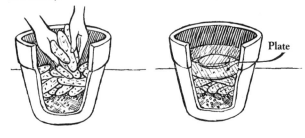

You can either leave the vegetables in the container and store in a cool place or process them in a canner. If you leave them in the container through the winter, cover surface with ¼ inch of vegetable oil to keep them from spoiling. To remove the salt from the vegetables before eating, cover with hot water and let stand 1 hour. Drain and repeat. Rinse. Use in your favorite pickling solution.

To process vegetables, remove from brine and remove salt by soaking in hot water. Pack in hot sterilized jars, leaving ¼ inch headspace. Prepare a solution of ½ cup salt, 4 cups vinegar, and 1 gallon water. Pour over vegetables. Add desired seasonings. Seal and process in boiling water for 15 minutes.

Sauerkraut can be made the same way. Keep it in the brine in which it was cured. Process pints for 15 minutes and quarts for 20 minutes.

Continual Pickle Jar

Fresh vegetables, any assortment
6 quarts vinegar
1 pound salt
2 tablespoons whole cloves
2 tablespoons whole allspice
2 tablespoons ground ginger
2 tablespoons pepper
2 tablespoons celery seed
¼ cup mustard seed
4 cups brown sugar
1 tablespoon cayenne pepper
½ cup dry mustard
2 tablespoons turmeric
Vinegar

Wash and drain fresh vegetables. Place vegetables in a 4- to 6-gallon crock or container. Combine the next 10 ingredients in a large pan. Bring to a boil and cook 8 minutes; cool. Make a thin paste of dry mustard, turmeric, and vinegar. Add to cooled vinegar-spice mixture. Pour brine over vegetables and cover. Leave undisturbed for 5 days. Store at room temperature. As vegetables are removed, others may be added. This brine can be kept up to a year.

Sweet Pickles

1 cup salt
2 quarts boiling water
1 gallon cucumbers, whole or sliced

First week: Dissolve salt in boiling water. Pour over whole or sliced cucumbers. Let stand 1 week.

Day 8: Drain, and add 1½ teaspoons alum dissolved in 2 quarts boiling water. Leave 24 hours.

Day 9: Drain. Add 1 gallon boiling water.

Day 10: Drain. Prepare a solution of 6 cups vinegar, 3 cups sugar, 2 teaspoons celery seed, 4 cinnamon sticks, and 1 teaspoon pickling spice (see index). Bring to a boil, and pour over pickles.

Day 11: Drain, reserving solution. Add ½ cup sugar to solution and bring to a boil. Pour over pickles.

Day 12: Drain and repeat same process as day 11.

Day 13: Drain and repeat same process as day 11.

Day 14: Drain and pack into clean jars. Cover with boiling syrup, leaving ¼ inch headspace. Seal.

Note: Omit the first week if you are using brine-cured pickles.

Dill Pickles

Pack whole or sliced cucumbers or brine-cured pickles in quart jars. Add 1 tablespoon salt and ½ cup vinegar to each jar. Add 1 tablespoon pickling spice (see index) and 1 head of dill. Fill jar with boiling water, leaving 1 inch headspace. Seal.

Bread and Butter Pickles

12 cups thinly sliced cucumbers
3 large onions, sliced thin
2 green peppers, diced
1 red pepper, diced
½ cup pickling salt
4 trays ice cubes
6 cups sugar
4 cups vinegar
2 teaspoons turmeric
2 teaspoons celery seed
2 teaspoons mustard seed

Combine cucumbers, onions, and green and red peppers in a large container and stir in salt. Add ice cubes and let stand 3 to 4 hours. Drain and discard any unmelted ice. Combine remaining ingredients in a large pan and bring to a boil. Add vegetables and return to a boil. Remove from heat and pack in sterilized jars. Makes 6 pints.

Zucchini Pickles

2 pounds zucchini
2 large onions
¼ cup pickling salt
2 cups white vinegar
½ teaspoon dry mustard
1 cup sugar
1 teaspoon each celery seed, mustard,
    turmeric

Wash and slice zucchini and onions. Cover with water and add pickling salt; let stand 1 hour. Drain, reserving liquid. Add remaining ingredients to reserved liquid. Bring to a boil and pour over zucchini and onion slices. Let stand 1 hour. Bring to a boil a second time and cook 3 minutes. Pack in hot jars and seal. Makes 3 pints.

Cheerful Sweet Pickles

9 cups overripe cucumbers, peeled,
    seeded, and cut in cubes
½ cup salt
3½ quarts water
3½ cups sugar
2 cups vinegar
1 teaspoon whole cloves

2 sticks cinnamon
1 jar (4 ounces) maraschino cherries
2 teaspoons red food coloring

Sprinkle cucumbers with salt and cover with boiling water. Let stand overnight. In the morning, bring cucumbers to a boil. Drain, reserving liquid. To liquid, add sugar, vinegar, and spices tied in cheesecloth; bring to a boil. Pour over drained cucumbers and let stand overnight. In the morning bring cucumbers to a boil and simmer until tender. Add cherries and food coloring. Put into jars and seal. Makes 4 or 5 pints.

Cucumber Relish

2 quarts chopped cucumbers
1 cup chopped onions
2 cups chopped sweet red peppers
2 cups chopped green peppers
1 tablespoon turmeric
½ cup salt
8 cups cold water
1 tablespoon mustard seed
2 teaspoons whole cloves
2 teaspoons whole allspice
1 teaspoon celery seed
4 cups vinegar
1½ cups brown sugar

Combine vegetables and sprinkle with turmeric. Dissolve salt in cold water and pour over vegetables. Let stand 4 hours. Drain and rinse vegetables. Combine spices in cheesecloth bag and add to vinegar and sugar. Heat to boiling and pour over vegetables. Let stand overnight. Bring vegetables to a boil and pack into sterilized jars. Seal at once. Makes 5 or 6 pints.

Country Hot Dog Relish

4 cups ground cabbage
4 cups ground onions
4 cups ground green tomatoes
12 green peppers, ground
4 sweet red peppers, ground
½ cup salt
6 cups sugar
1 tablespoon celery seed
2 tablespoons mustard seed
1½ teaspoons turmeric
4 cups vinegar
2 cups water

Sprinkle ground vegetables with salt. Let stand overnight. Rinse and drain. Combine remaining ingredients and pour over vegetables. Heat to boiling. Place in hot sterilized jars and seal. Makes 6 to 8 pints.

Sandwich Spread

2 cups finely chopped green tomatoes

2 cups finely chopped sweet red
  peppers

2 cups finely chopped green peppers

2 tablespoons salt

1 cup water

½ cup vinegar

¾ cup sugar or ½ cup honey

3 eggs

1 teaspoon mustard

2 tablespoons flour

1 cup sour cream

Add salt to chopped vegetables and let stand for 30 minutes. Drain and add 1 cup water. Simmer until vegetables are tender. Combine remaining ingredients and add to vegetables. Boil until thick. Put into hot sterilized jars and seal. Sandwich spread keeps indefinitely.

Curing Meats

Curing refers to preserving and flavoring meat through dry salt packing, brine submersion, pickling, or corning. Corning is a process of preserving meat without the addition of smoking, while brine and salt curing are usually associated with smoking or drying.

Commercially cured meats today are made to be stored in the freezer or refrigerator. They have added preservatives so they do not need a strong curing solution; thus they are not as salty as the home-cured meats.

Because the curing solution of home-cured meats is strong, the meat is salty. To desalt home-cured meat, simmer it in a pan with water for 10 to 12 minutes or until you have the desired taste. The liquid in which the meat is cooked may be used for cooking beans. (Do not add extra salt to the beans.) The cured meat can be sliced and eaten as is or sliced and fried. Meats that are home-cured have a much nicer flavor than do those cured comercially.

Any meat that is taken from the freezer must be thawed before curing. To thaw frozen meat, leave it wrapped and let it stand in the refrigerator. Do not put meat back in the freezer after thawing. Meat that has been frozen and then cured will not have as good a texture or flavor as fresh meat.

The following are the standard ingredients in curing:

Salt is the most essential ingredient. It inhibits bacteria growth and preserves the meat by drawing the moisture from the cells while at the same time entering the cells by osmosis. Meat can be cured in salt alone, but it will not have as good a flavor or texture. Never use iodized salt in curing.

Sugar tenderizes the meat and improves the flavor, texture, and color. Honey is sometimes used in place of sugar in the same proportions.

Saltpeter (nitrate of potassium) inhibits certain bacteria, adds to the flavor, and gives cured meat its color. Do not use more than called for.

Spices give aroma and flavor.

Water should be boiled before it is used in brine.

There are basically two types of curing: dry salt or brine. With the dry-salt method, the curing takes place faster and there is less chance of spoilage. This is a good method for warmer climates or where the temperature cannot be kept cool. The meat from the dry-salt cure will be saltier. Because it takes longer to cure using the brine method, the temperature of the meat must be kept cool to prevent spoilage. Brine curing results in a milder-flavored meat.

All meats to be cured or smoked must be cooked. The curing and smoking process does not destroy trichinae larvae, which cause trichinosis.

Brine Cure

100 pounds meat

8 pounds salt

2 pounds sugar

2 ounces saltpeter

4½ to 6 gallons water

Dissolve salt, sugar, and saltpeter in water. Pack hams, shoulders, or bacon into clean 1-gallon containers. (Eight pounds of meat can be cured in a 1-gallon container. Use glass containers, earthenware crocks, or plas-

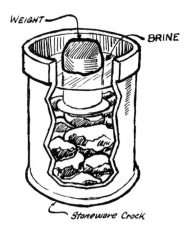

WEIGHT

BRINE

Stoneware Crock

tic buckets.) Pack bacon sides flat, with skin side down.

Put a clean weight over the meat, and cover completely with brine, making sure all surfaces are fully covered.

On the 5th, 13th, and 15th days, remove the meat and repack it, putting meat that was on top on the bottom, and meat that was on the bottom on the top. Cover with same brine, making sure meat is fully covered. If a thin scum of white mold forms and brine becomes ropy (drips from fingers like syrup), remove meat and wash it. Discard the old brine solution and make up a new one.

Hams and shoulders will take 4 days per pound to cure, and bacon will take 1½ days per pound.

Dry Salt Cure

100 pounds meat
8 pounds salt
1½ to 2 pounds sugar
2 ounces saltpeter

Mix salt, sugar, and saltpeter thoroughly. Put each ham or shoulder into a pan of curing mixture. Rub mixture into meat, coating all surfaces well and massaging the mixture into the meat. Rub hams 3 times, shoulders 2 times, and bacon once.

Put a layer of cure in the bottom of a barrel or box that has been drilled with holes in the bottom as a drain. (Keep the container raised from the ground or floor.) Pack the meat in the box and cover it with remaining cure, making sure all surfaces are covered. Repack the meat every 6 to 8 days. Cure hams and shoulders 2 days per pound of meat and smaller pieces 1½ days per pound. Allow meat to hang two weeks after curing before smoking.

Tender-Quick Cure

Tender-Quick, obtainable at grocery stores, is an easy-to-use combination of ingredients (including preservatives) that produces a fast cure, delicious flavor, and tender meat. It also helps prevent excess saltiness.

Brine Cure: Combine 1 cup Tender-Quick for each 3 cups water. Place meat in a clean container and pour enough brine over meat to completely cover it. Weight meat down. Place in the refrigerator or store in cool place, not over 40° F.

Dry Cure: Rub 2 heaping tablespoons Tender-Quick into each pound of meat, making sure all surfaces are completely covered. Place meat in a plastic bag and store it in the refrigerator or in a cool place, not over 40° F.

Curing Time: Cure slices and thin pieces for 1 to 3 days; 6- to 8-pound pieces for 10 days; 9- to 12-pound pieces or larger for 15 days.

Pickle Cure

Use fresh beef that has been chilled but not frozen. Dissolve 2 tablespoons Tender-Quick in 1 gallon pure or boiled water. Place meat in a clean crock or container. Pour in cooled Tender-Quick solution. Place a weight over meat to keep it covered, and pour in additional Tender-Quick. Cure 2 days for each 1 pound of meat.

Corning Beef

Eight pounds of salt will corn 100 pounds of meat. Cut meat into 5- to 6-inch squares of uniform thickness. Sprinkle a layer of salt ¼-inch deep over bottom of a clean container. Add alternate layers of salt and beef. Top with a liberal amount of salt, covering meat completely. Allow meat to set overnight.

Dissolve 4 pounds sugar, 2 ounces baking soda, and 4 ounces saltpeter in 1 gallon warm water. Pour over meat and add 3 gallons additional water. Weight down meat. If brine becomes ropy, discard and add new brine. Cure 28 to 40 days at 38° to 40° F. Drain meat thoroughly before wrapping or smoking.

Spiced Corned Beef Brine

2 pounds onions, chopped
3 garlic bulbs, minced
6 tablespoons Pickling Spice (see index)

Add onions, garlic, and spice to brine when curing 100 pounds of meat and follow directions for corning beef.

Dried Beef

Use only leanest, most tender beef, such as the tender part of the round. For every 20 pounds of beef, combine 2 cups salt, 1 teaspoon saltpeter, and ¼ pound brown sugar. Mix together. Each day for three successive days, rub the beef well with ⅓ of the mixture. Let beef set in cure for 6 days; then hang to dry.

Jerky

Cut away the fat and gristle from meat, and cut the meat on the bias in long, thin strips. Soak meat in a brine made from 1½ cups pickling salt and 1 gallon cold water. Cure 4 to 7 days. Remove meat from brine and roll in a mixture of salt, pepper, garlic powder, and herbs, if desired. Dry in food dryer, sun, or smokehouse.

Quick Beef Jerky

1½ pounds meat, cut into thin strips

1 teaspoon seasoning salt

⅓ teaspoon garlic powder

1 teaspoon pepper

¼ cup soy sauce

1 teaspoon monosodium glutamate (Accent)

1 teaspoon onion powder

¼ cup Worcestershire sauce

Few drops of smoke flavoring

Combine seasonings and sauces. Marinate meat 12 to 24 hours. Dry meat in oven 8 to 12 hours at 140° F. Turn meat halfway through the drying process. Meat may also be dried in dehydrator.

Pastrami

4 pounds beef brisket or flank

½ cup pickling salt

2 tablespoons brown sugar

1 tablespoon ginger

2 teaspoons black pepper

3 cloves garlic, finely minced

4 teaspoons coriander seed

Mix salt with remaining ingredients. Rub mixture into meat surface, coating well. Rub twice, massaging mixture into meat. Wrap meat in aluminum foil or put in a plastic bag. Place in refrigerator 10 to 12 days, and turn every day. Remove meat and hang to dry for several days before smoking. Smoke 2 to 4 hours in cold smoke method (p. 110). Cool, wrap, and refrigerate.

Salt Pork

Cut fatback into pieces approximately 1 inch wide and 3 to 4 inches long. Place in any brine with cured meat. Cure up to 1 month.

Deviled Ham

1½ cups cooked ham and trimmings, cubed

½ teaspoon horseradish

1 teaspoon mustard

2 teaspoons vinegar

Tabasco sauce to taste

1 clove garlic, minced

Pinch each of nutmeg, cloves, pepper, ginger, and thyme

Grind ham fine in a meat grinder or food processor. Add remaining ingredients and process in blender or food processor. Refrigerate overnight.

Making Sausage

Sausage making is one good way to use leftover scraps of pork or fat. Homemade sausages do not contain the additives that go into commercial sausages, and you will be able to choose the meat you wish to put into them. Salt and spices act as the curing agents. Curing refers not only to the ingredients, but also to the passage of time in which the ingredients do their job. All fresh sausages need to cure for a certain length of time.

Sausages fall into two groups: fresh sausage and cured sausage. Fresh sausage must be cooked before being eaten and should be stored the same as fresh meat. Cured sausage is preserved with ingredients such as salt or saltpeter, and dried or smoked to prevent spoilage. It can be eaten with or without cooking.

To prevent spoilage in making sausage, sterilize all utensils. Keep the work area clean, and wash your hands thoroughly. Refrigerate the meat as soon as possible. When making your own recipes for sausage, a good rule to follow is to use two-thirds chilled, fresh, lean meats and one-third fresh fat.

Steps in Making Sausage

1. Cube the meat and fat and put through a food chopper or meat grinder. Mix together. Add seasonings. Use less spice if meat is to be smoked. Put through a chopper or meat grinder again. The meat is then ready to be put into casings.

2. Case the meat, using natural hog casings about 1¼ inches in diameter, obtained from a butcher or meat packer. Keep the casings in the refrigerator, packed in salt, and cut off only what you need. For ease in handling, use a sausage horn to stuff the meat mixture. Soak casings in water 3 to 4 hours to make them more pliable. Ease the casing onto the narrow end of a funnel, pushing gently

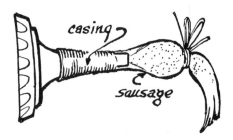

until only 2 inches of casing remains. Push meat mixture through the funnel into the casing with your fingers or a spoon. Tie the sausages at desired lengths with a cotton string or strong thread.

Breakfast Sausage

2 pounds ground pork
2 teaspoons salt
½ teaspoon dried thyme
½ teaspoon pepper
¼ teaspoon garlic salt
¼ teaspoon onion salt

Combine all ingredients and mix well. Stuff in casings or form into patties. Cure 3 or 4 days in the refrigerator or freeze up to one month in the freezer. Pan fry slowly, cooking thoroughly.

Italian Sausage

2 pounds ground pork
½ teaspoon pepper
1 to 2 teaspoons crushed red peppers
  (optional)
1 teaspoon paprika
½ teaspoon thyme
1 teaspoon fennel seed
½ teaspoon finely minced garlic
1 teaspoon finely chopped onion
2 teaspoons salt

Combine all ingredients and mix well. Stuff in casings. Cure in refrigerator 3 days or freeze. Cook in boiling water or pan fry until cooked through.

Chorizo

2 pounds ground pork
1 teaspoon dried red pepper flakes
¼ teaspoon ground cloves
2 teaspoons salt
2 teaspoons paprika
½ teaspoon pepper
1 large clove garlic, minced
1 teaspoon chili powder
1 teaspoon cayenne pepper (optional)

Combine all ingredients and mix well. Stuff in casings or form into patties. Cure 3 or 4 days in the refrigerator. Pan fry until cooked through.

Frankfurters

2 pounds raw pork or beef (or a
  mixture of both)
½ teaspoon pepper

½ teaspoon mace
2 teaspoons ground coriander
1 tablespoon salt
1 clove garlic, minced
¼ cup finely chopped onion
¼ teaspoon mustard
¼ teaspoon marjoram

Combine all ingredients and mix well. Stuff into casings. Refrigerate 2 or 3 days. To cook, simmer in water 20 to 30 minutes or until cooked through. Use within a week or freeze.

Pepperoni

4 pounds pork, cubed
1 pound salt pork, cubed
3 pounds beef, cubed
2 chili peppers, crushed
1 tablespoon pepper
3 cloves garlic, crushed
1 teaspoon saltpeter
2 teaspoons sugar
4 teaspoons paprika
2 teaspoons cayenne pepper
½ pound pork casings

Grind meat in a meat grinder. Add remaining ingredients and mix well. Stuff into casings. Hang to dry in a cool, airy room for 6 to 8 weeks. Store in refrigerator.

Salami

2 pounds lean beef, cubed
2 pounds lean pork, cubed
4 tablespoons salt
2 teaspoons pepper
2 teaspoons sugar
1 clove garlic, minced
¼ teaspoon nutmeg
½ teaspoon coriander
1 teaspoon fennel
½ teaspoon saltpeter

Grind meat. Add remaining ingredients, and put in refrigerator for 24 hours. Pack into casings and hang to dry in a cool, airy room for 8 weeks. Store in the refrigerator.

Summer Sausage with Tender-Quick

2 pounds ground pork or beef (or
  a mixture of both)
2 tablespoons Tender-Quick
1 teaspoon onion powder

½ teaspoon dry mustard

½ teaspoon seasoned pepper

½ teaspoon liquid smoke

½ teaspoon garlic powder

2 teaspoons whole peppercorns
(optional)

Mix ingredients well and form into 2 long rolls that will fit into a 13″ x 9″ cake pan. Wrap each roll in foil. Refrigerate for 24 hours. Add 2 cups hot water to pan and bake 1½ hours at 350° F. Drain each roll and rewrap in plastic or clean foil. Sausage can be frozen.

Smoking Meats

Cured meats are preserved further by smoking before they are stored. Smoking dries the meat and furnishes some protection against bacteria, but its primary purpose is for flavor and color.

Meat that has been cured in salt or brine should be removed from the brine, rinsed off, and hung in the smokehouse (see illustrations) to dry overnight. Hang with a strong cord inserted into a hole in the meat, and be sure pieces of meat do not touch.

To smoke, make a fire from hardwoods such as hickory, birch, oak, sassafras, cherry, or apple. Never use soft woods or paper. Most meats are smoked with the cold-smoke method for flavor and long-term preservation. With this method the meat is hung at least 6 feet away from the smoke. The ideal temperature is 70° to 90° F.

The hot smoke method, which requires a temperature of 160° to 210° F., is used to cook meats and smoke them at the same time. The fire can be built directly under the smokehouse. Meats smoked by this method should be eaten soon after smoking and not stored for long periods.

A good average time to smoke ham is either 24 hours a day for two days or 5 to 6 hours a day for six or seven days. Smaller pieces will take from 48 to 72 hours. Be careful not to smoke meat too long.

After smoking, meat can be sprinkled with black or red pepper and stored in a loosely woven bag or refrigerated or frozen.

To keep flies from meat, make a bag of muslin. Put a little straw in the bottom of the bag. Place meat in the bag and stuff straw all around it to prevent flies from depositing eggs on the surface of the meat. Hang in a cool place.

Inspect the meat occasionally. Mold on the outside does not indicate spoilage. Scrub it off or trim it. Brush meat with vegetable oil or lard to delay mold. Do not keep hams over a year. Bacon should be cooked and eaten soon, not stored for any length of time.

Smoked Salt

Put some table salt in a shallow pan and place on a rack in the smokehouse. Use the cold-smoke method. Stir occasionally. Leave for 3 to 4 hours.

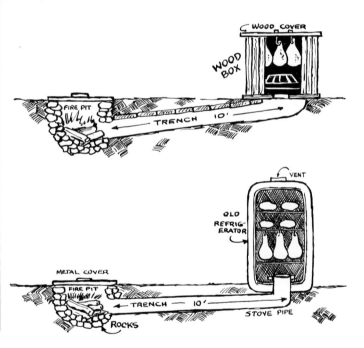

Gravies, Soups, and Sauces

Making Your Own Stock

Collect any fat scraps, bones, or bits and pieces of meat and put them in a bag in the freezer until you have enough to make a stock. If you have an animal butchered, have the butcher save the bones and left-over fat for you. When you cook a roast, scrape all the browned bits in the bottom of the pan into a container and save them.

For chicken soup base, save any fat or skin from the chicken, and any neck or wing that you might not desire to eat. Save any unused broth from broiled chicken. These can all be kept in the freezer until you are ready to use them.

Homemade Beef or Chicken Soup Base

6 pounds meat, bones, trimmings,
    scrapings, and fat from fresh beef,
    poultry, veal, or lamb
2 large onions
3 stalks celery (optional)
3 carrots (optional)

1 turnip (optional)
½ teaspoon pepper
½ teaspoon mace
½ teaspoon thyme
2 or 3 sprigs parsley
1 clove garlic
1 bay leaf
2 tablespoons butter

1. Heat oven to 450° F. Put bones, meat, fat, onions, and vegetables in a roasting pan. Brown ingredients in oven for 50 to 60 minutes, stirring occasionally. This will give you a good brown color and add to the flavor of your extract. This step can be omitted if you are making poultry soup base.

2. Grease stock pot or electric slow-cooking pot with butter. Remove ingredients from roasting pan and put them in stock pot. Add 2 cups water to roasting pan and dissolve all brown bits and pieces. Pour into stock pot with other ingredients.

3. Simmer very gently in a partially covered pot for 8 hours. Skim off any foam or scum that rises during this time. Strain broth through a fine sieve or through a cheesecloth. Set in the refrigerator to cool. Remove any fat that solidifies on top of the broth. (This is important, for fat can cause soup base to go rancid.) *(Continued)*

Basic Onion Soup (p. 113) with assorted soup toppings

4. Resume simmering until mixture will coat a metal spoon. Strain again and set aside to cool, uncovered. When soup base is cool, cover and put in the refrigerator. The cooled soup base should be firm and almost rubbery. The exact yield of the soup base depends on the amount of collagen present in the bones and meat.

A tablespoon of this bouillon and ¼ teaspoon salt to 1 cup boiling water will give you a better-tasting soup base or bouillon than you can buy. You can add it to soups, stews, gravies, and sauces. Keep it in the refrigerator for as long as you wish, or freeze it. You can also dry it and make it into cubes.

Bouillon Cubes

Pour the extract jelly soup base into a loaf pan or shallow pan ½-inch deep and let set until cool. Cut the jelly into cubes. One ½-inch cube equals 1 tablespoon soup base. Dry in oven or dehydrator at 100° F. Pack into jars or cover with foil. Keep in a dry place. Bouillon cubes need not be refrigerated.

Gravies

Chicken Gravy

1½ tablespoons butter or margarine
1½ tablespoons Chicken Soup Base
1 teaspoon onion powder
½ teaspoon garlic powder
¼ cup instant nonfat dry milk
¼ teaspoon turmeric
1¼ cups water
1 tablespoon flour

Place butter or margarine and soup base in saucepan. Stir over heat until combined. Add onion powder, garlic powder, dry milk, turmeric, and 1 cup water. Bring to a boil. Mix ¼ cup water and 1 tablespoon flour together and stir until combined. Add to boiling gravy and cook, stirring constantly, until thick.

Beef Gravy

1½ tablespoons butter or margarine
1½ tablespoons Beef Soup Base
1 teaspoon onion powder
½ teaspoon garlic powder
½ teaspoon Kitchen Bouquet
1 teaspoon Worcestershire sauce
1 tablespoon flour
1¼ cups water

Place butter or margarine and soup base in a saucepan. Stir over heat until combined. Add onion powder, garlic powder, Kitchen Bouquet, Worcestershire sauce, and 1 cup water. Bring to a boil. Mix ¼ cup water and 1 tablespoon flour together and stir until combined. Add to boiling gravy and cook, stirring constantly, until thick.

Mushroom Gravy: Add ¼ cup canned or cooked mushrooms.

Brown Gravy

1½ tablespoons butter or margarine
1½ tablespoons Beef Soup Base
1 tablespoon minced onion
1¼ cups water
½ teaspoon Kitchen Bouquet
1 teaspoon soy sauce
1 tablespoon flour

Place butter or margarine and soup base in saucepan. Stir over heat until combined. Add onion, 1 cup water, Kitchen Bouquet, and soy sauce. Bring to a boil. Mix ¼ cup water and 1 tablespoon flour together and stir until combined. Add to boiling gravy. Cook, stirring constantly, until thick.

Onion Gravy

¼ cup butter or margarine
3 cups chopped onions
1 tablespoon Beef Soup Base
2 cups boiling water
1 teaspoon Kitchen Bouquet
¼ cup cold water
2 tablespoons cornstarch
Salt and pepper to taste

Sauté onions in butter or margarine until tender. Add soup base, boiling water, and Kitchen Bouquet.

Combine cold water and cornstarch. Stir into sauce and cook until clear and thickened. Add salt and pepper.

Soups

Basic Onion Soup

5 medium onions, sliced thin
2 tablespoons margarine
1 teaspoon olive oil
5 cups beef broth or 5 teaspoons Beef
    Soup Base dissolved in 5 cups
    water
Salt to taste

Sauté onions in margarine and olive oil until limp. Cover and simmer for 10 minutes. Add beef broth or soup base and simmer 1 hour. Salt to taste. Makes about 1½ quarts.

Cream of Celery Soup

2½ cups chopped celery tops and stems
½ medium onion, chopped
2 tablespoons butter or margarine
2 cups water
1 quart milk
1 teaspoon dried parsley
1 teaspoon salt
¼ cup flour

Sauté celery and onion in butter until limp, not brown. Add water and boil over medium heat until tender. Add milk and simmer 10 minutes. Add parsley and salt. Mix flour with a little water and add to soup; simmer until thick. Makes 6 to 8 servings.

Cream of Tomato Soup

2 cups tomato juice
¼ cup chopped onions
1 teaspoon sugar
1 bay leaf
Salt and pepper to taste
3 tablespoons butter
3 tablespoons flour
1½ cups milk
Dash of cayenne pepper

Mix tomato juice, onions, sugar, bay leaf, salt, and pepper in a saucepan and simmer 15 minutes. Remove bay leaf. Melt butter, add flour, and blend. Stir milk into butter and flour mixture and add tomato mixture and cayenne pepper. Cook until thick. Makes 4 servings.

Cream of Chicken Soup

1 tablespoon chopped onion
3 tablespoons cooking oil
¼ cup flour
1 quart chicken broth
1 cup chopped cooked chicken
½ cup milk or half and half
½ teaspoon parsley
Salt and pepper to taste

Sauté onion in oil; add flour, and stir until smooth. Add chicken broth, chicken, milk, parsley, salt, and pepper. Cook until thick. Makes 6 servings.

Cream of Mushroom Soup

1½ cups fresh mushrooms, chopped
2 tablespoons chopped onions
3 tablespoons butter
3 tablespoons flour
3 cups chicken or beef broth, or 3
     teaspoons Soup Base dissolved in
     3 cups water
½ cup cream or canned milk
¼ teaspoon nutmeg
Salt and pepper to taste

Sauté mushrooms and onions in butter. Add flour, stirring until smooth. Add broth, cream or milk, nutmeg, salt, and pepper. Cook until thick. Makes 4 servings.

Sauces

White Sauce

Thin	*Medium*	*Thick*
1 Tbsp. butter	2 Tbsp. butter	3 Tbsp. butter
1 Tbsp. flour	2 Tbsp. flour	3 Tbsp. flour
¼ tsp. salt	¼ tsp. salt	¼ tsp. salt
1 cup milk	1 cup milk	1 cup milk

Melt butter over low heat in a saucepan. Stir in flour and salt. Add milk and heat, stirring constantly, until thick.

Cheese Sauce: Add ½ to 1 cup grated cheese and ½ teaspoon mustard.

Curry Sauce: Add ½ teaspoon curry powder and ½ teaspoon Worcestershire sauce.

Browned Butter

Put butter in a hot frying pan and toss it about until it is brown. Stir in browned flour (below), and cook until sauce is smooth and begins to boil. Use for coloring gravies and sauces for meats.

Browned Flour

Spread flour on a baking pan and set it under the broiler in a very hot oven. Or brown in a hot skillet on top of the stove. Stir until it is browned through. Keep on hand for thickening gravies or sauces.

Tomato Sauce

1 quart canned tomatoes
1 onion, sliced
2 whole cloves
Salt and pepper to taste
1 tablespoon flour
2 tablespoons butter

Combine tomatoes, onion, cloves, salt, and pepper in a saucepan. Boil 20 minutes. Strain through a sieve. Cook flour in butter until browned. Stir browned butter into tomato mixture, and cook until thick.

Catsup

1 bushel tomatoes
6 red peppers, chopped
6 onions, chopped
2 cloves garlic, minced
1 cup chopped celery
2 quarts vinegar
1 cup salt
2 tablespoons mustard
4 tablespoons Pickling Spice (see index)
1 tablespoon celery seed
1 tablespoon whole allspice
1 tablespoon whole nutmeg
4 cups sugar
⅛ teaspoon bottled hot sauce

Wash and drain tomatoes. Cook tomatoes, peppers, onions, garlic, and celery for 1 hour. Press through a sieve. Put Pickling Spice, celery seed, allspice, and nutmeg in a spice bag. Add vinegar, salt, mustard, and spice bag to tomato mixture. Cook until thick. Remove spice bag and add sugar and hot sauce to taste. Fill sterilized jars, leaving ½ inch headspace. Process pints 15 minutes.

Chili Sauce

2 dozen tomatoes, peeled
2 small green peppers, chopped
1 onion, chopped fine
2 tablespoons sugar

2 cups vinegar
1 tablespoon salt
1 teaspoon each ginger, allspice, cloves,
    and cinnamon

Combine tomatoes, peppers, onions, and sugar, and boil until thick. Stir in vinegar and strain through a sieve. Return to heat and add remaining ingredients. Simmer until thick. Fill sterilized jars and seal.

Chili Salsa

5 fresh tomatoes, chopped, or 1 can
    (16 ounces) tomatoes
1 medium onion, chopped
¼ teaspoon parsley
½ teaspoon mild crushed red peppers
½ teaspoon sugar or honey
Salt and pepper to taste
Pinch of oregano

To prepare fresh tomatoes, cut each in half and grate on large grater or chop in small pieces. Combine all ingredients in a bowl; chill and serve.

Picante Sauce

2 quarts tomatoes, peeled
1 large onion, chopped fine
¼ cup jalapeño pepper, chopped
    fine
½ chili pepper, chopped
¼ teaspoon black pepper
1 teaspoon salt
1 tablespoon garlic powder
¼ teaspoon allspice
1 teaspoon oregano
1 tablespoon sugar

Combine all ingredients and cook 1 hour or until desired consistency.

Guacamole Sauce No. 1

2 large ripe avocados, mashed
½ teaspoon lemon juice
½ teaspoon salt
1 tablespoon chopped onion
1 small fresh tomato, chopped
½ clove garlic, minced
½ jalapeño pepper, chopped

Combine all ingredients and mix well. Chill and serve.

Guacamole Sauce No. 2

1 tomato, chopped or grated
4 green onions, chopped fine
2 tablespoons lemon juice
1 teaspoon soy sauce
3 avocados, mashed
Tabasco sauce or Picante Sauce to taste
¾ teaspoon salt
Dash of cayenne pepper

Combine all ingredients; mix well. Chill and serve.

Teriyaki Sauce

1 cup soy sauce
¼ cup brown sugar
¼ teaspoon garlic powder
¼ teaspoon onion powder
2 tablespoons vinegar
1 teaspoon ground ginger

Combine ingredients and mix well to dissolve sugar. To use as a marinade, pour over meat and marinate 2 hours or longer. As meat cooks, brush it with marinade. To use as a sauce, simmer teriyaki sauce mixture 10 minutes; serve hot. Sauce may be used for dunking shrimp or meat pieces, or served over rice.

Sweet and Sour Sauce

½ cup brown sugar
2 teaspoons soy sauce
1 teaspoon Soup Base (see index)
2 tablespoons cornstarch
1 cup water
½ teaspoon salt
3 tablespoons vinegar
1½ cups pineapple juice

Mix brown sugar, soy sauce, Soup Base, and cornstarch in a saucepan. Add remaining ingredients. Cook, stirring constantly, until thick.

Tartar Sauce

¾ cup mayonnaise
3 tablespoons pickle relish
1 teaspoon minced onion
1 tablespoon lemon juice or vinegar
¼ teaspoon dry mustard
¼ teaspoon celery salt

Combine ingredients and mix well. Refrigerate. Serve with fish, salmon, or croquettes. Makes 1 cup.

Basic Barbecue Sauce

1 can (8 ounces) tomato sauce
⅓ cup vinegar
⅓ cup brown sugar
1 tablespoon prepared mustard

Combine ingredients and mix well.

Zingy Barbecue Sauce: Add ½ cup chili sauce and ⅛ teaspoon bottled hot pepper sauce.

Peppy Barbecue Sauce: Add 2 tablespoons Worcestershire sauce, ½ teaspoon garlic powder, and ½ teaspoon pepper.

Onion Barbecue Sauce: Add ½ cup chopped onion, ½ cup soy sauce, ¼ cup Worcestershire sauce, and ¼ cup steak sauce. Bring mixture to a boil and cool.

Hickory Barbecue Sauce: Add 1 teaspoon liquid smoke, 2 tablespoons soy sauce, 2 tablespoons Worcestershire sauce, and 2 tablespoons steak sauce.

Presto Marinade Sauce: Add ½ cup olive oil, 1 tablespoon pepper, ⅔ cup wine vinegar, ½ teaspoon meat tenderizer, and 2 teaspoons salt. Marinate meat 3 to 4 hours.

Sweets and Confections

Making Your Own Candies

There is nothing like a good, old-fashioned candy-making session and homemade sweets. The real pleasure of homemade candy is in the making.

Here are a few money-saving, old-fashioned recipes. Some of the recipes came from grandmother's cookbook. Have fun experimenting, and be sure to include the children.

To test candy without a thermometer, remove candy from heat and drop ½ teaspoon in a cup of cold water. Remember that both humidity and altitude affect candy. If you live at an altitude of 3,000 feet or higher, check with your county extension agent for temperature adjustment recommendations.

Temperature	Cold Water Test	Stage
234–240° F.	Firm enough to hold together	Soft ball
250–268° F.	Forms a firm ball	Hard ball
270–290° F.	Separates into hard threads	Soft crack
300–310° F.	Separates into brittle threads	Hard crack

Candied Pineapple

2 cans pineapple chunks or slices
2 cups sugar
¼ cup corn syrup

Drain pineapple, reserving 1 cup juice. In a 2-quart saucepan, combine reserved juice, sugar, and corn syrup. Bring to boil and cook for 5 minutes. Add pineapple and cook until pineapple is translucent, approximately 45 minutes.

Remove from heat and let stand overnight at room temperature. Bring back to a boil and boil 2 minutes. Remove from heat and drain pineapple on a fine screen or rack. Let pineapple dry in a warm place for 3 hours. When it is almost dry, roll in sugar. Continue to dry. Store in a tightly covered container.

Variation: Use canned cherries instead of pineapple.

Candied Citrus Peel

4 oranges or 2 grapefruits or 6 lemons
2 cups sugar
Water
¼ cup corn syrup

Score citrus fruit and peel in quarters. Cover peelings with water and bring to a boil. Simmer 30 minutes. Drain and scrape off membrane. Cut peelings into strips or chunks.

Combine sugar, corn syrup, and 1 cup water and bring to a boil, stirring until sugar is dissolved. Add peelings and simmer 45 minutes or until peelings are translucent. Stir frequently. Drain in a strainer or on a fine screen 2 to 3 hours. Roll in sugar and let stand until dry (approximately 3 hours). Store in tightly covered container.

Horehound Drops

2 cups horehound leaves
2 cups boiling water
3 cups brown sugar
¼ cup butter

Steep horehound leaves in boiling water for 1 hour; strain. Add brown sugar and bring to a boil. Add butter and continue cooking until mixture reaches the hard-ball stage. Pour into a well-greased pan and mark into sticks or small squares with a knife as soon as candy is cool enough to retain its shape.

Soy Nut Toffee

¼ cup corn syrup
2½ cups sugar
½ cup water
1 pound butter or half butter and half
    margarine
2 cups Soy Nuts (see index)
4 squares milk chocolate, melted
Soy Nuts for garnish

Cook corn syrup, sugar, water, and butter to 275° F., stirring constantly. Add nuts and remove from heat. Pour into an ungreased shallow pan. Cool. Melt chocolate and spread on toffee. Sprinkle with finely chopped soy nuts.

Soy Nut Brittle

1 cup water
2 cups sugar
1 cup light corn syrup
2 cups Soy Nuts (see index)
½ teaspoon salt
1 tablespoon butter
1 teaspoon baking soda

Mix water, sugar, and corn syrup in a heavy saucepan and heat, stirring until dissolved. Bring to a boil and cook over medium heat to 234° F. (soft ball). Add nuts and salt. Cook to hard-crack stage (305° F.). Remove from heat and stir in butter and soda. Pour at once into well-buttered pan. Cool, then break into pieces.

Soy Nut Clusters

¾ cup white or dark chocolate
⅔ cup Soy Nuts (see index)

Melt chocolate over low heat and stir in nuts. Mix well. Spoon into clusters on waxed paper. Cool. One 12-ounce package semisweet chocolate pieces may be substituted for chocolate.

Salt Water Taffy

2 cups sugar
1½ cups water
1 cup corn syrup
1½ teaspoons salt
2 teaspoons glycerin
1 teasoon vanilla
2 tablespoons butter

Combine all ingredients except butter in a 2-quart saucepan. Stir over low heat until sugar dissolves. Cook without stirring to hard-ball stage (265° F.). Remove from heat and add butter. Pour onto a buttered slab or cookie sheet. When cool enough to handle, pull taffy until satiny, light in color, and stiff. If taffy becomes sticky, butter hands. Pull into long strips ½-inch wide and cut with scissors. Wrap in plastic wrap or waxed paper.

Caramels

2 cups sugar
1½ cups cream
1½ cups corn syrup
½ cup butter
1 teaspoon vanilla

Combine all ingredients and cook to soft-ball stage, stirring occasionally. Pour mixture onto a well-buttered cookie sheet or pan. Cut into squares and wrap in plastic wrap.

Caramel Corn

2 cups brown sugar
½ cup corn syrup
1 cup butter
½ teaspoon baking soda
¼ teaspoon salt
Pinch of cream of tartar
4 to 5 quarts popped corn
1 to 2 cups peanuts or Soy Nuts
    (see index)

Combine brown sugar, corn syrup, and butter. Heat to boiling over medium high heat and boil for 5 minutes.

Candied Citrus Peel (p. 117); Colored Marshmallows (p. 120); Soy Nut Clusters made with white and dark chocolate (p. 118)

Remove from heat; add baking soda, salt, and cream of tartar. Pour over popped corn and nuts and stir to coat evenly. Put in a roaster and bake in oven for 1 hour at 200° F. Stir every 15 minutes.

Marshmallow Squares

2 cups sugar

¾ cup water

2 envelopes (2 tablespoons) unflavored gelatin dissolved in 8 teaspoons water

1 teaspoon vanilla

2 egg whites

Dash of salt

Cook sugar and water to soft-ball stage. Pour softened gelatin into sugar and water mixture and add vanilla. Whip for 20 minutes. Beat egg whites until stiff and gradually fold into sugar-water mixture. Pour into buttered shallow pan to cool. To remove from pan, dip pan

quickly into hot water and turn upside down on waxed paper; cut candy into squares. Roll in powdered sugar, coconut, or finely chopped nuts, chopped Soy Nuts, or Oat Topping (see index).

Toasted Snow Squares

1 envelope (1 tablespoon) unflavored gelatin

2 tablespoons cold water

1 cup boiling water

⅔ cup granulated sugar

3 egg whites

¼ teaspoon salt

1 teaspoon vanilla

Toasted coconut or Oat Topping (see index)

Soak gelatin in cold water for 5 minutes. Add boiling water and stir until dissolved. Add sugar and let cool slightly (about 20 minutes). Beat egg whites; add salt and vanilla. Add to gelatin mixture. Beat with beater until mixture resembles thick cream. Pour into pan or ice cube trays and chill. Cut and roll in toasted coconut or Oat Topping.

White Marshmallows

½ cup cold water
2 envelopes (2 tablespoons) unflavored
    gelatin
½ cup sugar
1 cup light corn syrup
1½ teaspoons vanilla
½ cup cornstarch
½ cup powdered sugar

In a saucepan dissolve gelatin in cold water. Add sugar and heat until dissolved. Let cool one minute, then add corn syrup and vanilla. With electric mixer, beat at high speed until mixture thickens to a smooth marshmallow. Mix together cornstarch and powdered sugar. Butter a small cake pan and sprinkle with part of sugar-cornstarch mixture. Pour in marshmallow mixture and let set in refrigerator overnight. Remove from pan and cut into squares; powder with remaining sugar-cornstarch mixture.

Honey Marshmallows

2 envelopes (2 tablespoons) unflavored
    gelatin
1 cup raw brown sugar
Pinch of salt
⅓ cup water
¾ cup honey
1 teaspoon vanilla
½ cup powdered sugar
½ cup cornstarch

In medium saucepan, combine gelatin, raw brown sugar, salt, and water; heat until dissolved. Remove from heat and let cool. Add honey and vanilla and beat at high speed until thick. Combine powdered sugar and cornstarch. Butter a small cake pan and powder with part of sugar-cornstarch mixture. Pour candy into cake pan and let stand overnight in the refrigerator. Remove from pan, cut into squares, and powder with remaining sugar-cornstarch mixture.

Colored Marshmallows

1 package (3 ounces) fruit-flavored
    gelatin
½ cup sugar
⅓ cup water

3 tablespoons light corn syrup
1 teaspoon vanilla
½ cup cornstarch
½ cup powdered sugar

In a saucepan, combine gelatin, sugar, and water and heat until dissolved. Let cool in the refrigerator for 5 minutes. Remove, then add corn syrup and vanilla. Beat at high speed until thick. Combine cornstarch and powdered sugar. Butter a small cake pan and powder with part of sugar-cornstarch mixture. Pour candy into cake pan and let set overnight in refrigerator. Remove from pan, cut into squares, and powder with remaining sugar-cornstarch mixture.

Chocolate Sauce

½ cup water
½ cup sugar
½ cup corn syrup or honey
¾ cup unsweetened cocoa
1 teaspoon vanilla
3 tablespoons butter

Bring water, sugar, and corn syrup or honey to a boil. Cook 2 minutes. Add cocoa, vanilla, and butter. Beat until smooth.

Butterscotch Sauce

1 cup brown sugar
3 tablespoons butter
½ cup corn syrup
2 tablespoons water
⅓ cup cream
1 teaspoon vanilla

Combine brown sugar and butter in a saucepan. Add corn syrup, water, and cream and cook to 240° F. Remove from heat and stir in vanilla.

Strawberry or Raspberry Sauce

2 packages (10 ounces each) frozen
    strawberries or raspberries
¼ cup cornstarch
½ cup sugar
¼ teaspoon salt
⅛ teaspoon allspice
¼ teaspoon mace
⅛ teaspoon nutmeg
2 tablespoons butter

Thaw fruit enough to drain syrup. Add enough water to syrup to make 1½ cups. Mix cornstarch, sugar, salt, and spices. Add fruit syrup and cook over medium heat, stirring constantly, until sauce is thick. Add fruit and simmer 3 minutes longer. Remove from heat and add butter. Serve over vanilla or rice pudding, ice cream, cheesecake, angel food cake, pound cake, chiffon cake, pancakes, or crepes.

Recipes Using Kool-Aid

Kool-Aid Jelly

1 package unsweetened Kool-Aid (any flavor)
1 package pectin
3 cups water
3 cups sugar

Combine Kool-Aid, pectin, and water and bring to a boil. Add sugar. Follow directions on pectin package. Put in jelly glasses and seal.

Imitation Strawberry Jam

1 package unsweetened strawberry Kool-Aid
1 package pectin
3 cups tomatoes, puréed
3 cups sugar

Combine Kool-Aid, pectin, and tomatoes and bring to a boil. Add sugar. Follow directions on pectin package. Put into canning jars and seal.

Lemon Kool-Aid Pie

1½ cups sugar
⅓ cup plus 1 tablespoon cornstarch
1½ cups water
1 teaspoon unsweetened lemon Kool-Aid
½ cup water
3 tablespoons butter or margarine
Rice Pie Crust (see index)

Mix sugar and cornstarch in a saucepan. Gradually stir in 1½ cups water. Cook over medium heat, stirring constantly until mixture thickens. Add Kool-Aid dissolved in ½ cup water. Stir in butter. Pour into pie crust and refrigerate. Serves 6.

Kool-Aid Sherbet

1¾ cups sugar
2 packages unsweetened Kool-Aid (any flavor)
6 cups warm milk or soy milk

Dissolve sugar and Kool-Aid in milk. Cool, pour into freezer tray, and freeze until mushy. Remove to a bowl and beat until smooth. Return sherbet to tray and freeze until firm. Makes 1½ quarts.

Soaps and Cosmetics

Soap Making

Soap making takes no special talent. It is easy, the benefits are rewarding, and it is a thrifty way to make something from an almost wasted by-product: leftover kitchen grease. It takes few ingredients and a few hours of work to make a month's supply or more of soap.

Most of the ingredients in soap are readily available. The basic ingredients are animal fat, lye, water, and borax. Other ingredients are added to improve the cleaning power, soften the skin, or create a pleasant odor or color.

When fat and lye come into contact with each other, they form a chemical reaction (saponification) that converts the mixture into soap and glycerin. In most commercial soaps the glycerin is removed and sold separately for a high price. Homemade soap retains the glycerin that comes from the animal fat. Most commercial toilet soaps are 80 percent fat and 20 percent coconut oil.

Fat

Many types of fat can be used in making soap. The most common are beef fat and lard. Fats will differ in the hardness of the soap produced.

Mutton fat (sheep) or goat fat makes a hard, dry soap. It is best when mixed with a soft fat.

Beef fat (tallow, suet) is next in hardness.

Lard (pig fat) makes nice soap. Mix with hard fat.

Poultry fat makes soap too soft. Mix with hard fat.

Fat can be obtained free or at a small charge from your butcher, meat packer, or the meat department at your local market. When our grandparents had an animal butchered, they saved everything: the meat for eating, the hide for tanning, the heat and intestines for sausage, and the fat for cooking and making soap and candles.

The rendering process involves melting down and clarifying solid fats. Not all the fat can be rendered. The small pieces of meat tissue left in the fat are called cracklings (crumbly, they resemble coarse graham cracker crumbs). These can be seasoned with salt and pepper and eaten like bacon, added to cornbread in place of the shortening, or used to flavor beans. To render the fat:

1. Cut the fat particles into small pieces or have the fat ground, and place in a pan large enough to prevent spilling. Porcelain or glass is ideal.

2. Put the pan in a 275° F. oven and slowly melt the fat. This will take several hours. Every hour or so remove the melted fat and strain into a container.

3. To remove as much of the scrap and granular matter as possible, strain the melted fat through several layers of cheesecloth or a milk filter.

To clarify the animal grease or vegetable shortening drippings, mix the fat with an equal amount of water. Bring to a boil. Remove the fat from the heat and add 1 quart cold water for every gallon of fat. This will cause the mixture to separate into three layers: solidified fat on top, gray impurities next, and water last. Take off the layer of fat and scrape off any meat proteins that might have gelled on the bottom. Refrigerate until ready to use.

If fat is rancid, use 1 part vinegar to 5 parts water in the clarifying process. Rancid fat will not affect the soapmaking process, nor will it have a rancid smell.

Refrigerate or freeze the clarified fat until needed. If fat is to be stored a long time without freezing, all the moisture should be removed. To remove moisture, place fat in a pan and heat to 275° F. Continue stirring and cooking until all the moisture is removed. Test by placing a lid on the kettle. If no moisture accumulates on the lid, the fat is ready to be put in airtight containers. Cool and seal, and store in a cool place. Fat will keep for several years without going rancid. If you add 1 pound commercial lard, it will keep 5 to 7 years.

Lye

To make soap, either commercial lye or homemade lye may be used. Commercial lye is available at most supermarkets (look for it in the section where you find drain cleaners) or at hardware stores. Be sure the label indicates it is pure lye. Most commercial lyes are caustic soda, a poisonous substance that burns, so store the container safely away from children and animals. Cover your working area with newspaper and wear plastic gloves. Do not make soap in an aluminum or stainless steel container.

Lye is made by pouring rainwater over ashes and letting it drip into a container. You can make your own lye from any hardwood ash, such as oak, walnut, hickory, sugar maple, or fruitwood.

You will need a large wooden barrel, tub, or vat. The larger the container, the more concentrated the lye will be. Drill a hole near the bottom of the container and place the container on bricks or other support so that the lye can run out the hole. Place a plastic or enamel pail below the hole to catch the lye.

Put a layer of straw in the bottom of the barrel or vat for drainage. Cover the straw with ashes, filling to a few inches from the top of the tub. Add a few quarts of boiling rainwater and let the water seep through the ashes. It should take a few days for the water to trickle through and empty into the container. Add more ashes and boiling water.

To test the concentration of the lye, put an egg or potato in the solution. If it floats, the lye is strong enough for soap making; if it sinks, put the lye solution through the ashes again or boil it down until it is strong enough to float an egg.

Lye can be made in a plastic container if a wooden one is not available. Fill the container with ashes and add boiling rainwater, stirring to wet the ashes. When the ashes settle, add more water and stir again. Let the solution stand in the ashes a day or two until the liquid is clear. Carefully pour or dip the lye from the pail.

When the liquid lye is strong enough, it can be used to make soap or it can be crystallized into potash. To make potash, boil the lye water in an enamel or heavy iron kettle. A dark residue called black salts will form. Maintain heat until the impurities are burned away and a grayish white potash remains.

Water and Borax

Soft water or rainwater give a softer, better-lathering soap. If you use hard water, treat it with a commercial softener or borax. This will help soften the water and aid in the cleaning action of the soap.

Coloring Soap

One of the easiest and best ways to color soap is to melt a crayon with the fat. Food coloring, chlorophyll, or a candle dye may also be used; add just before you pour the soap into the molds. Herbs that will color your soap include turmeric (yellow), alkanet root (red), hollyhock flowers (blue), and

Colorful soaps, granulated soap, and cleansing cream, all made at home

parsley (green). Colors may be extracted from fresh vegetables by pouring boiling water over them and letting them steep until the water reaches the desired color. Use the dye water in place of soft water in dissolving the lye.

The color you use will be changed somewhat by the lye. The color will continue to change until the chemical reaction has stopped and the soap is hard. A marbleized effect is achieved by swirling the coloring into the soap after the soap is poured into the mold.

Scenting Soap

The best way to scent soap is to add essences of fragrances, found in hobby shops, health food stores, or drugstores. Commonly used fragrances include oil of rose, oil of lavender, oil of carnation, oil of peppermint, lemon oil, oil of cloves, and cinnamon oil. Do not used alcohol-based perfume, as it will cause the soap to separate. Add small amounts of the fragrance just before pouring the soap into molds (use 2 to 4 teaspoons for a large batch of soap), and mix well.

You can also experiment with different flavorings that have strong odors, as well as candle scents.

All the scents will be changed somewhat once the soap has hardened and aged for two weeks.

You can scent your lard or fat by melting it and adding spices, citrus peel, or fresh flower petals; let it stand 24 hours. Remelt the fat and remove the petals, replacing them with fresh ones. Repeat this process for 3 or 4 days or until fat has the fragrance you desire.

Equipment for Making Soap

To dissolve the lye and mix the ingredients, use an enamel, iron, glass, earthenware, or hard plastic container that can withstand heat. Do not use aluminum or stainless steel.

Always stir the soap with a wooden paddle or spoon, and use a dairy thermometer for accurate temperatures.

Any convenient-size container made of plastic, glass, enamel, earthenware, or ceramic can be used as a mold. Some examples are custard cups, gelatin molds, sugar molds, candle molds, air-freshener containers, egg cartons, and plastic or paper cartons or trays. Plastic molds work well because they are flexible and it is easy to remove the soap from them. Molds that are nonflexible or have intricate detail should be greased with petroleum jelly (such as Vaseline), vegetable nonstick spray, or mineral oil. Boxes should be lined with plastic wrap or a damp cloth; be careful to remove all wrinkles.

Basic Bar Soap

To make 9 pounds:	*To make one bar:*
6 pounds clean fat (about 13 cups)	1 cup clean fat
¼ cup borax (optional)	1 teaspoon borax
1 can lye (13 ounces)	5 teaspoons lye
5 cups soft water	½ cup soft water

Warm fat until melted, and cool to 95° to 100° F. Dissolve lye in cold water, add borax, and cool to 95° to 100° F. Pour lye solution into the fat in a thin, steady stream with slow, even stirring. Continue stirring until soap mixture has a creamy, thick, honeylike texture. This should take 20 to 30 minutes. Then pour into molds.

If the soap mixture does not become thick within 30 minutes, set the pan in cool water and continue stirring. If the mixture is lumpy, it is probably too cool. Set the pan in warm water and stir until the lumps dissolve.

If the soap has streaks of grease in it or is crumbly, it can be reclaimed by adding a small amount of water and dissolving it over low heat. Stir occasionally. When the soap appears thick, pour it into molds.

Cooked Soap Using Solid Fat

1 can (13 ounces) lye or 4 cups ash lye
5 cups soft water
6 pounds solid fat

Dissolve lye in water and bring to a boil, stirring to prevent boiling over. Avoid breathing the fumes. Add fat and continue cooking until lye has consumed the grease.

To test the liquid, let the soap mixture drip off the spoon. If it is ready, it will string and bead like jelly. Pour into molds.

Granulated Soap

3 quarts cold soft water
1 can (13 ounces) lye
2 quarts warmed fat
2 tablespoons borax
2 tablespoons Sal Soda
1 cup ammonia or liquid
    laundry bleach (Clorox)

Dissolve lye in water and let stand until warm. Combine remaining ingredients and add to lye; stir for 5 minutes. Let set, stirring every 15 to 20 minutes, until mixture curdles and granulates. This will take several hours or possibly all day.

Toilet Soap Made with Lime

1 pound washing soda
½ pound unslaked lime
3 quarts boiling water
1 pound lard or tallow
1 tablespoon salt
Scent (optional)

Place washing soda and lime in a large pan; add boiling water, and stir until dissolved. Add grease and salt, and boil for 4 hours. Pour into shallow pans to cool. If soap should be inclined to curdle or separate, indicating the lime is too strong, add a little more water and boil again. Perfume and pour into molds.

Oatmeal Soap

11 cups cleaned fat
1 can (13 ounces) lye
5 cups soft water
⅓ cup sugar
½ cup powdered borax
½ cup ammonia
2 ounces lanolin (optional)
3 ounces glycerin
¼ cup ground oatmeal
Scent (optional)

Warm fat until melted or consistency of warm honey. Dissolve lye in cold soft water with sugar. Add borax and continue stirring until mixture is cool. Pour lye solution into fat in a steady, slow stream. Add remaining ingredients, and stir until thick and creamy. Pour into molds. (This makes a nonalkaline soap for soothing and softening the skin.)

Variation: Use cornmeal or ground almonds in place of oatmeal.

Castile Soap

To make approximately 9 pounds:	*To make 1 bar:*
10 cups tallow	⅔ cup tallow
3 cups olive oil	⅓ cup olive oil
1 can (13 ounces) lye	5 teaspoons lye
5 cups soft water	½ cup soft water

Follow directions for making Basic Bar Soap, mixing the olive oil with the tallow. (This makes a hard but simple soap.)

Variation: Add 4 tablespoons cocoa butter (1 teaspoon for 1-bar recipe).

Vegetable Soap

3 pounds vegetable shortening
16 ounces (2 cups) coconut oil
32 ounces (4 cups) olive oil
1 can (13 ounces) lye
5 cups soft water

Follow directions for making Basic Bar Soap, mixing the oils and shortening together. For a dry-hair shampoo, add 3 tablespoons glycerin and 3 tablespoons castor oil. (This makes an excellent soap or shampoo—soft and gentle.)

Coconut Soap

To make approximately 9 pounds:	*To make 1 bar:*
4 cups tallow	**⅓ cup tallow**
32 ounces (4 cups) olive oil	**⅓ cup olive oil**
32 ounces (4 cups) coconut oil	**⅓ cup coconut oil**
1 can (13 ounces) lye	**5 teaspoons lye**
5 cups soft water	**½ cup soft water**

Follow directions for making Basic Bar Soap, mixing the oils and tallow. (This makes a creamy soap, nourishing to the skin. The coconut oil enhances the foam.)

Cold-Cream Soap

To make approximately 9 pounds:	*To make 1 bar:*
6 pounds fat	**1 cup fat**
¼ cup cold cream	**1 teaspoon cold cream**
1 can (13 ounces) lye	**5 teaspoons lye**
5 cups soft water	**½ cup soft water**

Follow directions for making Basic Bar Soap, adding cold cream just before pouring soap mixture into molds. Mix well.

Milk and Honey Soap: For 9-pound recipe, add 2 tablespoons instant nonfat milk and 2 tablespoons honey. Mix well and pour into molds.

Rose-Water Soap: For 9-pound recipe, add ½ cup rose water and decrease soft water to 4 cups. For 1-bar recipe, add 1 teaspoon rose water.

Cornmeal Soap: For 9-pound recipe, add 3 tablespoons cornmeal. For 1-bar recipe, add 1 teaspoon cornmeal.

Almond Soap: For 9-pound recipe, add 3 tablespoons ground almonds. For 1-bar recipe, add 1 teaspoon ground almonds.

Cocoa-Butter Soap: For 9-pound recipe, add 4 tablespoons melted cocoa butter to the fat. For 1-bar recipe, add 1 teaspoon melted cocoa butter.

Castor Oil Soap

2 pounds tallow
2¾ cups coconut oil
2¾ cups olive oil
1 cup castor oil
1 can (13 ounces) lye
4 cups soft water

Follow Basic Bar Soap recipe, mixing the oils and tallow together.

Shampoo Bar

3 cups coconut oil
3 cups castor oil
5 cups olive oil
1 can (13 ounces) lye
4 cups soft water

Follow Basic Bar Soap recipe, adding lye water to the oils.

Herbed Soaps

Soap can be made with your favorite herb or spice. Herbs can be added in the powdered form or made into a strong herb tea and added in place of the soft water in any recipe.

Herbs recommended for different conditions are:

Dry skin: red clover, elder flower, citrus peel, slippery elm.

Oily skin: witch hazel, peppermint, cucumber, rose.

Dandruff or dry hair: sage, citrus peel, comfrey, clover, elder flowers.

Oily hair: orrisroot, peppermint, witch hazel.

Astringent: strawberry, camomile.

Light hair (blondes): camomile, mullein flowers, orange flowers, marigold, nettle, turmeric.

Dark hair (brunettes): rosemary, raspberry, sage, cloves, sassafras, mint, marjoram.

Red hair: cloves, witch hazel, hibiscus flowers.

Soapy lather: yucca, soapwort, leaves of papaya.

Shampoos and Hair Rinses

Lemon or Citrus Shampoo

Grind lemon or any citrus peel in a food grinder, blender, or processor. Place ground rind in a saucepan and cover with water. Simmer 15 to 20 minutes; *do not* boil. Strain liquid. The liquid, which contains the oils from the rind, can be used in place of water when making soap, or it can be used in shampoo, dish soap, or bubble bath. It can also be added to your bath water.

Soybean Whey Shampoo

The whey left over from making tofu makes an excellent shampoo. The oils in it contain lecithin, which has the ability to cut through oils and grease. The shampoo will not lather like commercial shampoos, but it will clean your hair and leave it shiny and soft.

Lemon Rinse

Lemon juice makes an excellent rinse and adds golden highlights to the hair. Juice one lemon and mix juice with 2 cups water. Rinse hair with lemon water, then rinse with warm water.

To lighten hair, squeeze 2 or 3 lemons and apply juice to hair. Leave on 15 to 30 minutes (sit in the sun for a lighter shade). Rinse thoroughly with warm water.

Herbal Rinse

Make a rinse by adding ½ cup herbs to 1 quart boiling water. Let set for a few hours, then strain. For golden highlights, use camomile. To darken hair, use sage. Or use any of the herbs listed for Herbed Soaps.

Gelatin Set

Dissolve 1 teaspoon plain gelatin in 1 cup boiling water. Cool and apply to hair. This will add protein to your hair.

Cleansers and Cold Creams

Cold Cream

2 tablespoons beeswax
¼ cup petroleum jelly
2 tablespoons witch hazel
6 tablespoons rose water

Melt beeswax and petroleum jelly. Add witch hazel and rose water. Beat until cool and creamy.

Cleansing Cream

1 tablespoon white wax
¼ cup coconut or almond oil
1 tablespoon rose water
2 tablespoons aloe gel
Fragrant oil (optional)

Melt wax. Warm the oil, rose water, and aloe gel; add to melted wax. Beat until cool and creamy. Add a few drops of fragrant oil, if desired.

Cocoa Butter Cleansing Cream

½ cup safflower oil
1 tablespoon cocoa butter
1 tablespoon beeswax
1 tablespoon rose water
⅛ teaspoon borax

Melt wax and add remaining ingredients. Beat until cool and creamy.

Fruit Cleansing Cream

2 tablespoons fruit juice, strained
    (strawberry, cucumber, or citrus)
⅛ teaspoon borax
6 tablespoons coconut oil or vegetable
    shortening

Dissolve borax in hot fruit juice and add to oil or melted shortening. Beat until cool and creamy.

Create your own cold cream or cleansing cream with 8 parts of oil or petroleum jelly to 1 part beeswax or white wax. Petroleum jelly is good for oily skin.

Rose Water

Boil rose petals in water a few minutes. Let steep 20 minutes. Use water to wash face.

Fresheners, Masks, and Astringents

Lemon Freshener

Combine ½ cup lemon juice, 2 cups soft water, and 1 teaspoon rose water. Use to freshen skin.

Citrus Freshener

Chop ¼ cup citrus peelings and add to ½ cup alcohol. Let steep for 3 days.

Lime Freshener

Combine ¼ cup witch hazel, ¼ cup alcohol, ⅛ teaspoon alum, ⅛ teaspoon borax, and 2 tablespoons lime juice, strained (or other citrus juice). Shake well.

Apple Freshener

Combine ¼ cup pure apple cider vinegar and 2 tablespoons witch hazel. Shake well.

Strawberry or Cucumber Freshener

Combine 6 tablespoons fresh strawberry or cucumber juice, ¼ cup witch hazel, and ¼ cup rose water. Shake well.

Elder Flower Astringent

Boil elder flowers in water and let steep 20 minutes. Strain. Add 1 teaspoon alcohol and 1 teaspoon glycerin; mix well. Apply to face, leave for a few minutes, then rinse.

Cucumber Astringent

Peel and quarter 1 cucumber and place in blender. Add a small amount of water, and blend. Apply to face; leave for a few minutes, then rinse.

Strawberry Astringent

Press ripe strawberries through a sieve to obtain the juice. Apply juice to face, leave for a few minutes, then rinse.

Cucumber Mask

Blend ½ cucumber in a blender. Add 1 egg white and 1 tablespoon dry milk powder; blend until smooth. Apply to face, leave for 30 minutes, and rinse.

Mint Mask

Add 2 tablespoons peppermint or spearmint to 1 cup boiling water and steep for 20 minutes. Strain. Dissolve 1 envelope (1 tablespoon) unflavored gelatin in hot mint mixture and cool. Apply to face and leave on for 15 to 20 minutes. Rinse.

Oatmeal Mask

Blend ½ cup oatmeal in blender. Add enough milk to make a thick paste. Blend until smooth. Apply to face and leave on for 20 to 30 minutes.

Lipsticks and Eye Shadows

Create your own lipstick or salve by using 1 part beeswax or white wax to 6 parts oil. Use more oil for a softer salve. To add color, soak a piece of alkanet root (available at herb shops) in oil until desired color is obtained, about 2 weeks.

Lip Salve

Combine 1 teaspoon jojoba oil and 2 tablespoons almond oil or olive oil. (If color is desired, add a piece of alkanet root and let stand 2 weeks. Strain.) Melt wax. Warm oils and add to wax. Beat until cold. Place in small jars.

Chapped Lipstick No. 1

Melt 1 tablespoon beeswax and 2 tablespoons petroleum jelly over low heat. Add 2 tablespoons warmed olive oil and beat until cool and creamy.

Chapped Lipstick No. 2

Melt 1 tablespoon beeswax and 1 teaspoon cocoa butter. Warm 2 tablespoons olive oil and 1 teaspoon almond oil. Combine oils with wax mixture, and beat until cool and creamy.

Chapped Lipstick No. 3

Melt 1 teaspoon beeswax. Warm 1 tablespoon olive oil and 1 tablespoon coconut oil. Add warmed oils to melted wax, and beat until cool and creamy.

Lip Gloss

Melt 1 teaspoon beeswax. Warm 1 teaspoon olive oil and 6 tablespoons jojoba oil. Add warmed oils to melted wax, and beat until cool and creamy.

Eye Shadow

Heat 4 teaspoons coconut oil or other pure oil and add herbs or flower petals (below). Let stand until desired color is obtained; strain. Melt 1 teaspoon beeswax and add to warmed oil. Beat until cool and creamy. Store in small jars.

Lavender: malva flowers mixed with alkanet
Green: parsley or hyssop
Blue: corn flowers or hollyhock flowers
Brown: juniper berries or hibiscus flowers

Cosmetics, astringents and fresheners, creams and lotions, and potpourri

Deodorants and Toothpastes

Lemon Deodorant

One of the best of nature's deodorants is lemon juice. Fill a spray bottle with lemon juice and spray on underarms. You can also apply lemon juice with a cotton ball.

Powder Deodorant No. 1

1 tablespoon alum
½ cup talc
½ cup cornstarch or rice starch
2 teaspoons chlorophyll
1 tablespoon isopropyl alcohol
½ teaspoon peppermint extract

Place alum, talc, and cornstarch in blender. Mix chlorophyll, alcohol, and extract, and gradually add to blender. Blend well. Add a few drips of liquid chlorophyll, if desired.

Powder Deodorant No. 2

Combine ¼ cup powdered boric acid, ¼ cup alum, and ¼ cup cornstarch; mix well. Add a few drops of liquid chlorophyll, if desired.

Liquid Deodorant No. 1

Put 2 tablespoons powdered alum in a 13-ounce spray bottle. Fill with warm water and mix well. Add a few drops of liquid chlorophyll, if desired.

Liquid Deodorant No. 2

Put 2 tablespoons baking soda in a 13-ounce spray bottle. Fill with water and mix well. Add a few drops of liquid chlorophyl, if desired.

Toothpowder No. 1

Combine ¼ cup precipitated chalk, 1 teaspoon salt, 1 teaspoon baking soda, and 2 whole cloves, crushed. Mix well.

Toothpowder No. 2

Combine equal amounts of soda and salt.

Toothpaste

Combine ¼ cup baking soda and 1 tablespoon salt. Add enough glycerin to make a paste. Add a few drops of peppermint oil.

Creams, Powders, and Lotions

Lemon Hand Cream

Melt 1 teaspoon beeswax. Warm together 2 tablespoons coconut oil, 2 tablespoons lemon juice, 1 tablespoon Lemon Rind Water (see index), and a few drops oil of lemon. Beat until cool and creamy.

Enriched Dry-Skin Hand Cream

Melt ¼ cup cocoa butter and ¼ cup lanolin, blending well. Remove from heat and beat until mixture begins to thicken. Add 4 teaspoons warmed almond oil or coconut oil and beat until cool and creamy. Add ½ teaspoon almond extract and beat again. Place in jars.

Hand Cream

1 cup flaked stearic acid
12 ounces glycerin
½ ounce paraffin wax
½ ounce ammonia (not soapy ammonia)
¼ teaspoon powdered borax
2 cups distilled water

Place stearic acid, glycerin, and wax in an enamel or glass double boiler. When stearic acid is dissolved, add ammonia and beat with mixer until milky. Dissolve borax in warm distilled water (water must be warm to prevent wax from setting). Combine both mixtures and continue beating until white and creamy. Coloring and cologne may be added, if desired.

Facial Powder or Blush

Finely chop 3 medium carrots and ½ beet. Place in a muslin bag and squeeze to obtain the juice, or use a juicer. Add the juice to 6 tablespoons cornstarch and mix well. Spread in a flat dish or pan and dry in the sun or in a very warm oven, stirring occasionally until a dry powder is formed. Blend in blender, if necessary, to get a fine powder with no lumps. This produces a pretty tinted powder. If you prefer a blush, increase amount of beets and decrease amount of carrots.

Eggshell Powder

Clean and wash eggshells thoroughly to remove all the albumen. Dry shells in a low oven. Crush the shells with a rolling pin or in the blender. Sift and crush again. When you have a fine powder, add a few drops of perfume and allow to dry. When the powder is dry, blend and sift again.

Baby Powder

Mix 2 cups talc and 2 tablespoons zinc oxide powder in a blender. Gradually add 1 teaspoon cod liver oil and 1 teaspoon liquid chlorophyll. Blend into a smooth powder.

Toilet Powder

Combine 1 cup finely powdered wheat starch, 8 drops oil of rose, 30 drops lemon oil, and 15 drops oil of bergamot. Rub together thoroughly. The French throw this powder into alcohol, shake it, let it settle, then pour off the alcohol and dry the powder. Add perfume last, if desired.

After-Shave Lotion

Combine ¼ cup witch hazel, ¼ cup alcohol, 1 teaspoon peppermint extract, and a few drops of favorite scent. Mix thoroughly.

Coconut Butter Suntan Oil

Melt 5 tablespoons cocoa butter and ¼ cup coconut oil together in a double boiler. Add ½ cup warmed sesame oil and beat until cool. Refrigerate.

Perfumes and Fragrant Oils

Creating your own perfumes and fragrances can be fun. Almost all highly perfumed flowers and leaves have their own essential oils. Fragrant oils and perfumes are made from herbs and an oil base, such as olive, safflower, corn, or almond.

Essential Oil

1. Gather fragrant leaves, flowers, or herbs.
2. Put in a jar and cover with olive, safflower, corn, or almond oil. Let stand for 24 hours in a warm place or in the sun.
3. Strain the liquid, pressing to release the oils from the flowers or herbs.
4. Repeat this process every day for several days or a few weeks until the oil is strong enough. Boil the oil and flowers or herbs together until the juice is consumed (flowers or herbs will become crisp). Strain while hot. Store in glass.

Perfume

Combine equal parts of fragrances and pure ethyl or rectified alcohol. If you want the fragrance to last, add a fixative, such as musk, civet, ambergris, or castoreum (available at drugstores), sandalwood, patchouli, orrisroot, benzoin (derived from plants). Shake every day for 2 weeks. Allow oil and alcohol to separate. Pour off the oil. Pour alcohol (perfume) into bottle and cap tightly.

Potpourri

Long before air fresheners, homemakers used potpourris to freshen their homes. These were made from fragrant leaves, petals, seeds, roots, bark, and spices with a fixative to preserve the essential oils. Whenever she wanted her home to smell good, the homemaker would lift the lid off a can of potpourri. The fragrance would last 2 to 3 weeks before the potpourri had to be revitalized. Then the homemaker would close the lid and shake the can well. Some potpourris lasted a lifetime.

Create your own potpourris by collecting ingredients all through the garden season. Pick flowers as soon as the dew is off the petals and before it gets hot. Red flowers have a stronger smell than white or pale colors. Dry flowers in the sun or a dryer. Store in jars until ready to use. Look for flowers and leaves that smell good. The following are suggested ingredients that may be collected.

Leaves: rose, geranium, bee balm, lemon, verbena, lavender, sweet myrtle.

Flowers: roses, lavender, orange blossoms, violets, jasmine, lilac, lily of the valley, jonquil, narcissus, dianthus.

Essential oils: rose, patchouli, jasmine, geranium, lilac, sandalwood, bergamot, lavender, lemon.

Spices: anise seed, bay leaves, allspice, cloves, cinnamon, nutmeg, cardamom seed, mace, sage, rosemary, thyme, ginger.

Fixatives: benzoin, orrisroot, calamus, storax, ambergris.

Dry Potpourri

2 cups rose petals, dried
1 cup dried geranium leaves, crushed
2 tablespoons orrisroot, crushed
1 1-inch vanilla bean, crushed
4 sticks cinnamon, broken
1 tablespoon allspice, crushed
1 teaspoon mace
Dried orange peel with cloves stuck in it
1 teaspoon sage leaves, crushed
Several drops of rose oil

In a small box or tin, alternate layers of rose petals with layers of noniodized salt; let set for one week.

Stir petals and add remaining ingredients. Shake container every few days for about six weeks.

Wet Potpourri

2 cups rose petals
½ cup lavender flowers
½ cup fragrant leaves
1 cup sandalwood
½ cup coarse, noniodized salt
½ cup orrisroot or 2 tablespoons powdered orrisroot

¼ cup brown sugar
1 1-inch vanilla bean, crushed
2 tablespoons allspice
2 tablespoons cloves
4 cinnamon barks, crushed
3 bay leaves, crushed
2 tablespoons alcohol-based perfume

Dry petals until leathery but not crisp. Layer with salt and let set 6 weeks. Add remaining ingredients and place a weight on top to bring out oils. Open the container, remove weight, and stir once a day for 1 month. Pack into containers. Add perfume if mixture begins to dry out. Keeps indefinitely.

Equivalents, Substitutes, and Miscellaneous Tips

Equivalent Measures

3 teaspoons	= 1 tablespoon
4 tablespoons	= ¼ cup
5⅓ tablespoons	= ⅓ cup
16 tablespoons	= 1 cup
2 cups	= 1 pint
2 pints	= 1 quart
4 quarts	= 1 gallon
16 ounces	= 1 pound
8 quarts	= 1 peck
4 pecks	= 1 bushel

Butter or margarine

1 ounce	= 2 tablespoons
¼ pound	= ½ cup
1 pound	= 2 cups

Cheese, grated

1 pound	= 5 cups

Rice, raw

1 pound	= 2⅓ cups

Flour

4 cups	= 1 pound

Sugar

1 pound granulated	= 2¼ cups
1 pound brown, packed	= 2¼ cups
1 pound powdered	= 3½ cups

Substitutes

Substitutes in Baking

1 tablespoon cornstarch = 4 teaspoons quick-cooking tapioca

1 tablespoon flour = ½ tablespoon cornstarch

1 tablespoon arrowroot starch = 3 tablespoons flour

1 tablespoon arrowroot starch = 1 tablespoon plus 1 teaspoon cornstarch

1 square unsweetened chocolate = 3 tablespoons cocoa plus 1 tablespoon butter

1 teaspoon baking powder = ¼ teaspoon baking soda plus ½ teaspoon cream of tartar

2 cups cake flour = 1¾ cups all-purpose flour

⅔ cup honey = 1 cup plus ⅓ cup liquid

1 cup sour milk = 1 tablespoon lemon juice or vinegar mixed with 1 cup milk

1 cup cream = ¾ cup milk plus ⅓ cup butter or margarine (do not use for whipping)

Substitutes for Wine

When a recipe calls for wine, the following may be substituted:

Red wine: water, beef bouillon, broth, consommé, tomato juice, cider vinegar

White wine: water, ginger ale, chicken bouillon, beef broth, consommé, white grape juice, white wine vinegar (diluted)

Beer or ale: ginger ale, chicken broth, white grape juice

Champagne: ginger ale

Creme de Menthe: spearmint extract (diluted with water)

Brandy: peach or apricot syrup

Rum: pineapple juice or almond extract (diluted with water or syrup)

Sherry: pineapple or orange juice

Substitute for Nuts

½ cup nuts = ½ cup crushed cornflakes and ⅛ teaspoon almond flavoring

Substitute for Powdered Sugar

Put in blender 1 cup granulated sugar and ½ teaspoon cornstarch. Blend until powdered.

Substitute for Whipped Cream

Beat egg white until stiff. Add one slice banana and 1 teaspoon vanilla per egg white. Beat until banana dissolves.

Substitute for Cake Flour

For every ¾ cup flour, add ¼ cup cornstarch. This makes a nice, fluffy cake.

Cream for Fruit

1 cup milk
2 egg whites
1 tablespoon sugar
⅛ teaspoon butter
1 teaspoon cornstarch
½ cup cold milk

Heat 1 cup milk to boiling point. Beat together egg whites, sugar, and butter, and add cornstarch and ½ cup cold milk. Stir until very light and smooth. Stir into boiling milk; remove from heat, and cool. Sauce should be the consistency of fresh cream. Serve it as you would serve fresh cream on fruit and other desserts.

Mock Mincemeat

1 cup raisins
1 cup cold water
½ cup molasses
½ cup brown sugar
½ cup cider vinegar
⅔ cup butter, melted
1 egg, beaten
½ cup cracker crumbs
1 tablespoon cinnamon
1 teaspoon each cloves, allspice, nutmeg, salt, and black pepper

Cook raisins in water for 5 minutes. Add remaining ingredients and mix well. Use in place of mincemeat.

Cooking Tips

1. Vegetables that grow underground should be cooked in a pan with the lid tightly in place.

2. Vegetables that grow above ground should be cooked without a lid.

3. To peel tomatoes, plunge them into hot water for 3 to 4 minutes, then into cold water. Drain and peel. You may also place them in a flat baking pan and set in a hot oven for 5 minutes. The skins will readily slip off.

4. Boil potatoes 5 minutes before baking them in the oven. They will bake in only half the usual time.

5. A pinch of sugar brings out the flavor in beets, carrots, tomatoes, and mashed potatoes.

6. Add a little milk to the water while boiling potatoes to prevent the potatoes from going dark and to improve the flavor.

7. If soup has been salted too much, add raw grated potatoes to neutralize the salt.

8. When making vegetable soup, add an old wrinkled apple to bring out the flavor.

9. To bring out a good flavor in spinach, add a clove of garlic.

10. Add ½ cup milk and 1 teaspoon sugar when you cook corn on the cob.

11. Add a few drops of almond extract to canned cherries for a fresh taste.

12. To sweeten sour fruit without sugar, add 1 teaspoon soda for every 2 pounds fruit while cooking.

13. Mix overripe bananas with a small amount of lemon juice. Freeze in plastic bags and use in cooking.

14. To get more juice out of citrus fruits, put the fruit in a warm oven or plunge in hot water until fruit is warm. Roll until soft. Cut and juice.

15. When lemons are in season, put whole lemons in sterilized canning jars and cover with cold water. Screw down the rubber screw-seal lids tightly. Lemons should stay fresh for several months.

16. Rub a little olive oil on the sides of the cooker before making jam to prevent sticking.

17. When canning peaches or making jam, add peach stones to your syrup and let boil for 5 minutes or so. Remove the stones and add the liquid to the peaches. This will add flavor and color.

18. To save sugar when canning fruit, stir the sugar into the fruit after the fruit is cooked. Sugar that is boiled with an acid will convert to glucose, which has less than half as much sweetening power as sugar.

19. Don't throw away bacon that has mold on it. Dip a clean cloth in vinegar and sponge off the mold.

20. To prevent sausage from breaking up when cooking, roll it in flour.

21. Add a little soda or vinegar to the water when boiling fowl to tenderize the meat.

22. Roast meats with the fat side up. This will keep the roast from drying out and will also enhance the flavor.

23. Add an egg white to cream that won't whip. Refrigerate until chilled and whip again.

24. Whipped cream made ahead of time will not separate if you add ¼ teaspoon gelatin dissolved in a little water for each cup of cream.

25. To keep foods from sticking together during freezing, spread food pieces on a cookie sheet and freeze. Remove to an airtight container and return to freezer.

26. Grate rinds of lemons and oranges and freeze. Use as needed.

27. Keep popcorn in the freezer to preserve freshness and decrease the numbers of hard kernels when popping.

28. Add a pinch of baking powder to egg whites before beating to give a high meringue.

29. When cooking hard-boiled eggs for deviled eggs, stir the water to keep the yolks centered.

30. Add a small amount of salt to the water while boiling eggs. This will make shells harden for easier peeling.

31. Sprinkle salt in the pan while frying to keep grease from splattering.

32. Rose hips are high in vitamin C. The hips can be gathered any time after the first frost. Dry and store in an airtight container.

33. To make crisp waffles, use cold water instead of milk.

34. Mix a pinch of soda with cream before serving the cream, to prevent curdling.

35. To keep olive oil from going rancid, add a teaspoon of sugar.

36. When making pumpkin pie, brush pie crust shell with egg white or melted butter before filling. This prevents pie crust from becoming soggy.

37. To make lemon meringue pie easier to cut, sprinkle meringue with granulated sugar.

38. Add a tablespoon of tapioca to fruit pie fillings that are juicy. The tapioca keeps the filling from bubbling over while cooking.

39. To sweeten rancid butter or soured cottage cheese, work in ½ cup sweet milk to every pound of butter or cottage cheese and wash it out. This will take the rancid taste out and make the butter or cottage cheese taste fresh again.

Miscellaneous Tips

Storing Potatoes in Winter

Potatoes keep best when stored thirty bushels at a time. Dig a pit and place potatoes in layers, with straw between each layer to cushion and insulate. Place a flue at one end of the pit to permit gasses to escape. Cover with dirt at least 2 feet deep. Potatoes will keep all winter in this manner.

Treating Frozen Potato or Beet Roots

Potato or beet roots that have been frozen may be restored to their normal condition by immersing them in cold water until the frost is removed.

Storing Cucumbers in Winter

Layer cucumbers with rock salt in a barrel or other container. Cover with a cloth (do not add water). Rinse cloth every time you add more cucumbers, as the scum will rise and settle on it. Cucumbers will keep up to a year.

Purifying Water

Sprinkle alum into a barrel of water, stirring as you add it. This will, after a few hours, purify the water and give it nearly all the freshness and clearness of spring water. Add 1 teaspoon for every 4 gallons of water.

Cementing China and Glass

Add 1 cup vinegar to 1 cup milk in order to curdle the milk. Separate the curd from the whey, and mix the whey with the whites of 4 eggs. Beat together. When well mixed, add a little quicklime, through a sieve, until cement has acquired the consistency of a thick paste. Broken vessels and cracks of all kinds can be mended with this cement. It dries quickly and resists the action of fire and water.

Making Your Own Glue

Mix a handful of quicklime with 4 ounces linseed oil and boil until thick. Spread on tin plates and set in the shade. Glue will become hard but will dissolve over heat by boiling 1 pound glue in 2 quarts skim milk.

Lighting Tips

1. To prevent lamps from smoking, soak lamp wicks in vinegar and dry well. This will keep lamps burning sweet and bright.

2. To replace broken chimneys, tie around the bottom of a canning jar a string soaked in coal oil, turpentine, or kerosene. Light the string. When it has burned all the way around, plunge the bottle into cold water. The bottle will crack where the string was tied. Rub the edges smooth with a sandstone. Use small-mouthed bottles for lamps and large-mouthed bottles for lanterns.

3. To temper lamp chimneys, place the chimney glass in cold water and gradually bring water to boil. Remove from heat and cool slowly. Chimney will then resist cracking.

4. When candles or oil lamps are not available, fill a lid or saucer with lard and roll a string in it. Light the string and it will burn for hours.

5. To make wicks, soak cotton yarn or string for 12 hours in 1 cup water, 1 tablespoon salt, and 2 tablespoons boric acid. Dry yarn and braid it.

6. To harden tallow for candles, add ½ pound alum and ½ pound saltpeter to each pound of melted tallow. For firmer, brighter candles, add 3 tablespoons powdered stearin or stearic acid to 1 pound paraffin.

To Make Candles

Method 1: Melt wax or tallow in a double boiler. Add coloring and scent, if desired. Pour wax into molds with the wick in the center.

Method 2: If you prefer to dip candles, heat wax or tallow to 160° to 180° F. Cut wicks 4 or 5 inches longer than desired length. Tie top of wick to a stick or dowel. Tie a weight on the bottom end of the wick. Dip in paraffin or tallow and pull straight out. Let dry and dip again. Dip until you have desired width. Roll candles occasionally to straighten them. On last dip, add 1 tablespoon stearic acid or stearin. This will harden the outer layer and make it dripless. Trim the wicks, and cut candle base straight.

Homemade Pectin

Wash and cut up 8 large, unpeeled tart apples. Add 4 cups water and 2 tablespoons lemon juice. Boil 40 minutes and strain through several thicknesses of cheesecloth. Boil the juice for 15 minutes. Pour into small sterilized jars and seal.

The skins and cores of apples may also be used to make pectin. Add 4 cups water to 2 pounds skins and cores, and follow same procedure as with whole apples. *Note:* The more tart the apples, the more pectin you will get.

Jelly with Homemade Pectin

Cook fruit and put it through a jelly bag. To every cup of fruit juice (which will be weak in pectin), add 1 cup homemade pectin and ¾ to 1 cup sugar. Boil 5 minutes, remove scum, and pour into sterilized jars.

Jam with Homemade Pectin

Mix 4 cups mashed fruit with 4 cups sugar and let stand 1 hour. Add 4 cups pectin and boil hard for 5 minutes. Remove scum from top. Stir jam for 5 minutes and pour into sterilized jars and seal.

Homemade Gelatin

Gelatin is a strained, clarified meat stock made from the bones, joints, feet, and ligaments of an animal or fowl. Homemade beef or pork gelatin is mild. Chicken gelatin tends to have a slight chicken taste.

Cover bones with water and simmer until water is reduced by one-half. Strain through several thicknesses of cheesecloth. Chill until firm. Remove fat from top and scrape off the sediment on the bottom of the jelly.

If you want to clarify, beat 2 or 3 egg whites for every quart of gelatin. Add to gelatin and boil 15 minutes. Remove from heat and cover. Let stand 30 minutes. Strain through several thicknesses of cloth.

To substitute homemade gelatin in recipes, use 2 cups gelatin for every envelope of commercial unflavored gelatin.

Household Cleaning Hints

Cleaning Jewelry

Use a mixture of equal parts of water and ammonia. If the jewelry is very dull or dirty, rub a little soap on a soft brush, dip in ammonia mixture, and brush on jewelry. Rinse in cold water, and dry with a soft cloth.

Cleaning Silver

Make a paste of ashes and water. Apply with a soft cloth. You will be amazed at how easily silver is cleaned!

Removing Machine Grease

Add 1 tablespoon ammonia to cold water and soap. This will take out machine grease without causing colors to run.

Removing Rust from Steel

Apply a paste of salt and hot vinegar. Scour and rinse. Dry with a flannel cloth, and polish with a little sweet oil.

Removing Ink from Carpets

Use cotton batting to soak up all the ink that it will receive, being careful not to let stain spread. Then take fresh cotton, wet in milk, and blot stained area. Repeat this process, changing cotton and milk each time; continue until all ink disappears. Wash the spot with clean warm water and a little soap. Rinse in clear water and rub until almost dry.

Removing Tar from Fabrics

Saturate the spot and rub it well with turpentine.

Removing Ink or Fruit Stains

Saturate the stain with tomato juice. Then wash with warm water and a little soap. Ink stains from ballpoint pens can also be dissolved by spraying them with hair spray.

Removing Paint

Equal parts of ammonia and turpentine will take paint out of clothing, no matter how dry or hard it may be. Saturate the spot two or three times, then wash with soap and water.

Removing Paint from Window Glass

Rub paint with hot vinegar.

To Soften Water

Method 1: Place 1 quart bran in a strong cloth bag. Place bag in 10 gallons water and boil. Remove bag of bran. The lime in the water will rise to the top of the water and can be skimmed off.

Method 2: Add 2 ounces quicklime, dissolved in water, to every 25 gallons water. Let stand a short time so the lime will unite with the carbonate of lime and sink to the bottom of the container.

Laundry Cleaning Fluid

Dissolve 4 pounds washing soda and ¼ pound baking soda in one gallon water. Heat water to boiling; boil about 5 minutes. Pour water-soda solution over 2 pounds unslaked lime. Let it bubble and foam until it settles. Remove from heat and bottle for use. This fluid is used in professional laundries for whitening linen and is called "javelle water." Use 1 tablespoon for every 3 gallons water. It will remove fruit, grass, and almost all ordinary stains, and will brighten colored clothes. However, it should not be left long in any water.

Window Cleaner

Mix 1 quart water, 2 tablespoons vinegar, ¼ cup ammonia, and 2 teaspoons liquid detergent.

Removing Yellow Stains from Tubs and Sinks

Mix equal amounts of cream of tartar and peroxide and rub the stains thoroughly. Rinse with warm water.

Index

About the Authors

Cooking has always been a favorite avocation of Kay Martineau, Marlynn Phipps, and Sally Hornberger. All three have given many demonstrations and taught classes in preparing and using the recipes and techniques described in this cookbook.

Kay and Marlynn are sisters who, as they grew up, took a special interest in watching their mother and grandmother prepare meals. They were taught never to throw anything away. This knowledge was put to good use when they married and started their own families. When hard times came, they could still feed their families appetizing and nutritious meals at little or no cost, with the help of their food storage and garden. They now reside in Arizona.

Sally has a bachelor of science in home economics education, with knowledge of food preparation that came in handy in preparing recipes for the cookbook. She lives in Missouri.